SWAN ON A
BLACK SEA

SWAN ON A BLACK SEA

A STUDY IN AUTOMATIC WRITING: THE CUMMINS-WILLETT SCRIPTS

transmitted by

GERALDINE CUMMINS

edited by

SIGNE TOKSVIG

with a Foreword by

C. D. BROAD

www.whitecrowbooks.com

For

JOHN N. EAST

'Is there an entity called a soul that rises like a swan above the Black Sea of Death?'

FOREWORD

BY PROFESSOR C. D. BROAD

Fellow of Trinity College, Cambridge

As I have agreed, after considerable hesitation, at the request of the Publishers and of others, to write an Introduction to this book, I will begin with a few relevant personal statements. I have never met either the automatist, Miss Geraldine Cummins, or the editor, Signe Toksvig. Miss Cummins is an Irish lady, well known as the producer (in automatic script) of a number of interesting writings, some of which purport to contain detailed information, not available from normal historical sources, about incidents in the early history of Christianity. As a good example of these writings I would mention her well-known book *The Scripts of Cleophas* (1928). The reader will find a full account of her and her psychic activities in the interesting essay 'Personal Background', which she has written for the present volume. Signe Toksvig is a Danish lady whom I first came to know of through reading and reviewing her excellent book Emmanuel Swedenborg, *Scientist and Mystic* (1948). I have derived much instruction from this, and have expressed my indebtedness to it in some of my published writings. Since then I have found that she and I have mutual friends in Sweden. This has served as a kind of personal introduction to her; and, though we have never met, we have exchanged occasional letters.

The typescript was submitted to me, to some other senior members of the Society for Psychical Research, and to some other persons. Since then I have read the proofs. I found them of great interest, and I believe that these automatic scripts are a very important addition to the vast mass of such material which *prima facie* suggests rather strongly that certain human beings have survived the death of their physical bodies and have been able to communicate with certain others who are still in the flesh.

I think that these scripts are of special interest for the following reason. They purport to be communications from the surviving spirit of Mrs. Charles Coombe Tennant, who died on Aug. 31, 1956. Now that lady had herself had the gift of automatic writing and speech. Under the pseudonym of 'Mrs. Willett' she had been the vehicle for ostensible communications of a most remarkable kind, purporting to come from the surviving spirits of F. W. H. Myers, Edmund Gurney, and others of that distinguished group of friends who were among the founders and the most active early members of the Society for Psychical Research. Her automatic scripts and trance-utterances, together with others which were produced contemporaneously by certain other automatists, and which appear to be significantly inter-connected in their content, have been intensively studied by experts, and they form the subject of a number of extremely important papers in the *S.P.R. Proceedings*. Moreover, the phenomenology of Mrs. Coombe Tennant's mediumship was carefully studied by Gerald Balfour (the second Earl of Balfour), who had had innumerable sittings with her and had been intimately acquainted with most of the persons who were ostensibly communicating through her. He contributed in 1935 a highly elaborate and very valuable paper on this topic to the *S.P.R. Proceedings* (Vol. 43), entitled 'A Study of the Psychological Aspects of Mrs. Willett's Mediumship'.

I have two and only two qualifications, beside my interest in the subject, for writing this Introduction. In the first place, I have been a member of the S.P.R. 'establishment' (if only on its outer fringes) for a great many years. I have met, in my early middle age and their extreme old age, some of the Old Guard, such as Mrs. Sidgwick and Gerald Balfour, with whom Mrs. Coombe Tennant was on terms of personal friendship. I have known well and have co-operated with Mr. and Mrs. W. H. Salter, who were from their youth in the confidence of this group, and who may be said to have carried the torch received from them. And I have been, for most of my adult life, a Fellow of Trinity College, Cambridge, with which nearly all these persons have been intimately connected, in one way or another, at some time in their lives.

Secondly, it so happens that Mrs. Coombe Tennant's youngest son, Henry, who entered Trinity College as an undergraduate in 1932 and read Moral Sciences (in which he displayed outstanding ability), was my pupil during the whole of his time at Cambridge. We soon became very good friends, and we have kept in touch with each other from that day to this. While he was up at Trinity I met his mother occasionally when she visited him in Cambridge, and I still possess a collection of Emily Bronte's poems which she gave me. Soon after he went down I met her once or twice at her London home (then in Portland Place), when calling on him. While he was a prisoner of war in Germany I had some correspondence with her about sending books to him. That is the extent of my acquaintance with her.

She struck me (if I may say so) as a somewhat formidable lady, and I admired the way in which Henry, as it seemed to me, combined perfect politeness and respect towards her with complete refusal to be dominated by her.

I had not the slightest idea at the time, or indeed until it was made public after her death, that she had mediumistic gifts and had regularly exercised them. Still less did I suspect that she was the famous 'Mrs. Willett', whose mediumship had played so important a part in the history of psychical research in the first quarter of this century. I knew, both from Henry and from Mr. W. H. Salter, that she and her family were close friends of the Gerald Balfours and frequent visitors at the latter's home, Fisher's Hill, Woking. I knew also that Mrs. Coombe Tennant's sister-in-law, Eveleen Tennant, had married F. W. H. Myers and had survived him by many years. So I connected Mrs. Coombe Tennant closely with what I may call the 'S.P.R. Cambridge Group', though I had no idea that she was interested in or concerned with their activities as psychical researchers.

Mrs. Coombe Tennant's mediumship was, in fact, a most carefully guarded secret. She herself had a very great shrinking from any publicity in such matters. Her son Alexander has described her to me as an 'extremely discreet person', and he has quoted to me as a favourite saying of hers: 'Never give unnecessary information!' She was, moreover, busily engaged for many years in public work of various kinds, and she must have well known that the faintest hint of 'spookiness' would excite irrational prejudice and would be used without scruple to hamper her activities and to cast doubt on her judgment. The Countess of Balfour states ('The "Palm Sunday" Case'. *S.P.R. Proceedings*, Vol. 52, Part 189, Feb. 1960) that Mr. Coombe Tennant was fully aware of his wife's psychic activities, and had no apparent objection to them, but that some other members of the family disapproved strongly. The facts were, of course, known to the Balfours, to certain friends and colleagues closely associated with them in psychical research (notably Sir Oliver Lodge, Mr. Piddington, Mrs. Verrall, and Miss Alice Johnson), and to Mr. W. H. Salter and his wife (nee Helen Verrall). All these were by nature or by training eminently reticent. One other person who must have been well informed was Dame Edith Lyttelton, who married the Conservative statesman Alfred Lyttelton after the death of his first wife. Dame Edith was, from 1915 onwards, a close friend of Mrs. Coombe Tennant. She developed the gift of automatic writing after her husband's death in 1913, and she played a prominent part (under the pseudonym of 'Mrs. King') in the 'cross-correspondence' phenomena, in which Mrs. Coombe Tennant's scripts were also involved. She was an active and valued member of the S.P.R. up to her death in 1948. I should be surprised if anyone, outside the small circle of friends and relatives mentioned above, was aware, during Mrs. Coombe Tennant's lifetime, of the identity of the 'Mrs. Willett', whose scripts and whose mediumship had been the subject of so much discussion in the *S.P.R. Proceedings.*

There is ample material in various publications for an account of the main outlines of the non-mediumistic aspects of Mrs. Coombe Tennant's life. And there is an immense mass of information in the *S.P.R. Proceedings* about her mediumistic activities under the pseudonym of 'Mrs. Willett'. I propose now to treat in turn those two topics.

Winifred Margaret Pearce-Serocold (for that was her maiden name) was born on November 1, 1874. She was the only child of George Edward Pearce-Serocold by his second wife, Mary Richardson, of Derwen Fawr, near Swansea. The double surname originated in the eighteenth century through the marriage of William Pearce (1744-1820) with Anne Serocold. He was a Cornishman, who in 1789 became Master of Jesus College, Cambridge. She was the eldest child of the Rev. Walter Serocold of Cherryhinton, a village now almost swallowed up in the horrible proliferation of Cambridge. Anne was co-heiress with her brother, Walter Serocold, a captain in the Royal Navy, who fell in action at the siege of Calvi in Corsica, and to whose memory there is a tablet in Cherryhinton church. Her son, Edward Serocold Pearce (1786-1849) changed his surname in 1842 to 'Pearce-Serocold'. He was Mrs. Coombe Tennant's paternal grandfather. There are numerous monuments and tablets to members of the family in the church at Cherryhinton.

Mrs. Coombe Tennant's father, George Pearce-Serocold (1828-1912), joined the Royal Navy at the age of thirteen, and saw service in the first China War. At the signing of the Treaty of Nankin (1842) he, as the youngest midshipman in the Fleet, carried the document on a silver salver to be signed. Later on he served on the West Coast of Africa in the suppression of the slave trade. Still later he spent ten years sheep-farming in Australia, where Mount Serocold in Central Queensland is named after him.

On December 12, 1895, Winifred Pearce-Serocold married Charles Coombe Tennant of Cadoxton Lodge, Glamorganshire. He was born on July 31, 1852, and was thus twenty-two years older than she. The Tennants of Cadoxton (who are not to be confused with another famous family of that name, to which Margot Asquith and her sister Laura Lyttelton belonged) are of purely English origin. But they had for some generations been settled at Cadoxton, and occupied a very important position in the Vale of Neath. Charles Coombe Tennant was the only son in the family of four children born to Charles Tennant, M.P., of Cadoxton (1796-1873), and his wife Gertrude Barbara Rich Collier (1819-1918). The latter was a most notable personage in her time. She was a descendant of Oliver Cromwell, through his daughter Frances. She had spent the first twenty-four years of her life in France, and had known Flaubert, Gambetta, Renan, and many other eminent Frenchmen. After her marriage she held a salon at her house at Richmond Terrace in London, which was for long a meeting-place for such eminent Victorians as Gladstone, Ruskin, Tennyson, Thomas Hardy, Herbert Spencer, George Eliot, G. F. Watts, and Burne-Jones. She kept her faculties and her interests almost up to her death in 1918 at the age of ninety-nine.

The Tennants sprang originally from the neighbourhood of Dent in Yorkshire, and in the early eighteenth century some of them moved to Lancashire. The first of them to settle in Glamorganshire was Charles Coombe Tennant's paternal grandfather, George, who died in 1832. He was a man of great energy and business ability. He purchased first the Rhydding estate, near Neath, and later the adjoining property of Cadoxton. In the period 1817 to 1824 he constructed the Tennant Canal from Swansea to the Brecon Hills.

Mrs. Coombe Tennant had thus married into a remarkable family. Of her husband's sisters one, Eveleen, married in 1880 F. W. H. Myers (1843-1901), the author of that posthumously published classic of psychical research *Human Personality and its Survival of Bodily Death*, and one of the founders and the most active early members of the S.P.R. Another sister, Dorothy, married the explorer, H. M. Stanley.

Cadoxton is named after the sixth-century Welsh saint and martyr Cadoc, who is commemorated in a number of Welsh place-names, e.g., Llangattock. It became the country home of Mrs. Coombe Tennant. She has given a very full description of the house and of its beautiful surroundings in the memoir which she contributed to the book *Christopher*, compiled by Sir Oliver Lodge with her co-operation, and published by Messrs. Cassell in 1918. This book is a moving biographical tribute to the memory of her eldest child, Christopher, who fell in Flanders on September 3, 1917, shortly before his twentieth birthday. It contains much factual information, and indirectly throws much light on her character, ideals, and beliefs.

Christopher was born at Cadoxton Lodge on October 10, 1897. He was at school at Winchester from 1911 until July, 1916, when he passed into Sandhurst as a prize cadet. He was gazetted to the Welsh Guards and joined that regiment early in May, 1917. He crossed to Flanders with a draft on August 9, 1917, and was killed by a shell in the trenches near Langemark on the morning of September 3 of that year. His letters, his actions, and the many moving tributes paid to him after his death by persons of all ranks of society, show him to have been an extremely fine character, gentle, sensitive, and highly intelligent, yet courageous and spirited, with a deep appreciation of beauty in nature, in human character, in literature, and in art. As with so many of his contemporaries,

Ostendent terris hunc tantum fata, neque ultra
esse sinent...

The vast majority of the letters in *Christopher* are between him and his mother. His are generally signed 'Cruff'. It is plain from them that there was an extremely close link between mother and son. The father is very little in the picture, and one might be inclined to infer from the contents and the emphasis of the book that he played a somewhat minor role in a predominantly matriarchal household. Lodge states, however, that Charles Coombe Tennant had much to do with Christopher when the latter was young, and that their relations remained intimate and almost fraternal up to the end. They used to play chess, billiards, and picquet together; and Christopher, who became a devotee of the classics and had intended to pursue his studies at Trinity College, Cambridge, was initiated into Greek by his father.

Christopher used to call him 'Deedoge'.

In 'The "Palm Sunday" Case' (*S.P.R. Proceedings*, Vol. 52, Part 189) the Countess of Balfour remarks that 'Mrs. Willett was a lady who had a very strong predilection for maternity'. The birth of Christopher had been difficult, and he himself states that he was born 'almost inanimate' and had to be brought to life by 'judicious flapping with wet towels', on the doctor's orders. Mr. W. H. Salter, in 'The Rose of Sharon' (*S.P.R. Proceedings*, Vol. 54, Part 194), states that Mrs. Coombe Tennant has recorded that early in 1905, i.e. some eight years after Christopher's birth, she suddenly began, for no discernible reason, to find herself longing for another child. That desire persisted and became a daily thought. She consulted a doctor in August, 1905, and he gave the opinion that there would be no special risk in her having a second child. On January 6 (Epiphany), 1907 she gave birth to her second child and only daughter, Daphne, whose brief life and tragic death were a turning point in Mrs. Coombe Tennant's spiritual development.

Daphne was born at Cadoxton and christened there. She died in London, after a sudden and short illness, in the early morning of July 21, 1908. During her lifetime she was known in the family as 'The Darling'. Though she lived only one year and seven months, she had clearly become a considerable personality by the time of her death. Lodge writes of her: 'From the testimony of those who knew the infant I judge that nothing less than genius will account for the impression she made'. Her mother wrote and privately printed a memoir of the child in August, 1908, and from this Lodge quotes, among other sentences, '. . . her one attitude towards outward objects seemed to be love, and her chief desire to express all the love her little heart held . .

The loss of such a child was naturally a shattering blow to her mother, and it had a profound influence on Christopher, who was nearly eleven years old when Daphne died, and had been devoted to her. I shall describe in the appropriate place below its sequel in Mrs. Coombe Tennant's psychical development.

Here it will suffice to say that she became convinced, on what appeared to her adequate personal evidence, of Daphne's survival, and in general, to quote her own words, that death is 'no more than a doorway admitting to a fuller and freer life'. That conviction came to be shared by Christopher, and it led to the following compact between mother and son when he was on leave at Cadoxton shortly before going out to Flanders. They considered together what action should be taken on each of the following alternative possibilities, viz., that he should be wounded, that he should be reported missing, and that he should be killed. Since it was the third of these which was fulfilled, we need consider only what they agreed to do in that event.

As regards Christopher himself, they decided that, if he should find himself suddenly in the next world, he should start with the expectation of meeting Daphne and his uncle by marriage, F. W. H. Myers. If he were not at once to be in touch with them, he was to inquire for them. Thereafter he was to concentrate on getting his bearings in his new and unfamiliar situation. He was to keep constantly in mind that his mother would be all right, that she would know that he was essentially unchanged, and that she would be trying to help him telepathically. As regards Mrs. Coombe Tennant, they agreed that she would try to avoid excessive grief, as a disturbing factor in their relations; that she would hold on to the belief that a period of deeper intimacy between them had now begun; and that she would strive to make Cadoxton 'a happy hunting-ground for him'.

As a result of this, the news of Christopher's death, when it came on the evening of September 6, 1917, though naturally grievous, was not shattering. In a letter written by his mother on the following day she remarks: 'He is to me as if just out of a severe operation—my steady hand in his is what he needs now ... He will soon get his bearings there, and whether he does it happily and easily depends on what telepathic impressions he gets from us—especially from me.

Mrs. Coombe Tennant had two other children after Christopher and Daphne. They were Alexander, born in 1909, and Henry, born in 1913. Her husband died on November 5, 1928, in his seventy-seventh year, shortly after Alexander had entered Trinity College, Cambridge, as a freshman. Henry came up to Trinity four years later. Their mother long survived her husband, dying in her eighty-third year on August 31, 1956 at her home in London. An obituary notice of her appeared in *The Times* for Saturday, September 1, 1956. This dealt with her public life and activities. In the S.P.R. Journal (vol. 39, No. 694) for December of next year there appeared the *Obituary Notice of Mrs. Coombe Tennant*, which made public for the first time her identity with 'Mrs. Willett'.

From these and other published sources one sees something of her public spirit and her energy. She had very early become an enthusiastic supporter of the extension of the suffrage to women, and had worked to that end with Mrs. Fawcett. During the 1914—18 war she was Vice-chairman of the Glamorganshire Women's Agricultural Committee, and from 1917 was Chairman of the Neath and District War-Pensions Committee. In 1920 she was appointed a Justice of the Peace, and sat on the Glamorganshire County bench, being the first woman to be a

magistrate there. From 1920 to 1931 she was one of the Visiting Jus-
tices at Swansea prison. She took that duty very seriously, and was in-
strumental in effecting some highly sensible and practical reforms in
the treatment of prisoners. She was a strong Liberal in politics, and
an admirer of Lloyd George, and in 1922 she unsuccessfully stood as
Liberal candidate for the Forest of Dean constituency. She shared the
high hopes, felt by so many fine spirits immediately after the First
World War, in the newly formed League of Nations, and she was the
first woman to be appointed by the British Government as a delegate
to its Assembly.

As we have seen, Mrs. Coombe Tennant was of Welsh descent on
the side of her mother, Mary Richardson of Derwen Fawr. She became
a very keen Welsh Nationalist. For many years she played an active
part in the 'Gorsedd' or 'Circle of Bards', in the capacity of 'Mistress of
the Robes', and she had the official title of 'Mam-o-Nedd' ('Mother of
Neath'). She was Chairman of the Arts and Crafts Section of the National Eisteddfod in 1918, and, in recognition of her services, the Arch
Druid conferred on her the honorary Eisteddfodic degree of 'Ovate'. She
was one of the twenty original members elected in May, 1918 to form
an Executive Committee for introducing self-government on federal
lines into Wales. For many years she was an active member of the Art
Committee of the Swansea Borough Council. Not only was she a dis-
criminating patron of specifically Welsh painting; she had also made
for herself a fine collection of modern French pictures.

We may sum up all this side of Mrs. Coombe Tennant's personality
and life by remarking that she was one of the many conspicuous counter-instances to the silly popular belief that a person with mystical or
mediumistic gifts must *eo ipso* be 'moony' and incompetent in practical affairs. Other notable counter-instances, within the circle of the
S.P.R., were Mrs. Verrall, her daughter Helen (Mrs. W. H. Salter), and
Dame Edith Lyttelton. And, if we care to go further afield and to look
higher, we might mention St. Birgitta of Sweden, St. Teresa of Spain,
and Florence Nightingale, as women conspicuous for energy, business
ability, and outstanding practical achievement, who would have made
a very poor showing on the currently accepted tests for bodily and
mental normality and psychological integration.

Let us now turn to the mediumistic, or 'Mrs. Willett', aspect of
Mrs. Coombe Tennant's complex personality. This is abundantly doc-
umented in a number of important articles in the S.P.R. Proceedings.
At the centre of these is G. W. Balfour's comprehensive paper: 'A Study

of the Psychological Aspects of Mrs. Willett's Mediumship, and of the Statements of the Communicators concerning Process' (*Proceedings*, Vol. 40, Part 139; 1935). Mrs. Willett was first introduced in the literature of the subject, so far as I know, in two papers in *Proceedings*, Vol. 25, Part 63 (1911), viz., Sir Oliver Lodge: 'Evidence of Classical Scholarship and of Cross Correspondence in some new Automatic Writing', and Mrs. Verrall: 'Notes on Mrs. Willett's Scripts'. Then came in fairly quick succession two important papers by Balfour concerning automatic scripts in which Mrs. Willettt had played an essential part, viz., 'Some recent Scripts affording Evidence of Personal Survival' (*Proceedings*, Vol. 27, Part 69; 1914) and 'The Ear of Dionysius' (*Proceedings*, Vol. 29, Part 73; 1917). After Balfour's paper of 1935, on the psychological aspects of Mrs. Willett's mediumship and on the statements made by the ostensible communicators as to the processes involved, there is a long interval, extending well beyond the date of Mrs. Coombe Tennant's death in 1956. Then, in 1960, comes an important paper by Jean Balfour (the Countess of Balfour) entitled 'The "Palm Sunday" Case' (*Proceedings*, Vol. 52, Part 189). This is wholly concerned with certain scripts and trance-utterances of Mrs. Willett, which will be described below. That article was followed in 1963 by W. H. Salter's paper 'The Rose of Sharon' (*Proceedings*, Vol. 54, Part 194). This is not, indeed, concerned with Mrs. Willett's own scripts, but with certain scripts by Mrs. Verrall, by her daughter Helen, and by members of a Scottish family, known as 'The Macs'. But these, as Mr. Salter argues, appear to contain indubitable references, though in cryptic language, to the forthcoming birth and the early death of Daphne Coombe Tennant, at a time when the writers could have had no normal knowledge about those still future events.

Of the papers enumerated above, those up to and including Balfour's essay of 1935 have become classics in the literature of psychical research, and have been discussed from all angles. It would be out of place to attempt to discuss them in detail here. I think that most competent commentators, who have devoted serious attention to them, would agree that they involve, on the part of Mrs. Willett, knowledge of particular facts and incidents and of highly recondite classical lore, which cannot plausibly be traced to any source normally available to Mrs. Coombe Tennant, and which are often highly characteristic of the interests, the erudition, and the idiosyncrasies of the deceased scholars (e.g., Myers, Verrall, and Butcher) who were ostensibly communicating through her.

In Gerald Balfour's 'Study of the Psychological Aspects of Mrs. Willett's Mediumship' we learn in great detail what the ostensible communicators (purporting to be the surviving spirits of Myers and of Gurney) told, first to Lodge and later to Balfour, through Mrs. Willett's automatic script or trance-speech, about the use which they claimed to be deliberately making of her, of the methods which they employed, and of the difficulties which they encountered in attempting various kinds of communication through her. These seem to me to be some of the most interesting and the most intellectually impressive products of trance-mediumship of which we have any record. Mrs. Coombe Tennant was undoubtedly a highly intelligent woman, artistically gifted, practically efficient, and of excellent general education which she had never allowed to rust. But she had little interest in, or capacity for, psychological analysis or philosophical speculation. It is no insult to say (what, indeed, she often said herself) that these ostensible communications through her Willett personality were altogether above her head, or, as she once impatiently put it, 'all so much Greek to me'.

In 'The "Palm Sunday" Case' we have something quite different, but almost equally impressive and much easier for the ordinary reader to appreciate. Here Mrs. Willett, in a long series of automatic scripts and trance-utterances, seems to be referring, cryptically but in the aggregate unmistakably, to a very private and personal matter in the early life of Gerald Balfour's elder brother, the Conservative statesman A. J. Balfour (1848-1930). This was his love for Catherine Mary Lyttelton; her tragic death from typhus on Palm Sunday 1875, before he had declared himself; the very singular action which he took at the time, unknown to the other members of his family, to show his devotion; and certain incidents in his last illness, as a very old man in 1929, which seemed to suggest her continued existence and affection and her active intervention. Mrs. Willett was producing these scripts in sittings which she gave to Gerald Balfour, mostly in 1912, followed by others scattered over the years 1913-18. According to Jean Balfour, it was not until after a sitting held at A. J. Balfour's London house on June 19, 1916, in his presence, that Gerald Balfour learned, for the first time and from his brother, about the silver box which the latter had had made after 1875 to contain a tress of Mary Lyttelton's beautiful hair, cut off at her death in that year. It was then found that there had been repeated references to this in Mrs. Willett's earlier scripts and trance-utterances, long before the first of her few meetings with A. J. Balfour.

I pass now from this outline of Mrs. Coombe Tennant's main achievements as a medium to a brief account of the development of her mediumship.

It will be remembered that Mrs. Coombe Tennant's sister-in-law, Eveleen Tennant, had married F. W. H. Myers in 1880. Mrs. Coombe Tennant liked, respected, and admired Myers; but a family quarrel developed with his wife. The latter, indeed, would seem, from all accounts that I have ever heard of her, to have been a singularly egotistic and rather unscrupulous person. In partial mitigation of some of her conduct it is fair to say that even a less possessive woman might have resented the facts that she had been preceded in her husband's affections by a lady who had died tragically and to whom he remained passionately devoted; that he had tried repeatedly, and, as he believed, successfully, to get in touch with her surviving spirit; and that he was avowedly looking forward with confident longing to rejoining her on the astral plane immediately after his own death. (For the details of this I would refer the reader to Myers's posthumously published *Fragments of Inner Life* (S.P.R. Publication, 1961); to Mr. Salter's article T. W. H. Myers's Posthumous Message' (*S.P.R. Proceedings*, Vol. 52, Part 187; 1958); and to Dr. Alan Gauld's letter 'Frederic Myers and "Phyllis"' in the *S.P.R. Journal*, Vol. 42, No. 720; 1964.)

It was probably through her admiration for Myers that Mrs. Coombe Tennant became an Associate Member of the S.P.R. soon after his death in 1901. She had already met Mrs. Verrall casually in 1896, at the Myers's house in Cambridge, and she had met Mrs. Verrall's daughter Helen once or twice in 1898. She was, however, not greatly interested in psychic matters at that time, and she resigned her associate membership in 1905. It was the death of her daughter Daphne on July 21, 1908, that revived her interest and was the occasion of the beginning of her own mediumship.

On July 28, 1908, i.e., a week after Daphne's death, Mrs. Coombe Tennant wrote to Mrs. Verrall, who was then almost a stranger to her personally, as one whom she knew to have had ostensible communications in automatic script, purporting to come from the deceased F. W. H. Myers. She stated that she had lost her child Daphne a week before, and that she had decided to inform Mrs. Verrall at once, lest any allusion to Daphne that might occur in the latter's script might be overlooked.

In August and September, 1908, Mrs. Coombe Tennant read in the *S.P.R. Proceedings* a paper by Miss Alice Johnson entitled 'A Report on

Mrs. Holland's Script'. (The name 'Mrs. Holland' was a pseudonym for Mrs. Alice Macdonald Fleming, a sister of Rudyard Kipling, living in India, who was producing automatic writing.) On reading this Report Mrs. Coombe Tennant felt an impulse to try for herself. She described these early attempts in a letter of October 8, 1908, to Mrs. Verrall. The scripts purported to come from Myers. She was not much impressed by them, and she destroyed them.

Early in January, 1909, however, she received, in the course of a script ostensibly emanating from Myers, an order to stop writing, to try to apprehend the ideas that would be put into her head, and to record them in ordinary writing either at once or at the earliest convenient later moment. It was stated in the scripts that Edmund Gurney (who had died in 1888) was also involved in the experiments which were about to be made 'from the other side' with Mrs. Coombe Tennant.

The next stage was that the 'Myers-*persona*' and the 'Gurney-*persona*' (to use a strictly non-committal phraseology) expressed a wish, in their ostensible communications through Mrs. Willett, that she should sit in the presence of another person and should dictate to him the impressions which she would receive from them. The first person whom they proposed as a sitter was Sir Oliver Lodge, who had been an active member of the S.P.R. from its early days and had known and collaborated with Gurney during the latter's lifetime.

Lodge was at that time a complete stranger to Mrs. Coombe Tennant, though he had once met Charles Coombe Tennant, before the latter's marriage, through an introduction from Myers. After considerable resistance Mrs. Coombe Tennant consented to approach Lodge. He first met her on May 17, 1909, and afterwards had many sittings with her.

Next the Gurney-*persona* asked that G. W. Balfour should be introduced as a sitter and note-taker. That wish was expressed again and again in ostensible communications purporting to come from Gurney. Balfour had been a close friend of Gurney's, and they had co-operated in psychical research up to the time of the latter's death. He was a man of keen philosophic interest and deeply read in philosophy. So it was highly appropriate that the Gurney-*persona* should say (as he did) that his reason for wanting Balfour to become a sitter with Mrs. Willett was that Balfour would be interested in the processes involved in communication rather than in the *products*.

Balfour at that time was a complete stranger to Mrs. Coombe Tennant, and he was a distinguished member of a very distinguished family. She therefore hesitated very much to approach him with this strange request. She must, however, have known of Balfour's sister Norah (Mrs. Henry Sidgwick) through Myers, and she may well have met her occasionally at the Myers's house in Cambridge. Anyhow, Mrs. Coombe Tennant eventually gave her consent, an introduction was effected, and Balfour had his first sitting with her on June 4, 1911. Thereafter Balfour became almost the only sitter with Mrs. Willett, and hundreds of sittings were held in the next twenty years, sometimes at Cadoxton and sometimes at Balfour's house, Fisher's Hill, Woking.

Mrs. Coombe Tennant soon became a close friend of Gerald Balfour and his family. She and her children, and sometimes one or another of the children without her, would often stay at Fisher's Hill. The boys knew Lady Betty Balfour (*nee* Lady Elizabeth Lytton) as 'Aunt Betty'. Christopher spent some of his last days in England there in July, 1917, with 'the beloved "Aunt Betty" ', as he calls her in a letter to his mother of July 16.

The community at Fisher's Hill, with which Mrs. Coombe Tennant thus became intimate, was a most remarkable one in the annals of psychical research. Beside Gerald Balfour and his wife and children, there was living there from 1916 onwards his sister Mrs. Sidgwick. She was the widow of Professor Henry Sidgwick, one of the 'founding fathers' of the S.P.R.; was one of the ablest women of her own or of any other time; and herself played a great part in the organization of the S.P.R. and contributed papers of outstanding importance to its *Proceedings*. Another resident there was Balfour's old friend, Mr. J. G. Piddington (*ne* Smith), who was living at Fisher's Hill from 1919 to 1940. Piddington had been a businessman, and in that capacity he rendered valuable service to the S.P.R. in the conduct of its finances. But he was also, like Balfour, a fine scholar, with immense patience and pertinacity in tracing obscure allusions and unravelling literary puzzles. The two of them together devoted all their skill and learning, and most of the energies of their later years, to a minute study of the immense mass of script material, written by various automatists (including Mrs. Willett.), which seems *prima facie* to suggest the survival and the deliberate post mortem collaboration of the group of Cambridge friends and contemporaries, Myers, Gurney, Sidgwick, Verrall, and Butcher.

Gerald Balfour died in 1944, at the age of ninety. He had been preceded by his brother Arthur in 1930 at the age of eighty-two, and by his sister Eleanor (Mrs. Sidgwick) in 1936 in her 91st year. He was followed by his friend Piddington in 1952 at the age of eighty-three. With them ended the 'old guard' of the S.P.R. Of the next generation, their spiritual heirs, Dame Edith Lyttelton died in 1948, and Mrs. Coombe Tennant (as we have seen) in 1956 at the age of eighty-two. Mrs. Verrall's daughter Helen (Mrs. W. H. Salter) died in her sleep, *felix opportunitate mortis*, while still in good bodily health and full mental vigour, in 1959 at the age of seventy-six. And, lastly, it should be recorded that Myers's son Leopold, who became a distinguished novelist, died 'by his own hand' (to quote the *Dictionary of National Biography*) on April 8, 1944, at the age of sixty-three. Of all these, and of all that has been narrated above about their doings and sufferings, we may fairly say, confining ourselves to this life:

> *Hi motus animorum, atque haec certamina tanta,*
> *pulveris exigui iactu compressa quiescunt.*

I think it will be useful, at this point, for the reader to have before him, for reference, the following chronological table, which summarizes the main relevant biographical and bibliographical facts up to and including Mrs. Coombe Tennant's death:

CHRONOLIGICAL TABLE
UP TO MRS. COOMBE TENNANT'S DEATH

Year	Mrs. Coombe Tennant and her Relatives	Background Events
1838		Henry Sidgwick born (d. 1900)
1843		F. W. H. Myers born (d. 1901)
1845		Mrs. Sidgwick (née Eleanor Mildred Balfour) born (d. 1936)
		Mrs. Annie Eliza Marshall (née Hill), 'Phyllis', born (d. 1876)
1847		Edmund Gurney born (d. 1888)
1848		A. J. Balfour (1st Earl of Balfour) born (d. 1930)
1850		Mary Catherine Lyttelton born (d.
1850		Palm Sunday, 1875)
1851		Francis Maitland Balfour, 'The Dark Young Man', born (d. 1882)
		A. W. Verrall born (d. 1912)
1852	Charles Coombe Tennant born (d. 1928)	
1854		G. W. Balfour (2nd Earl of Balfour) born (d. 1944)
1855		Oliver Lodge born (d. 1940)
1857		Alfred Lyttelton born (d. 1913)
1859		Mrs. A. W. Verrall (née Merrifield) born (d. 1916)
		Henry Sidgwick elected Fellow of Trinity College, Cambridge
1865		F. W. H. Myers elected Fellow of Trinity College, Cambridge
1866		Anne Eliza Hill ('Phyllis') married Walter James Marshall
		J. W. Strutt (3rd Lord Rayleigh) elected Fellow of Trinity College, Cambridge
1869		J. G. Piddington (né Smith) born (d. 1952)
1872		Edmund Gurney elected Fellow of Trinity College, Cambridge
1873		F. W. H. Myers falls in love with Mrs. Annie Marshall ('Phyllis')

Year	Mrs. Coombe Tennant and her Relatives	Background Events
1874	MRS. COOMBE TENNANT (*née* WINIFRED MARGARET PEARCE-SEROCOLD) born 1/11 (d. 31/8/1956)	F. M. Balfour, S. H. Butcher, and A. W. Verrall elected Fellows of Trinity College, Cambridge
1875		Mary Catherine Lyttelton died (Palm Sunday, 21/3)
1876		Mrs. Annie Marshall ('Phyllis') died by drowning (29/8)
1877		G. W. Balfour elected Fellow of Trinity College, Cambridge
1880	Eveleen Tennant married F. W. H. Myers	W. H. Salter born
1881	Myers's son L. H. Myers born (d. 1944)	
1882		F. M. Balfour ('The Dark Young Man') killed on the Alps
1883		Mrs. W. H. Salter (*née* Helen de G. Verrall)born (d. 1959)
1888		Edmund Gurney died
1892		Dame Edith Lyttelton (*née* Balfour) married Alfred Lyttelton as his second wife
1893		F. W. H. Myers' *Fragments of Inner Life*, privately printed
1895	W. M. Pearce-Serocold marries Charles Coombe Tennant (12/12)	
1896	Mrs. C.T. meets Mrs. Verrall for first time at the Myers's house	
1897	George Christopher Serocold Coombe Tennant born (10/10) (d. 3/9/1917)	
1898	Mrs. C.T. meets Helen Verrall for first time	
1900		Henry Sidgwick died

Year	Mrs. Coombe Tennant and her Relatives	Background Events
1901	Mrs. C.T. becomes Associate Member of S.P.R.	F. W. H. Myers died
1902		Dame Edith Lyttelton joins S.P.R.
1905	Mrs. C.T. ceases to be Associate Member of S.P.R.	
1907	Daphne Coombe Tennant born (6/1)	
1908	Daphne C.T. died (21/7) Mrs. C.T. writes to Mrs. Verrall for advice	
1909	Alexander John Serocold C.T. born	Oliver Lodge first made acquaintance with Mrs. C.T. (17/5)
1911	Mrs. C.T.'s first contact with Gerald Balfour and with Piddington	First published accounts of 'Mrs. Willett's' scripts. [S.P.R. *Proceedings*, Vol. 25—Lodge: 'Evidence of Classical Scholarship', and Mrs. Verrall: 'Notes on Mrs. Willet's Scripts'.]
1912		A. W. Verrall died
1913	Augustus Henry Serocold C.T. born (9/4)	Alfred Lyttelton died. Dame Edith began automatic writing
1914		S.P.R. *Proceedings*, Vol. 27—G. W. Balfour: 'Some recent Scripts affording Evidence of Personal Survival'.
1915	Mrs. C.T. becomes a friend of Dame Edith Lyttelton	Oliver Lodge's son Raymond killed in action
1916		Mrs. Verrall died Lodge's book *Raymond* published
1917	George Christopher Serocold killed in action (3/9)	S.P.R. *Proceedings*, Vol. 29—G. W. Balfour: 'The Ear of Dionysius'
1918	*Christopher* (by Oliver Lodge) published (Cassell)	

Year	Mrs. Coombe Tennant and her Relatives	Background Events
1918	Mrs. C.T.'s mother-in-law, Gertrude Tennant, died at age of 99 Mrs. C.T. chairman of Arts and Crafts Section of National Eisteddfod	
1919	American edition of *Christopher*	
1928	Charles C.T. died (5/11) A.J.S.C.T. entered Trinity College, Cambridge, as freshman	Dame Edith Lyttelton became member of S.P.R. Council
1930		A. J. Balfour (1st Earl of Balfour) died (19/3)
1932	A.H.S.C.T. entered Trinity College, Cambridge, as freshman	
1935		S.P.R. *Proceedings*, Vol 43—G. W. Balfour: 'A Study of the Psychological Aspects of Mrs. Willett's Mediumship'
1936		Mrs. Sidgwick died.
1937	Eveleen Tennant (Mrs. F.W.H. Myers) died (12/3)	
1939		Geraldine Cummins gave one sitting at Fishers Hill, Woking, to Gerald and Lady Betty Balfour
1940		Oliver Lodge died
1942	Mrs. C.T. took up residense as a paying guest with a friend (April)	
1944	L. H. Myers (son of F.W.H.M. and Eveleen Tennant) died by his own hand	G. W. Balfour (2nd Earl of Balfour) died
1948		Dame Edith Lyttelton died (2/9)
1952		J. G. Piddington died

Year	Mrs. Coombe Tennant and her Relatives	Background Events
1955		Geraldine Cummins read extracts from G. W. Balfour's 'Study of the Psychological Aspects of Mrs. Willett's Mediumship' in a book by Tyrrell and a book by Salt-marsh
1956	MRS. COOMBE TENNANT died (31/8)	Obituary notice of Mrs. C.T. in *Times* (1/9)
1957		Obituary notice of Mrs. C.T. in S.P.R. *Journal* (December)

With the above Chronological Table before him for reference, the reader is now invited to address himself to the following Synopsis of the main contents of the Scripts, in the order of their occurrence, with Notes on relevant circumstances at the dates in question:

SYNOPSIS, WITH NOTES, OF THE MAIN CONTENTS OF THE SCRIPTS

Note. In this Synopsis I shall refer to the ostensible Communicator as 'W.' This may be taken to represent both Mrs. Coombe Tennant's name 'Winifred' and the pseudonym 'Mrs. Willett' under which she was known in the literature of psychical research. It is to be understood as leaving completely open the question of the Communicator's identity.

The following abbreviations will be used:

A.J.B.	Arthur James, 1st Earl of Balfour
G.W.B.	His brother Gerald William, 2nd Earl of Balfour
Lady Betty B.	G.W.B.'s wife, *née* Lady Elizabeth Lytton
G.C.	Miss Geraldine Cummins
Mrs. C.T.	Mrs. Winifred Margaret Coombe Tennant
George (Christopher)	Her eldest child, G.C.S. Coombe Tennant
Daphne	Her daughter, Daphne Coombe Tennant
Alexander	Her second son, A.J.S. Coombe Tennant
Henry	Her youngest child, A.H.S. Coombe Tennant
E.G.	Edmund Gurney
F.W.H.M.	F.W.H. Myers
O.L.	Oliver Lodge
W.H.S.	Mr. W. H. Salter
Helen S.	Mrs. W. H. Salter (*née* Helen Verrall)
Mrs. V.	Her mother, Mrs. Margaret Verrall
A.W.V.	Her father, Dr. A. W. Verrall

Date	Script	Main Contents of Script	Notes on Relevant Circumstances
1956 Aug. 31 Sept. 1			Death of Mrs. C.T. Obituary notice of Mrs. C.T. in *Times*
1957 Aug. 7			First letter from W.H.S. to G.C. (received Aug. 9)
22			Second letter from W.H.S. to G.C.
28	1	Introduction of Communicator. Name 'Wyn' or 'Win'. Son killed at 19 or 20 in World War I. Another son alive, in his early forties. Name 'Harry' or 'Henry'	G.C. held W.H.S.'s letter to her forehead. All this is correct for Mrs. C.T. and her sons
29	2	Further description of Communicator. References to her automatic writing. Name of person 'Geraldine' or 'Gerald'; partly Scottish, English mother. Name of person 'Francis; died young from a fall in a foreign country. Message to W.H.S., lifting her ban on publication of certain papers	The mother of the Balfours was Lady Blanche Cecil. Francis Maitland Balfour was killed in a mountaineering accident on the Alps in 1882, at the age of 31
Sept. 10	3	Name of communicator 'Winifred'. Son 'Henry' (not 'Harry'), who fought in World War II. W. has been a magistrate	No use was made of specimens of his mother's handwriting provided by 'Major Tennant' (Henry), in obtaining the first three scripts

Date	Script	Main Contents of Script	Notes on Relevant Circumstances
Sept. 22	4	G.W.B. explicitly takes charge first, and communicates a message to W.H.S. as to how he will proceed. Then W. takes over, and begins reminiscences. Place-name 'Morganwg'. Met her husband there, but was herself brought up in England. Names 'Cadox Lodge', 'Dorothy', 'Eveleen', 'Fred', All connected with this and with husbands family	G.C. presented paper with fragment of what was in fact Mrs. C.T.'s handwriting, with a reference to the *Provost's Lodge at Eton*. The Tennants' home was Cadoxton Lodge, Glamorganshire. 'Dorothy' and 'Eveleen' were two of Charles Coombe Tennant's sisters. 'Fred' was Eveleen's husband, F.W.H.M.
24	5	Name 'Mrs. Wills'—'not quite right'. 'George, my son'. 'Cambridge, Cherry-' Had early dream experiences, and later automatic writing. Consulted a very wise woman, 'Portia'. Sends love to 'Portia's daughter. Gave sittings to a 'Scientist'. Then to 'Gerald'. Refers to Gerald's wife 'Betty'. Also to 'the Cambridge group', which includes 'Portia', 'the Scientist', and 'Gerald'	G.C. presented paper with fragment of what was in fact Mrs. C.T.'s handwriting, with a reference to a *memorial*. G.C. was reminded by the names 'Gerald' and 'Betty' of the one sitting which she gave to the Balfours, at their house, Fishers' Hill, in 1939. 'Portia' was Mrs. V. Her daughter was Helen S. The 'Scientist' was Oliver Lodge
26	6	W.'s reflexions on the dangers of possessiveness in family life, illustrated by the lives of Eveleen Tennant and her husband (F.W.H.M.) and their	G.C. was now practically certain that the communicator was the medium known as 'Mrs. Willet' Leopold Myers died by

Date	Script	Main Contents of Script	Notes on Relevant Circumstances
		son, Leopold Myers	his own hand in 1944 (see *D.N.B.*)
October			At the end of October, 1957 W.H.S. called on G.C. and confirmed that 'Mrs. Willett' had been Mrs. C.T.
Dec.			Obituary notice of Mrs. C.T. in S.P.R. *Journal*, revealing her identity with 'Mrs. Willett', and stating that she had been a magistrate and a delegate to the League of Nations
1958 January			G.C. reads obituary notice of Mrs. C.T. in *Journal*
Feb. 14	7	W.'s recollections of her experiences at G.W.B.'s house, in a room where A.J.B. lay resting as a very old man, and she had a vision of the spirit of Mary Lyttelton visiting him	Script addressed to W.H.S. and Helen S. G.C. was holding in her hand a letter from W.H.S. The date of this experience of Mrs. C.T.'s was Oct. 16, 1929. It is mentioned (but not explained in detail) in G.W.B.'s 'Study of the Psychological Aspects of Mrs. Willett's Mediumship' (S.P.R. *Proceedings*, 1935). It was first described in full in Jean Balfour's 'The "Palm Sunday" Case' (S.P.R. *Proceedings*, Feb. 1960

Date	Script	Main Contents of Script	Notes on Relevant Circumstances
Feb. 15	8	W. describes difficulties in communication, illustrated by her experiences with interpreters at League of Nations. Then describes A.J.B.'s union with Mary Lyttelton in the after-life	Continuation of Script 7, to the Salters
16	9	W.'s account of her experiences immediately after her death. First, uneasy dreams. Then, meeting first her father and mother; then her son George; then her husband and her half-sisters. Taken by parents through panorama of childhood, girlhood, and young womanhood. Mentions 'Cambridge' and 'Cherryhinting' (sic), where she was a baby with doll and pram. Mention of 'Derwen House' in Wales	G.C. had received a letter from Henry, saying that he, unlike his mother, had always believed in extinction at bodily death. The script is W.'s answer to this, addressed to her son Henry The Pearce-Serocolds had for long lived at Cherryhinton, near Cambridge. Mrs. C.T.'s mother's home was Derwen Fawr, near Swansea
17	10	Continuation of W'.s memories of her earthly life. Engagement to Charles Coombe Tennant. Disdainful attitude of his sisters, Dorothy (wife of H.M. Stanley) and Eveleen (Mrs. F.W.H.M.). Great change in W.'s personality in 1918, due to World War I. Suspects that she may then have	This script contains the first mention of Daphne, and of her death

Date	Script	Main Contents of Script	Notes on Relevant Circumstances
		neglected her husband and small sons for public work. Important changes connected with number 8: 1908, death of Daphne; 1918, immersion in public work; 1928, husband's death	
Feb. 18	11	Continuation of W.'s memories of her earthly life. Widowhood in 1938, and anxiety about Henry (then a boy of 15 at Eton). Enlarges on the essential identity of a human individual through great changes of personality, in earthly life; and hence argues for possibility of survival of bodily death	
Mar. 1	12	[Not reproduced in text]	In answer to a letter from Henry, asking his mother's advice on alternative possible careers
12	13	Begins by continuing discussion of possible careers. Then switches, by way of topic of personal relations, to Mrs. C.T.'s quarrel with a lady with whom she had lived as paying guest	Mrs. C.T. had gone, in April, 1942, to live as a paying guest with a lady with whom she had been on friendly terms. After nearly four years this arrangement ended in a violent quarrel
22	14	First, deals in detail with the processes involved in communication through a	The first part in response to a request by W.H.S. to G.C. to ques-

Date	Script	Main Contents of Script	Notes on Relevant Circumstances
		medium, and the conditions needed for success. Then reverts to the story of A.J.B.'s and Mary Lyttelton's love, as viewed from the after-life	tion W. about the process of communication. The Script was mislaid, and not sent at once to W.H.S. (see below, under Mar. 30, April 4, and May 9)
Mar. 30			Mrs. Sitwell, in course of conversation with G.C., informs G.C. of A.J.B.'s early love-affair, of the death of the girl, and of the fate of the intended engagement-ring, but does not mention the girl's name.
April 4			G.C. finds Script 14 (which she had mislaid), and is struck with the similarity to what Mrs. Sitwell had told her. She consults Mrs. Gay (of the S.P.R.) as to what to do with the script. Mrs. Gay consults W.H.S.
12	15	[Of no general interest]	Addressed to W.H.S.
13	16	W. claims to have seen W.H.S. and Helen S. together in a book-lined room in an ancient house, studying past records, in which W. had played a part. She lifts her former ban on their publication	The Salters' house, 'The Crown House', is an ancient one, with many books in it. They had been discussing the publication of the Willett scripts which eventually formed the basis of 'The "Palm Sunday" Case'

Date	Script	Main Contents of Script	Notes on Relevant Circumstances
April 19	17	W. introduces the Lytteltons, under the pseudonym of the 'Lobs'. She states, *wrongly*, that her son George was at the school (*Eton*) of which one of the 'Lobs', whom she disliked, was head-master. She mentions a 'Lob', who played an important part in politics, and was married to 'Edith'. Another 'Lob' married another 'Edith'; this one was 'Mrs. Bob'	George was in fact at Winchester, and Henry at Eton. The facts are correctly stated in Script 26. The politician was Alfred Lyttelton. His second wife was Dame Edith Lyttelton, an active member of the S.P.R., an automatic writer, and a friend of Mrs. C.T.'s. The head-master was Dr. Edward Lyttelton
20	18	More about the 'Lobs'. They held seances, very privately. At some of these A.J.B. was present, and there Mrs. C.T. first met him. W. comments on A.J.B.'s personality; and the unfavourable impression which, at that time, it had produced on her	It appears, from Jean Balfour's 'The "Palm Sunday" Case' (S.P.R. *Proceedings*, Feb., 1960), that such sittings were held by the Lytteltons, and that A.J.B. was present at some of them
May 3	19	More comments by W. on her early impressions of A.J.B. Then switches to description of her recent devastatingly disappoint-ing meeting, in the after-life, with Daphne. Finally, begins elaborate account of inception of the 'Mrs. Willett' mediumship	In the course of this sit-ting G.C. submitted a question from Henry as to the inception of the 'Mrs. Willett' medium-ship. The latter part of the script is in answer to this

Date	Script	Main Contents of Script	Notes on Relevant Circumstances
May 4	20	Inception of 'Willett' mediumship continued. Essential part played by the spirit of F.W.H.M. Reference to very private communications, received by her from him, about his matrimonial troubles with Eveleen. Mention of F.W.H.M.'s pre-marital love affair, of its tragic end, and of Eveleen's persistent jealousy	The relevant facts about F.W.H.M. and 'Phyllis' (Mrs. Annie Marshall) were first made public in Oct., 1958, in W.H.S.'s paper 'F.W.H. Myers' Posthumous Message' (S.P.R. *Proceedings*)
5	21	Inception of 'Willett' mediumship continued. Important part played by spirit of E.G.	For history of 'Willett' mediumship, compare G.W.B.'s 'Study of the Psychological Aspects of Mrs. Willett's Medium-ship' (S.P.R. *Proceedings*, 1935)
9			W.H.S., after being consulted by Mrs. Gay on G.C.'s behalf, writes to G.C., urging her not to destroy Script 14 (as she had thought of doing), but to let him and Henry see it
27	22	W.'s reminiscences of her life as a very young woman in Gloucestershire. Was painfully conscious of being rather stout and very shy	

Date	Script	Main Contents of Script	Notes on Relevant Circumstances
June 7	23	W's reminiscences of her life in Wales and in London as a young married woman	
8	24	W.'s account of her resistance to giving sittings in presence of a stranger; of the pressure put on her from 'the other side' to do so; and of her finally consenting to sit for O.L.	In answer to question put, on behalf of Henry, as to what W. can remember of her sittings with 'the Scientist'
11	25	Account of sittings for O.L. continued: Various forms in which messages came. Sittings with Mrs. V. as introduction to those with O.L.	
13	26	Account of sittings for O.L. continued: Her communicators now insisted that she should give sittings for G.W.B., which she at first strongly resisted. Mention of Daphne, whose death is stated to be the initiation of all these psychic experiments. W. had always longed for a daughter. Reference to the 'Lob', whom she disliked, who was Headmaster of Eton. Sent George to Winchester; but Henry went to Eton after that 'Lob' had retired	Cf. Script 17, and the Note thereon, in regard to the public schools of George and of Henry

Date	Script	Main Contents of Script	Notes on Relevant Circumstances
June 15	27	Account of O.L. sittings continued, and early sittings with G.W.B. described. W. used to treat her 'unseen guests' as a 'hostess', not as a mere passive reporter	
July 7	28	Account of sittings with G.W.B. continued. W.'s estimate of G.W.B.'s intellect and personality. Summary of conditions favourable to communication. Describes a mystical experience, in union with the spirit of F.W.H.M. Expounds, in this connexion, a theory of 'Group Souls'	For history of sittings with O.L., and with G.W.B., see G.W.B.'s 'Study . . .' (S.P.R. *Proceedings*, 1935), referred to in Note on Script 21. The ideas in the latter part of this Script occur in two books by G.C., viz., *Beyond Human Personality* (1935) and *The Road to Immortality* (1955). In both cases they are supposed to have been communicated by F.W.H.M.
11	29	(1) A human life is a play, in which the 'primary self' is the central character, and the others are 'aspects or units' of it. (2) The origin of W.'s public life was in her enthusiasm for women's rights, in which she was greatly inspired by Lady Betty B.'s sister, Constance Lytton. (3) W. gives three reasons why she has not mentioned anything about the last phase of her earthly life	Addressed to W.H.S. G.C. had been given a copy of Constance Lytton's book *Prisons and Prisoners* by Lady Betty B. in 1939, and had read it

Date	Script	Main Contents of Script	Notes on Relevant Circumstances
July 22	30	(1) For reasons, not divulged, W. has been angry with Henry for his intention to write the letter in question. (2) She relents, and relates in considerable detail a mystical experience, which she has lately had in Henry's company, though without his knowledge. (3) Ends with curious account of conversation with recently deceased medical man: 'Osmund' and 'psychedelic' occur in it, which puzzled her	G.C. had received from Henry a letter, written on 12 July, 1958, saying that his mother, if still existing and still able to follow terrestrial events, would certainly have been with him in his recent experiences. Henry had no recollection of any experience of his own, corresponding to that described in Script 30
Aug. 6	31	W.'s account of a recently remembered dream, had by her shortly before the above-mentioned mystical experience. In it she had seemed to see Henry and W.H.S. discussing records of sittings given by her for O.L. and for G.W.B.	There had in fact been such a meeting between W.H.S. and Henry
October			W.H.S.'s 'F.W.H. Myers' Posthumous Message' appeared in S.P.R. *Proceedings*, giving first published account of F.W.H.M.'s tragic love-affair with 'Phyllis'
29	32	W. states that she can at will re-live, in a kind of	

Date	Script	Main Contents of Script	Notes on Relevant Circumstances
		dream, any part of her earthly life: (1) Early married life in Wales, (2) Excitement over League of Nations, and fascination for Lloyd George. Yet in fact the only statesman she ever really helped or influenced (and that only in his inmost private life) was A.J.B.	
1959 April 11	33	W.'s account of her experiences when dying	
22			Death of Helen S. in her sleep
May 30	34	W. refers, in cryptic form, to recent sudden death of the daughter of her old friend 'Mrs. Margaret', who has herself been long in the after-world. W. proposes to call the deceased 'Mrs. X.' Her husband, 'Mr. X', is a friend of Henry's. 'Mrs. X' is represented as a relative of the Tennants	It is quite plain, from the context and the sequel, that the *daughter* is Helen S., that her *mother* is Mrs. V., and that 'Mr. X.' is W.H.S.
31	35	(1) Full account, from W.'s point of view, of 'Mrs. X.'s' death, its immediate sequel, and the active part played by the spirits of 'Mrs. X.'s' parents. (2) Message from 'Mrs. X.' to her	

Date	Script	Main Contents of Script	Notes on Relevant Circumstances
		husband. (3) Apologies by W. to Henry for certain sarcastic passages in the scripts, which, she says, are due to E.G.	
June 9	37 [sic]	Astor describes the 'interfering' communicator as a man dressed in typical Victorian fashion. An Englishman, intimately concerned with Ancient Greece and with drama. Suffered from a disease of the bones, which caused great pain and disablement, to which he refused to yield. He is accompanied by his wife. He gives a dramatic account of how he and she, acting for their daughter's good, frustrated the latter's desperate attempts to struggle back into her body; and how she is now resting and recuperating under their care	This Script occurred as an 'interference by a penetrating and unusual mind pushing in', in the course of scripts addressed to a 'Mrs. Flower' from her deceased husband. It was assumed to refer to someone connected with 'Mrs. Flower', and was sent to her accordingly. She failed to find anything relevant in it. But a later script suggested that it might be meant for W.H.S. So it was sent to him, and he recognized it as applying to his long deceased father-in-law, Dr. A. W. Verrall. (That it does so, is perfectly obvious to anyone familiar with A.W.V., his character and interests, and his martyrdom to arthritis.) The name 'Mrs. Flower' is a pseudonym for an active member of the S.P.R.
16	36 [sic]	W. describes the important part played by the	

Date	Script	Main Contents of Script	Notes on Relevant Circumstances
		spirit of E.G. in organizing her communications through G.C., and, in particular those concerning 'Mrs. X.' 'Mrs. X.' is now revealed as Mrs. W. H. Salter (*née* Helen Verrall), daughter of W.'s old friend and counsellor, Mrs. A. W. Verrall ('Margaret'). W. again apologizes for certain sarcastic passages, due to E.G., which she thinks in bad taste. Ends with latest news of Helen S., whom W. has now met	
July 24	38	(1) W. describes 'reliving' with Helen S. early Cambridge experiences. They exchange memories of difficulties with Eveleen (Mrs. F.W.H.M.), and W. once more enlarges on Eveleen's defects. (2) Helen S. then takes over, and describes her present life as a kind of dream-reproduction of her early home life. Comments on W.'s attitude to her husband, Charles C.T.	Addressed to W.H.S.; first from W., and then from Helen S.
Sept.			Obituary notice of Helen S. in S.P.R. *Journal*
Nov.			G.C. hears for first time of O.L.'s book *Christopher*, from Henry

Date	Script	Main Contents of Script	Notes on Relevant Circumstances
Nov. 23	39	W. apologizes to Alexander, for what she feels to have been her injustice to him as a small boy, and describes the psychological background of her attitude towards him and towards Henry. This has been brought home to her by meeting, and being repulsed by, the spirit of Daphne	Cf. Scripts 10 and 19
Dec. 3			G.C. meets Henry for first time, in a brief call which he makes at her flat
1960 Feb.			G.C. meets Alexander for first time, spending an evening with him and his wife
Feb.			Jean Balfour's 'The "Palm Sunday" Case' (S.P.R. *Proceedings*). First published account of A.J.B.'s love-affair with Mary Lyttelton, her death, and its sequels. [But cf. Note on March 30, 1958]
Mar. 6	40	(1) W. introduces herself as 'the former Mrs. Willett'. Then relates an incident when Helen S. called on her, in her extreme old age, and when she (W.) repelled Helen S.'s questions about her	This Script is an 'intrusion', in the course of a sitting given by G.C. for 'Mrs. Flower', (1) of W., on behalf of Helen S.; and (2) of Helen S. herself. W.H.S. confirms that

Date	Script	Main contents of Script	Notet on Relevant Circumstances
		sittings with the Balfours. (2) Helen S. now takes over; and (i) claims to have met all the old Cambridge and S.P.R. group (whom she names), and (ii) withdraws her former advice to W.H.S. to give up their house	there was such an interview as W. describes, between Helen S. and Mrs. C.T., shortly before the latter's death
1961 March			S.P.R. publishes, by subscription, for the first time, F.W.H.M.'s privately printed 'Fragments of Inner Life', which are concerned with the 'Phyllis' episode
1963 May			W.H.S.'s 'The Rose of Sharon' (S.P.R. *Proceedings*). Describes certain passages in automatic scripts which seem, on retrospect, to refer proleptically to Daphne, and to foreshadow her early death

The reader is now in possession of a fairly adequate account of the content of the Scripts, of the dramatic form in which it was presented by the automatist, and of the kind of relevant information which might have been available to her from normal sources at the time when each script was written. He must make his own reflexions and draw his own conclusions. I will end this Introduction with a few of mine.

The scripts are in the form of ostensible communications from the surviving personality of a certain deceased person. Any such material must in the first place be considered under the following two heads, viz., (1) *the factual information* conveyed in it, and (2) *the dramatic form* in which it is presented.

Under the first heading the following questions arise: (i) What proportion of the factual statements are *verifiable or refutable*, either with certainty or with high probability? (ii) Of these, what proportion are *specially relevant* to the known relationships experiences, interests, knowledge, and beliefs of the ostensible communicator? (iii) Of the testable statements which have this special personal relevance, what proportion are certainly or very probably correct? Under the second heading come the following questions: (i) Does the form in which the ostensible communications are couched suggest a *single, self-consistent, outstanding personality?* (ii) If so, does that personality seem, to those who were well acquainted with the deceased, *to bear a striking resemblance to hers?*

As regards the questions under heading (1), the following remarks may be made. Statements by the ostensible communicator about her experiences at the point of death or in the afterlife cannot be tested. Nor can some of her statements about the emotions which she felt towards certain persons and in certain situations in her earthly life. But, when all these are set aside, there remains a large mass of statements which can be tested. And, in marked contrast to the contents of many mediumistic utterances, they are not in the least vague, general, allusive, or oracular. They abound in extremely concrete detail about named persons and places, and about definite events in which these were concerned. Moreover, of the large mass of concrete testable statements, very nearly all are true. And, when a mistake in detail is made (as in Script 5, where the name 'Mrs. Wills' is given instead of 'Mrs. Willett', or in Script 17, where it is stated that George C. T. was at school at *Eton*), it is nearly always corrected in a later script. As regards the first question under heading (2), I should think that no reader could fail to get the impression of an extremely definite personality, with a rather unusual combination of characteristics. In one aspect, she is a typical Victorian *grande dame*, who treats even her 'unseen guests' as she was wont to treat ordinary mortals in her capacity of hostess; who likes to play her part in public life, and does so very efficiently; and whose political interests are rather surprisingly radical for a woman of her period and social position. In another aspect, she has very strong likes and dislikes towards certain individuals; and, in particular, she has an intense maternal instinct, and an uneasy feeling that this has not always been fortunate in its effects on her relationships with her children. In yet another aspect, she is a mystic, possessed of psychic gifts which she has for long been concerned to conceal, living in two

xlv

worlds. As regards the second question under the present heading, it is for those who knew Mrs. Coombe Tennant intimately, and, in particular, for her surviving sons, to decide whether the very marked personality which emerges in the scripts is that of the individual who is ostensibly communicating through G.C. All that I can usefully say is that it seems to me, as a largely but not wholly ignorant external observer, to fit like a glove.

Granted that the scripts contain much correct information of a highly detailed kind concerning Mrs. Coombe Tennant and her family and associates and activities, and that they give a strong impression of emanating from a highly personal source, and assuming (for the sake of argument) that those who knew Mrs. Coombe Tennant intimately find them redolent of her personality, the next question that arises is this: What is the least implausible way of accounting for the production of such scripts by a person whose *normal* sources of information were those available to Miss Geraldine Cummins at the times when her hand automatically wrote them?

We may classify conceivable explanations of such cases as follows: (1) Those which presuppose *nothing but normal* sources of information and nothing but normal and generally recognized powers of cognition, selection, and dramatization in the automatist. (Those normal powers may be supposed to be present to an abnormal degree, as, e.g., in the case of a calculating prodigy, a literary or dramatic genius, and so on. And they may be supposed to exhibit themselves only when the automatist is in the peculiar dissociated state in which she produces her automatic utterances, and not at all in her everyday life.)

(2) Those which presuppose in the automatist certain paranormal powers of cognition and selection, not generally admitted by contemporary scientists, applied only to existing records and to persons still alive in the flesh. Examples would be: (i) the alleged power of becoming *telepathically* aware of facts known, of beliefs held, and of emotions felt by other persons, and not conveyed from them by spoken or written utterances, by gestures, by changes of facial expression and so on. (ii) The alleged power of becoming *clairvoyantly* aware of physical things, events, and state of affairs (and, in particular, of written records) without the use of sense-perception, and without telepathic awareness of the normal knowledge of those objects possessed by someone still alive in the flesh. (3) Those which (without necessarily excluding the acquirement of information by paranormal means from persons still in the flesh and/or from existing records) presuppose the intervention

of some person or persons not at present alive on earth. This would, in theory, cover the two alternatives of intervention (i) by some human being who has survived bodily death, and (ii) by some non-human person. I will now consider very briefly, in turn, these three conceivable alternatives as applied to the present case.

We may begin with the following platitude. Corresponding to *any* statement that can be verified at a given moment, there must then exist on earth either some relevant accessible record or some living person who has a relevant recollection. What has to be explained is the occurrence, in a particular script produced under specified circumstances, of a certain set of highly specific and closely interconnected items, corresponding to a certain very small selection from all this immense mass of mainly irrelevant documentary or mnemonic material.

Now, suppose we accept, as I have not the slightest hesitation in doing from long personal acquaintance, the *bona fides* and the discretion of Mr. W. H. Salter and of Henry Coombe Tennant. And suppose that, without any positive evidence whatever, we were to ascribe to G.C. immense powers of cryptomnesia, or (to make no bones about it) deliberate, active, and dishonest rummaging in and collating published records. I do not see how we can explain, without postulating *something paranormal*, the amount and kind of detailed and correct information, highly relevant to Mrs. Coombe Tennant, that had already emerged by the end of the sixth script.

If that be granted, I would next maintain that access, whether by normal or by paranormal means, to printed records, does not suffice. A good deal of relevant factual information does exist in print. Burke's *Landed Gentry*, e.g., contains fairly full accounts of the history and genealogy of the Tennants and the Pearce-Serocolds. Still more of relevant material is contained in Lodge's long out-of-print memoir *Christopher*. But no printed source existing at the time contained anything about Mrs. Coombe Tennant's sister-in-law Eveleen's peculiarities; about F. W. H. Myers's matrimonial difficulties with her; and about her putting their son Leopold, with tragic results, against his father. Yet all this is explicitly referred to in Script 6, and it is a frequently recurring theme in later scripts. Nor, e.g., can the communicator's very personal reflexions about her relationships with her several children, or about the quarrel with 'Mrs. R.', or about 'the Lobs', have come from anything in print at the time. But some or all of them might conceivably have come to the automatist, either by the normal way of indiscreet chatter or in a paranormal telepathic way, from one or another of the very

few persons then in the flesh who had the relevant knowledge or beliefs. In view of the fact that G.C. did not meet Henry until late in 1959
or Alexander until early in 1960, and that neither of them would be in
the least inclined to chatter about intimate personal or family affairs,
I think it quite inconceivable that this part of the content of the scripts
can have come in a normal way from either of them.

It may be worthwhile to add a word at this point about the book
Christopher. G.C. states that she was unaware of its existence until
Henry informed her of it in November, 1959. It seems to me that there
are two facts which make against the possibility that it was an important source of the contents even of those parts of the scripts to which
it is relevant. One is the fact that Mrs. Coombe Tennant's eldest son is
referred to throughout the book as 'Christopher' or 'Cruff', and *never*
as 'George'; whilst, in the scripts, where he is unmistakably referred to
from the very first, he is always called 'George', and not 'Christopher'.
(This seems to me an extremely odd circumstance, on any view of the
case.) The other relevant fact is that the life and death of Daphne are a
very prominent feature in the book *Christopher*; whilst Daphne is not
mentioned in the scripts until Script 10, though it is true that she plays
a fairly important part later, e.g., in Script 19.

It seems to me, then, that we shall need to postulate *telepathy* with
persons still in the flesh, and not merely clairvoyance of existing records, if we are to attempt to explain the facts of the case in accor-
dance with the second of the three alternatives distinguished above. It
remains to consider whether any explanation is adequate which does
not go beyond this.

So far as concerns the *factual content* of the scripts, it seems to me
that most, though not perhaps all of it would have been within the
knowledge or belief of either Mr. Salter or Henry. Part of this might
have been confined to the former, and another part to the latter, whilst
part would be common to both. Now it was Henry who initiated, and
Mr. Salter who carried through, the process of consulting G.C. on behalf of the to her unknown 'Major Tennant'. The two had discussed the
matter together; and the thought of Mrs. Coombe Tennant, and of the
question of her survival and of the possibility of obtaining evidence for
it through G.C., must have been exercising their minds and focussing
their attention. We might suppose that this would serve to establish
some kind of telepathic 'rapport' between a certain sub-conscious lay-
er of G.C.'s mind, on the one hand, and the memory-traces of W.H.S.
and/or of Henry concerning Mrs. Coombe Tennant, on the other. And

we might suppose that this telepathic 'rapport' was activated, and that actual telepathic 'leakage' of relevant data took place, on each occasion when G.C. held a sitting with the thought of W.H.S. and his client 'Major Tennant' explicitly before her mind. In this connexion it is worth noting that both Mrs. and Mr. Salter had been devoting a great deal of thought and discussion to the question of the possible publication of the Willett scripts concerned with A.J.B.'s love-affair with Mary Lyttelton, for a long time before the appearance in February, 1960 of Jean Balfour's paper 'The "Palm Sunday" Case', which first revealed the whole story to readers of the *S.P.R. Proceedings*.

If we are prepared to swallow the possibility of *clairvoyance*, in addition to telepathy, we might suppose further, that the telepathic 'rapport' between G.C., on the one hand, and W.H.S. and Henry, on the other, in some way focussed G.C.'s clairvoyant attention on certain printed records containing details relevant to Mrs. Coombe Tennant which were outside their own range of knowledge or belief.

I think it is true to say that there is very little independent evidence for telepathy between persons still in the flesh on anything like the scale that would be required to explain the present case. And I am quite sure that there is practically no independent evidence for clairvoyant access to the contents of printed records by persons still in the flesh. But, even if we could safely take such telepathy and such clairvoyance as independently established possibilities, we should not be at the end of our difficulties.

We should still have to explain how the information, obtained telepathically from those still in the flesh or clairvoyantly from existing records, issues in a dramatic form *so characteristic of a certain deceased person*, whom the automatist has never met. For that purpose it would be necessary to ascribe to some subconscious level of the automatist the literary gifts of a novelist or a playwright. But that would not be sufficient. It would be necessary also to ascribe to some subconscious level of one or more persons still in the flesh, who had known the ostensible communicator, the power of telepathically influencing the automatist's subconscious creative gift so as to imitate the style of the particular deceased person in question. There is, undoubtedly, some independent evidence for the existence, in some few persons, of remarkable creative and dramatizing powers, which reveal themselves only when their possessor is in a dissociated state. (Cf. e.g., the achievements of 'Miss Hélène Smith', described in Professor Flournoy's famous book: *Des Indes au planète Mars*.) But, so far as I am aware, there is little or no independent evidence for the existence, in ordinary persons alive in the flesh, of the power of subconsciously and telepathically directing the exercise of those gifts of creation and dramatization.

We may pass, then, to the third of the alternative possible types of explanation enumerated above, viz., that an essential factor in the case is the intervention of some person or persons *not at present alive in the flesh*. Obviously much the simplest and most plausible hypothesis *prima facie* is that Mrs. Coombe Tennant, or some part or some aspect of her, survived the death of her body on August 31, 1956; that she was still actively in existence at least as late as March 6, 1960 and that during that period she from time to time controlled, directly or indirectly, the pen of the automatist G.C. On the other hand, it seems to most contemporary Westerners antecedently improbable, to the point of practical inconceivability, that a person should continue to exist and to function after the death and disintegration of his earthly body, with its brain and nervous system. It is only because of this that so many of the few who are aware of the kind of facts of which the present case is such a striking instance, and who are prepared honestly to face them, have recourse to the fantastic hypothesis, involving telepathy and clairvoyance on the part of those still in the flesh, which I have described in discussing the second alternative type of explanation.

I have discussed elsewhere, to the best of my ability, this very real dilemma, and I can only refer any reader who may be interested in my views to the relevant sections of my book *Lectures on Psychical Research*.

Suppose that one is willing to contemplate seriously the possibility that Mrs. Coombe Tennant may have survived bodily death, and that the scripts may in fact emanate from her. On that hypothesis, they come from someone who might reasonably be expected, in view of her experiences on earth as 'Mrs. Willett', to 'know the ropes' very much better than the average surviving spirit, in regard to communicating through a medium. On the same hypothesis, we can regard the untestable parts of the content of the scripts as 'travellers' tales'. I will conclude with a few remarks about them, viewed tentatively in that light. I will consider in turn: (1) Statements about a person's experiences at the point of death and immediately afterwards; and (2) Statements about conditions in the afterlife.

(1) Since we shall all die, and since some at least of us may possibly survive bodily death, it is of some interest to have what purports to be first-hand information about what to expect on that occasion. We have accounts in the scripts of two very different kinds of death, viz., that of

1

Mrs. Coombe Tennant herself in very old age and after a long period of bodily weakness, and that of Helen Salter, who died suddenly in her sleep when still active and vigorous in body and mind.

In the very special circumstances of the latter, it is claimed that the spirits of Helen S.'s parents actively and deliberately intervened. The communicator W. describes the scene, which she claims to have witnessed, and an ostensibly independent account is given by an 'intruding' communicator, who claims to have been one of the two main actors in it, and who is described in a way which obviously and strikingly fits Helen S.'s father, A.W.V., when alive in the flesh.

In both cases it is claimed that death is followed by a longish dream-like period of rest and recuperation, under the supervision of near relatives of the deceased. An essential feature of this is alleged to be a vivid hallucinatory re-living of the whole course of one's earthly life. It may be remarked that this agrees, so far as it goes, with statements made by Swedenborg, on the alleged basis of his own personal observation as a 'visitor' to the next world. But it should be added that Swedenborg insists on the largely delusive character of the ostensible reunions with relatives and friends, which play so important a part at this early stage.

(2) As to statements contained in the scripts about conditions in the afterlife, I will make only the following comments:

(i) I find W.'s statements in Script 19, about her devastatingly disappointing meeting with Daphne, very moving and very true to what might reasonably be expected to happen if people survive bodily death. Daphne's earthly life had lasted only a little more than eighteen months. On the hypothesis which we are now making, she had been in the afterlife for some forty-eight years of our time when her mother passed over to it. Those eighteen months, and their tragic ending, had been an outstanding and almost obsessive emotional experience in the life of the mother. But the daughter must presumably have gone through some process analogous to 'growing-up', and must have acquired her own interests and formed her own affections. In all this her memories of her eighteen months of infancy on earth, and of her relationship to her mother, might be expected to play a negligibly small part. The unreasonable expectations of the mother, the chilly reactions of the daughter, and the consequent feeling of emotional frustration, are, it seems to me, precisely what an impartial observer might have foreseen.

(ii) If there be an after-world, the scripts must present an extremely narrow and peculiar corner of it. All the persons whom we meet in them are particularly cultured and intelligent members of the English upper or upper-middle classes, whose earthly lives were lived in a certain brief period of English history. It is platitudinous, but not superfluous, to point out that most human beings are not Victorian English ladies and gentlemen, and that a good many of them are savages. Even if we quite arbitrarily confine our attention to our contemporary fellow-countrymen, we must remember that a certain proportion of them are actual or potential criminals; that a much larger proportion are feeble-minded or neurotic or downright crazy; and that the vast majority of the rest are more or less amiable nit-wits, with no intellectual or cultural interests whatever. If all or most human beings survive the death of their bodies, there must presumably be, among the many mansions of their Father's house, places prepared for such as these. And they must be very unlike those gentlemanly and academic English apartments to which alone the scripts introduce us.

(iii) Closely connected with this is the fact that so little pain and unhappiness, and so little passive selfishness, active cruelty, and sheer incompatibility of temperament, are depicted in the scripts. These play a very large part in our earthly life, and it seems to me quite incredible that the mere incident of dying and surviving bodily death should automatically cure them. Indeed, survival might be expected often to re-open emotional wounds which had been temporarily healed by the death of one or more of the parties concerned. It is fair to say that there is, in Script 6, a glimpse of these less cheerful aspects of life, in the account of the sufferings which Leo Myers has brought on himself, of his hostile and reproachful reception of his mother Eveleen, of the latter's sorrowful realization of the evils which her possessiveness has wrought on one whom she loved, and of her resolute attempts to make amends. So far, so bad; but I should suspect that even if there should be no predominantly evil non-human inhabitants of the astral world, enough of those human beings who have made hells on earth would be likely, if they survive, to make new hells in the afterlife. In all this, it seems to me, Swedenborg's account is much more plausible than the somewhat rose-tinted picture painted in the scripts.

With these comments I invite readers to study carefully for themselves the scripts and the notes on them, and to draw their own conclusions as to what is, rather literally, a 'question of life or death.'

CONTENTS

INTRODUCTION

BY SIGNE TOKSVIG

The title *Swan on a Black Sea*, taken from a phrase in the Cummins-Willett scripts, suggested to one reader the question: 'Is there an entity, sometimes called a soul, that rises like a swan from the black sea of death?'

The present book contains an attempt to answer that question by evidence obtained through mediumship of an unusually subtle kind. As an explanation seems still to be needed when one undertakes a study of mediumship, I must take a little space to account for the origin of my own interest in the subject.

I was making preparatory studies for a biography of Emanuel Swedenborg, the great Swedish scientist and mystic of the eighteenth century. In his diaries he confessed that at times his hand seemed to write 'of itself', often things with which he disagreed. Later on the messages through his hand claimed to come from the dead. In other ways too he seems to have been a so-called medium, or an interpreter between the living and the dead. He continued to acquire much of his information from the 'other world' by means of what we now call 'automatic writing', a technical term for it, though 'transmitted' would be better, since it is far from being as mechanical as 'automatic' implies.

The process is simple. Certain people can sit down before a blank sheet of paper, pencil in hand, and, after an interval, the hand, seemingly of its own volition and often at high speed, may write communications that claim to come from the spirits of the dead. Usually the result is far from inspiring, but a few such mediums have produced results impossible to attribute to their own store of knowledge. The deceased who is alleged to direct the pen or pencil may be entirely unknown to the medium, yet may identify himself so vividly that the personality can be recognised without any doubt by living relatives or friends.

Descriptions of dim historical periods may be given of which it seems most unlikely that the medium could have had any information, still with many details admittedly correct in the opinion of scholars.

In my researches among modern mediums, however, I could find none whose capacities approached those of Swedenborg's, either in matter or manner, until I came upon Gerald Balfour's 'Study of the Psychological Aspects of Mrs. Willett's Mediumship, and of the Statements of the Communicators concerning Process'. (*Proceedings of the Society for Psychical Research*, May, 1935). The similarities were striking between Mrs. Willett's form of mediumship and Swedenborg's. Naturally I tried to meet her. I soon found out that her name was a pseudonym, but not even past Presidents of the Society for Psychical Research knew her real name. Her anonymity was relentless.

I then, in the books of Miss Geraldine Cummins, came across other cases of transmitted writings (now technically known as 'scripts'). These also had similarities to those of Swedenborg.

Much of his early writings of this kind are hardly read by any except a small sectarian public. In these scripts he claimed that his hand was used by Jewish and Gentile Christians of the first two centuries of our era, fighting with each other, as well as with Jews and Pagans.

Several volumes of Miss Cummins's early-transmitted writings were *The Cleophas Scripts*. They too deal with the contentions of Jewish and Gentile Christians in those centuries, filling out details of the Acts of the Apostles. But, unlike Swedenborg's scripts on these topics, Miss Cummins's present a vivid and coherent narrative, thrilling even to one like myself with a minimal interest in the subject matter. Even to her normal interest and knowledge it was alien, yet, as mentioned, scholars have testified to the correctness of some of the obscure historical details.

In 1955 I succeeded in meeting Miss Cummins, and since then we have kept in frequent touch. She wrote to me in August, 1957, that an official of the S.P.R. had asked her—as an experiment and because he thought the case would interest her, to try to get a 'message' from a dead mother for her living son.

She was given only the name, unknown to her, of the son, and later on, some scraps of the mother's handwriting. As a compliment to the distinguished inquirer, she wrote to me, she intended to do only one or two scripts, but the personality of the communicator fascinated her, and she did six before her attention was called to an obituary that had just appeared in the *Journal of the S.P.R.*

In that notice it was stated that 'Mrs. Willett' of the famous Balfour Study had been the pseudonym of a certain English lady who, Miss Cummins had realised, was the very same woman from whom she was obtaining these vigorous scripts.

For personal reasons the lady will chiefly be referred to as Mrs. Willett, 'Winifred' for short, since—an oddity in the other world, first names seem to be used there as frequently as in modern America.

The six scripts received by Geraldine Cummins before she knew that the communicator and Mrs. Willett were identical had been, so she was assured by the experimenter, full of correct information about matters known to 'the absent sitter', who was the lady's younger son, Henry. Miss Cummins was urged to continue. When she stopped the stream there were forty-four scripts. Part of them are too correct about private affairs to be published, but enough are complete to make it inestimably worth while to study them from various points of view, even from that of considering that they go far to establish the survival of consciousness after death.

The notes at the end of each script will attempt to assess the correctness of the information given and of the likelihood that Miss Cummins could not have had normal knowledge of it.

That is one way of doing it, which must be done. Yet it brings up the question of kinds of mediumship. In one, although the medium is unacquainted with the deceased person, she is able to furnish a list of facts concerning him or her, even if the sitter or note-taker is equally unacquainted with the communicator. These are called proxy sittings.

My own experience with such a medium has been with Mrs. Bertha Harris, whose probity and excellence in such matters are most justifiably praised. I have had two proxy sittings with her, in which she was completely ignorant concerning my dead communicators, and in the first sitting my proxy, a member of the S.P.R. Council was equally ignorant. Still, out of about forty statements given as facts by Mrs. Harris, about thirty were correct and the rest non-verifiable. In the second sitting my proxy knew a couple of facts but naturally did not tell. Yet Mrs. Harris was able to give many correct pieces of information about my dead relative. They were far from commonplace, and some which were not even known to the absent sitter (that is myself) were highly relevant and helpful.

You might think this would settle the matter, but it does not. Some theorists hold that 'extrasensory perception', or the ability to obtain information without the aid of the known senses, can, in the case of certain gifted individuals, extend both backwards and forwards in time, and everywhere on the earth in space. Therefore the accomplishments of a good medium need not involve the survival of consciousness after death, so goes the theory. There is at present no real evidence of such omniscience on the part of any medium, and the supposition is thorny with difficulties greater, it would seem, than the belief in survival, but theoretically it is possible.

The so-called 'book tests' appear to support the mediumistic-omniscience point of view. Certain mediums have been able to tell, roughly, what was printed on, say, page seven in a book with a green cover, fourth from the end of the last Shelf in a book-case in a room where they'd never been, perhaps even in a far-away house.

This is pertinent to the Cummins-Willett scripts, because some of Mrs. Willett's communications deal indubitably with the same subject matters as those dealt with in the Balfour Study, sometimes in nearly the same words.

Miss Cummins has not read the Balfour Study, she has only read fragments from it, quoted in two other books which are far from covering the subjects in her own Willett scripts, but the possibility of subconscious extrasensory perception of the Balfour Study is there. I believe that several factors militate against this. Mrs. Willett was dictating to Miss Cummins a perfect stream of reminiscences from her youth (all verifiable but unknown to Miss C.) when questions were sent to her by her son about the very sittings she had had in her lifetime with Gerald Balfour and Oliver Lodge. Reluctant though she was to leave her reminiscing, what could she do (supposing her existence) other than answer and recount what happened then? Yet she did not do it in the words of the learned Balfour Study; she put the ideas in her own easy style, that of an unpedantic woman of the world.

Still more important, she sometimes introduced descriptions of scenes and events which were not made available to the public till 'The Palm Sunday Case' came out two years later. Did Miss Cummins's subconscious perception roam around till she found and put together various unpublished manuscripts?

Or did the same omniscience find these facts in the minds of those few people still living who knew them, and arranged the material for publication?

Possibly, but unlikely. Miss Cummins has done badly in telepathy tests of the quantitative kind. Out of the question is the supposition that she consciously hunted about in reference books for the facts or played the detective secretly in getting them from living people who might have known Mrs. Willett. That lady's anonymity was exceptionally well guarded, and Geraldine Cummins's utter sincerity is guaranteed by all who know her. I agree with Sir Oliver Lodge in calling her of 'transparent honesty'.

Even so, admitting this, the anxious doubter might say, she could have learned facts referring to Mrs. Willett and forgotten them, her subconscious then bringing them to the surface later on in the guise of communications from the 'living dead'.

So Protean and precognitive a subconscious is slippery to deal with, but, as has been mentioned, an attempt will be made in the Notes.

There is, however, another form of mediumship, which offers convincing proof of identity, especially when combined with verifiable statements.' It was certainly possessed by Mrs. Willett in her lifetime. Through her mediumship the personalities of her communicators emerged freshly and clearly.

Various published scripts by Miss Cummins demonstrate that she too is a channel that can convey the wholeness of a personality, as well as facts unknown to her that are often startlingly verified. Nowhere is this better shown than in the Cummins-Willett scripts, perhaps partly for the reason (one is permitted to speculate) that here a medium is communicating through another medium, each of them aware of the difficulties of the task. Note, for instance, the ingenious way in which Mrs. Willett manages to transmit proper names of people and places, one of the worst hurdles of mediumship.

The objection might finally be raised that Geraldine Cummins is an author in her own right, quite apart from her 'transmitted' writing, so why could she not simply be continuing this creativity in her subconscious mind, then in perfect good faith dubbing it 'transmitted' when it comes to the surface?

This objection certainly has to be taken into account, but I do not think it is valid. Her novels and plays date back to her youth. Since then she has, most unselfishly and unremuneratively, dedicated herself to psychic research with the best of all guinea pigs, herself. She might have developed into a genuinely creative conscious writer, but she did not give herself the chance. Some of her fiction makes it fairly obvious that she at least cannot draw credible characters if she is not dealing with those known to her in her native Ireland.

Yet in her transmitted writings one can discover some forty-odd personalities, differing markedly and convincingly from each other and from the people known to her.

Now, especially - from these Cummins-Willett scripts, a figure steps forward, completely unlike Miss Cummins or any of her compatriots, a lady who, one feels, is almost aggressively self-drawn. In fact she sometimes patronizes the 'little reporter' as she calls G.C., with so unsparing personal comments that one refuses to believe the most humble subconscious capable of such abasement. But it is not done with any malice; it's just the lady's way.

Lapses from verisimilitude do occur now and then, as Mrs. Willett herself points out in no uncertain terms. She cannot, for instance, battle against strong currents of opinion in the medium's mind. The Englishwoman is radical in her political point of view, the Irishwoman is Conservative, and hence, Mrs. Willett remarks, 'patches are yours and patches are mine.' But they are quite easily distinguishable and they are not many.

The reader must decide for himself how far this formidable yet sensitive and intelligent Englishwoman comes alive—in every sense of the word.

My husband, the writer Francis Hackett (author of *Henry VIII, Francis I* and other works) who died in April, 1962, wrote concerning the Cummins-Willett scripts to an American diplomat friend in February, 1960:

'Mrs. Willett is a massive Briton of the ruling class, and treats G. like an amanuensis. Her mind is disciplined, and the structure of her communications is dominated by her orderly, magisterial habit of mind, plus her dramatic and passionate intimacies, about which she is conscience-stricken as only a scrupulous, self-searching person could be. All this has welled over Geraldine like a tidal wave, and the corroborations have been astounding. No one could have known all that these scripts pour out, not even her sons. They give her sons a clue to themselves not hitherto suspected. Geraldine's authority has only come to her through the exercise of this force she has learned to obey, and to guide in its proper channel.'

Geraldine Cummins has many remarkable gifts, but I think few would consider that they include an 'orderly magisterial habit of mind'.

Francis Hackett had been interested in my interest in psychical research, which began about twenty years ago, mainly because of the Swedenborg biography, but he did not commit himself fully to a belief in the survival of personal consciousness after death, until he read and re-read the Cummins-Willett scripts.

'That settles it,' he said one day to me. 'Now I'm convinced. I've read Geraldine's fiction. She could not possibly have invented Mrs. Willett.'

NOTE

The Cummins-Willett scripts began in 1957 and ended in 1960. Not until they were far along was Miss Cummins told whether the facts stated in them were correct or not.

The first came on August 28, 1957, the second on August 29. Two days later, on August 31, Miss Cummins wrote to the editor, as an aside in a personal letter: I could not write sooner, being suddenly sunk in work. I had a challenge from the S.P.R. [The Society for Psychical Research, London], Mr. Salter [W. H. Salter the Hon. Secretary of the S.P.R.] wrote when I was in Bantry, asking me to do a test. He would send me the name of a sitter and I was to get a communication from sitter's mother who died recently. When I arrived here (her home in Glanmire, Co. Cork, Ireland) a letter and name of a Major in the army was awaiting me. The name meant nothing to me. But I realised I must tackle the job the next day. Otherwise these critical people would say I spent time making inquiries about this blasted major. Any leisure I had from household affairs, I expended on the task for the next two days. Astor (the "control") strove in vain to get the mother from this very ordinary name, then suggested my holding Salter's letter, which might give directive to mother, as he might have known the deceased mother. It worked in the sense that I then got two rather odd scripts, one quite dramatic. Either they're pure invention or there's something that hit the target as the statements were very definite—a kind of story with names. And I don't care if it's all wrong. It seemed to me an impossible task.'

On September 14, 1957, four days after her writing of script 3, and while she was still in Glanmire, Miss Cummins wrote as follows, again as an aside in a personal letter to the editor: 'Re Salter experiment, by holding Salter's first letter to me I got an alleged mother who wrote part of a name "Win". Well, one script was written to her son, whose surname was sent me, the second script contained a direct message to Salter. It was giving him permission and a free hand in writing a "memoir". Someone called "Gerald", it said, was urging this giving permission. Salter replied thanking me "very warmly for undertaking experiment ..." [See page insert, "The Beginning of the Willett Scripts"]. He then said he was passing on to the son the transcript of the scripts.'

Miss Cummins then adds, 'I'm sure the script message is a failure.' It can be seen that Miss Cummins is by no means an automatic believer in her automatic or transmitted scripts.

ORIENTATION

The names variously used in the Notes: 'Mrs. Wills, Mrs. Willett, Winifred', refer to the supposed communicator of the scripts, Winifred Margaret Coombe Tennant, born Serocold. 'A.T.' refers to her older living son, Alexander Coombe Tennant. 'H.T.' refers to her younger living son, Henry Coombe Tennant. 'Astor': if one accepts the reality of spirits, 'Astor' is a sort of pen-name for this spirit, who acts as Miss Geraldine Cummins's 'control', bringing the spirits who wish to communicate and sometimes interpreting for them. But 'Mrs. Willett' herself speaks in these scripts of that part of G.C.'s mind which calls itself 'Astor'.

THE BEGINNING OF
THE CUMMINS-WILLETT
SCRIPTS

I must explain that these scripts of mine have chiefly been investigated by Mr. W. H. Salter and 'Mrs. Willett's' younger son, Major H. Tennant, and her older son Mr. A. Tennant,[1] as well as, much later on, Miss Signe Toksvig.

I was not aware of Major Tennant's existence, nor of that of any of his relatives or friends. I was only informed of his initials and his surname when Mr. Salter wrote a second time to me, initiating the experiment. I had met Mr. Salter twice, a few months after the death of my friend and collaborator, Miss Gibbes. I had not met his wife. He had corresponded with me in regard to my publishing certain records of the Society for Psychical Research in my book Mind in Life and Death. (They had been selected for me by a member of the S.P.R. Council, since I on purpose had done very little reading of psychic literature.) I knew that Mr. Salter had devoted most of his working life to psychic research in the position of Hon. Secretary to the S.P.R., of which I have never been a member.

On August 9, 1957, I received the following letter from Mr. Salter:

The Crown House, Newport, Essex.
7 August, 1957.

---

[1] The surname Coombe Tennant is abbreviated throughout to Tennant or T.

Dear Miss Cummins,

A member of the S.P.R., who lost his mother some months ago, would like to give her an opportunity of sending him a message. I believe that this is a case that would interest you evidentially; I mean because the circumstances are peculiar. I am wondering whether you would be willing to consult Astor on his behalf.

I certainly should not wish to press on you any work that you might find a strain, but the facts so far known to me are definitely curious and of a kind to rouse your keenness in the search for convincing evidence. Would you let me know how you feel about it?

Perhaps you might feel moved to have a try while in Ireland. By the end of the year the evidential significance of the case will probably have declined through the publication of some facts at present known to very few persons, so that if you were so good as to try for a message you might feel disposed to do so fairly soon.

I should propose to restrict the information given you to the name of 'the absent sitter', so as to make a success all the more striking.

My wife joins in good wishes and hopes that your health will benefit from your stay in Ireland.

Yours sincerely,
W. H. Salter.

At the time of the receipt of this letter I was staying on holiday in a small cottage with a friend by the sea, near Bantry in S.W. Eire. I replied to it that I would be very pleased to undertake the experiment as soon as I returned home to Woodville, Glanmire, Co. Cork. But it was impossible to make an experiment where I was staying.

On my return I found a letter from Mr. Salter awaiting me at Woodville.

Letter 2.   Crown House, 22 Aug. '57.

Dear Miss Cummins,

The member about whom I wrote to you, Major A. H. S. Coombe Tennant, M.C., expresses himself as most gratified that you consent to try for a message from his mother. He has sent me four papers in her handwriting. Would you prefer to have these sent you open for inspection, or would you for evidential reasons wish to have them forwarded in a sealed envelope?

Yours very sincerely,
W. H. Salter.

Owing to my capacity for object reading, I preferred to try without the specimens of the mother's handwriting, and the first three scripts were obtained by me without them. So these three, which contained definite evidence of Mrs. Willett's surviving memory, with some correct indications of her character could not be said to be aided by psychometry.

Before I obtained script 4, the four papers, samples of the mother's handwriting, came by post to me to Woodville.

In script 4 Mrs. Willett makes some intimate and correct allusions to her background of Wales and the part it played in her life. It did not play a part in mine, as the following facts show.

I once stayed one night in Wales in a house about two miles from Swansea with a stranger to me, a lady very interested in my Cleophas Scripts, because of their value to her in their early Christian history. So our conversation was about this series of books. Otherwise my acquaintanceship with Wales consisted solely in my seeing it through a railway carriage window during my numerous journeys in a fast train between Fishguard and Paddington in the early morning or late evening. Since 1921, with the exception of the war years, I have travelled thus about twice a year between London and my home in Co. Cork.

Fortunately for this experiment Mrs. Willett and her family had no connection with Southern Ireland. Equally I was in the same position as regards Wales. It is true that for a number of years my uncle Professor Lyle Cummins was attached to Cardiff University and directed a fine crusade against tuberculosis in Wales. But he was a very over-occupied man, so our paths did not cross each other's except for one day in the nineteen-twenties, when he eloquently tried to persuade me wholly to abandon psychical research for my literary work.

The first six scripts of this series of Willett writings, conducted by post by Mr. W. H. Salter, were obtained when I was living in S. Eire in the country where I am busy with various occupations connected with my home and family.

In script 5 Winifred (Mrs. Willett) wrote of her psychic work and of Gerald and his wife Betty. These two names recalled to me that I and my friend Miss Gibbes at the request of Dame Edith Lyttelton had gone to Woking one day in June, 1959, where I gave Lord Balfour and his wife Lady Betty a sitting. The communicators were a relative of Lord Balfour and Lady Constance Lytton, Lady Betty's sister. I travelled to my home in Eire two or three days later, and, the war intervening, 3 we were not able to meet again for further sittings as proposed by Lord Balfour.

In script 5, obtained by me on September 24, 1951, at Woodville, my communicator Winifred (Mrs. Willett) described her early sittings and wrote 'I insisted on being called Mrs. Wills.' When staying in Bantry in August, 1957, with my friend Mrs. Smyth, I had seen a good deal of her friend, Mrs. Wills. Again in script 5, Winifred wrote, 'I am Mrs. Wills. *That is not quite right.* Never mind Wills, press on.'

I began to realise that the surname of Mrs. Wills had obviously blocked the writing of Mrs. Willett's name. I became almost certain that Major Tennant's mother was Mrs. Willett, the pseudonym of a remarkable transmitting writer, who had given sittings to Gerald, Lord Balfour. The information conveyed to me in script 6, written at Woodville, Glanmire, on September 26, 1957, strengthened to a certainty my view that Mrs. Willett was Mrs. Tennant. I had fairly recently read about her psychic work in a chapter in G. N. M. Tyrrell's book *The Personality of Man*, the only reading I'd done about it, besides a brief mention of it in H. F. Saltmarsh's *Evidence of Personal Survival from Cross-Correspondences*. This did not bring me any further information about the lady's life, as her identity was still a close secret, known only to a few people with whom I was not acquainted.

In mid-October I returned to my flat in Chelsea, and when Mr. Salter called on me at the end of October, I gathered that the object of his visit was to ask me to obtain further scripts from Mrs. Willett and to post them to her son Major Tennant. I refused to do so, as I was going to have a very occupied winter in London.

When I set out on this series of writings, Major Tennant and his family were completely unknown to me. I had, therefore, never heard of his initials and surname, which was all the information Mr. Salter had given me. There have been experiments made when a fictitious surname of an alleged deceased person has been imparted to a medium, and it has led to the medium weaving a fictitious narrative about it. In a cynical mood, most unfairly I had suspected that Mr. Salter might be playing the same game. All the better, I reflected. If my storytelling subconscious invents a yarn of this kind the game will be up after I have written two or three scripts. So as I had other affairs to attend to, the experiment would be fairly brief in character. I did not then reckon for a moment that Mrs. Willett would command my time to the extent of some forty-four scripts during the next couple of years.

In January, 1958, I read a first short obituary notice of Mrs. Tennant, which revealed that she was Mrs. Willett. The few facts revealed in it about her life were not enlightening as to her personality and family.

But in the early spring of 1958 I found that I had time to resume working on this case. So on February 14, 1958, I wrote script 7, which I posted to Mr. Salter.

It is to be noted that I did not meet either of Mrs. Willett's two sons until after script 40 had been written on November 23, 1959.

My first meeting with a son of Mrs. Willett took place when Major Tennant called on me in Chelsea on December 3, 1959. He could only stay a few minutes as he was leaving London that afternoon. Subsequently in February, 1960, I spent an evening with his elder brother and the latter's wife and made their acquaintance.

All the Cummins-Willett scripts were written when I was alone, and in most instances in the bright light of the early morning before I had met anybody. Nor does the theory that mediums obtain through telepathy from a presiding sitter the veridical communications given at a sitting need to be taken into consideration in any study of the Cummins-Willett scripts.

NOTE TO THE THIRD EDITION

Since the first printing of this book, a word for word comparison of the printed text with the original scripts of Miss Cummins was made by means of tape-recording. As a result, some inaccuracies, due to erroneous copying, have been corrected in this edition. They are not essential to the evidential value of the scripts.

THE SCRIPTS
AND NOTES

August 28, 1957. Script 1.

Astor comes. What a task you set me. You ask me to find the mother of a Major Tennant, but I cannot pick up a wavelength from a name. Oh, very well! I will try. Wait for a little while and suspend all thought but the desire that I find this soul who you say has recently died. It is useless; I cannot pick up any line. But hold the letter of W.H. If he has any contact with the mother, even in correspondence, I may through his vibratory field link up with her. Put the letter to your forehead.

Oh! I am sorry for W. H. He seems to have had some worry or argument in connection with someone who has to do with writing and secrets to be kept. People aren't in agreement. It has to do with things that happened many years ago. It is in a muddle to me. I can't make it out at present. But I have got on to another line. This is interesting. There is a lady who has come to me, not I to her. She decided she would look out for a light, (1). She understands that if she writes herself they won't accept what she records, so she is showing me her memories and her mind.

I see her as a very old woman in the eighties, very fragile. She lost a son when he was only a youth. He was killed when he was nineteen or twenty, I think. I see the memory of that agonising news. It is like a scar on the mind. Well, she has found him again after many, many years, so it was not in the last war he was killed; the First World War, she says. One can't have it both ways, by finding him I lost another very dear son. It is a middle-aged man, early forties. I think she is trying to show me his likeness. He was very good to her when she was old and ailing. She thinks now she may have been too possessive in her love for him. But there was some great bond between them. He was her youngest—only a little boy, and he was such a comfort, such a help, when the other grown-up son was killed. I see the picture of the mother watching her little boy playing and her fixing all her love on him, and her heart prays that he will never have to fight in any future war. It is because of the shock of the loss of her first son that she clings as it were to the little boy.

Her mind is going over these far-off memories now, and she shows them to me. You ask for a name. I hear the sound Wyn or Win . . . can't get more. Then there is someone still in the physical body. She shows me the name—hard to perceive—Henry, or is it Harry? I can't get more. It is fading. Perhaps Win or Wyn was her name. I think it is hers, but I may be mistaken. I think you had better call me tomorrow. You are tired. Tomorrow hold both of W.H.'s letters and perhaps I can get closer. It was very difficult, so faint today. I think Win or Wyn was too anxious. She was trying so hard to show me different memories, and I couldn't perceive them (2).

(1) In scripts of this sort the communicator often speaks of being attracted to the medium through perceiving a psychic light emanating from the person. This paragraph, which Astor finds 'a muddle', has a real significance that emerges later on. 'W.H.' are the initials of Mr. Salter.

(2) H.T., the communicator's younger, living son, comments on the statements by Astor: 'My mother died at 81. My brother, Christopher, was killed in action, 3.9.17, at the age of nineteen.' (Through finding him in the beyond after her own death the communicator of course 'lost' the living son, who is forty-four).

Her relationship with H.T. in her lifetime is said by him to have been correctly described by Astor. Her love was too possessive, yet there was a 'special bond' between them, this was the expression she generally used, in spite of their differences of opinion and temperament. She often used to say how good he was to her. He was only a little boy when the grown-up son was killed.

The three first letters of her name are, as stated, 'Win', but she was never called that. The name is correctly given in full later on.

The living son's name is Henry, he has never been called Harry, except a long time ago by an aunt. In regard to this mistake of Astor's, Miss Cummins adds this note:

'My favourite brother Harry was killed in Gallipoli. I had been talking of him with an old friend and thinking of him. He was always called Harry. Hence no doubt the difficulty in getting the name "Henry" through.'

August 29, 1957. Script 2.

Astor is here. Yes, it is quite different this time. There was too much emotion on the last occasion. I see again the old lady, or rather her mind, and she shows me the letter W. That means it is one of her initials. I use the word lady in her connection in the old-fashioned sense of the word. She was sensitive, cultured, but not learned and had a high code of honour during her lifetime, which extends back to the Victorian age. She grew up then, and the many conventions concerning girls in that period led her in part to have a fear or shrinking from the present age, in which the modern young woman so often observes no conventions. She was incapable of doing anything in bad taste. Despite her retiring disposition, she was a woman of the world and mixed with ease in the Society of her period (1).

But she was and is most unusual in one respect, and it is the fundamental reason for a mood that led her at times to want to be alone, to shrink from close contact with other minds. This was because of her extraordinary gift for penetrating into the deeper levels of the mind. To put it crudely, she would and often did live in two worlds. She tells me that when she was a child she began to get automatic writing. But she was doubtful about it and, being extremely sensitive, pursued the practice only occasionally when alone. Later on, years after she was married, the power greatly increased. She felt that she had better get advice about it, and she succeeded in obtaining wise guidance. She is very anxious to get a message through today about the work she did in the past (2).

Now Win is happy and lively. What a contrast from yesterday when she revealed to me a great sorrow in her past life. It was redeemed only by the little boy. Other people were kind, but there was a double burden. His father was suffering as she was (3). That little boy was her salvation, then and for the rest of her life, he loved and served her. She feels that she cannot write now of all she owes him. It is too intimate, too private a matter (4).

There are others here today. They have come about a matter that concerns W.H. There are several impressions. It is rather confusing. Wait.

I have dropped the threads, or rather only one presses on my attention. I will try and describe him. He is allowing me to look into his mind. He had in the past a capacity for close analysis, a metaphysical passion only perhaps to be found in a Scotsman. He was partly Scottish, I am sure. This was balanced by a steadiness, a shrewdness, inherited from ancestors on his mother's side. She was English, I think. They were distinguished people of great ability. Now I am hearing your name— Geraldine. No, it is the masculine equivalent. Yes, I have it—Gerald. Gerald says, 'I would like to show you my old disguise.' Now it rises up like the ghost of Samuel, when he appeared to the Witch of Endor. I see Gerald as he was in the last years of his life. He appears as a very old man: I would say he was on the verge of ninety, so frail, so stricken by the news of the outbreak of war. But he has an invincible courage. He is a scholar by nature. But he comes to London and though he has difficulty in walking he goes about, tries to get war work to do. At least he can advise, speak. It is all rather pitiable, his trying to do war work when he was near dissolution. He died during the war. It pleases him to show me his exit from the stage of earthly life (5).

Now he turns away and converses with Win. They are old friends. He draws from the shadows a young man. I see the name Francis. The young man's mind is like his own, scholarly. But his life was cut short in some sport. There is an accident, a crash. He died from a fall, away in some foreign country. Win is so pleased, so excited to meet him. 'I wasn't mistaken,' she says. 'Of course we knew each other quite well.'

I don't quite understand the connection between these two. They met and talked on a number of occasions in some odd, unusual circumstances (6).

Now Gerald is interrupting them. They have had consultations about some business or affair of a mundane character. He tells Win that she must not miss this opportunity. It is for her to convey her wishes, though no doubt they will be ignored, but he hopes that at least they will not be ignored by W.H. It seems to concern papers, writing a memoir to be published, I think. She always blocked the publication when on earth. Gerald would have liked at least some of these reminiscences to be published. But she was a very determined lady, (7). She forbade it. He considers that, though in part justified, it does not matter now. It all concerned people so long ago. He tells her that she has a morbid conscience.

'Very well,' she says, 'as in *Pilgrims Progress* the Pilgrim will drop that heavy burden. Oh, it was such a weight. I shall be brazen and wicked and shock.'

Now here is Win's brief message:

'Dear W.H. I lift my ban entirely. That is to say, I trust you absolutely. You have a free hand. Publish what you like. We are all forgotten and were, in any case, as I see now, people of little moment during our passage through life. My memory is still rather in tatters, but I seem to recollect that I left restrictions as to what should be published. Scrap them. I am convinced—no, I think it is "concerned", W.H.S.—that people should believe (8).

'There comes to me from the earth such a feeling of oppression, of worrying, of anxiety, of fear of death, and all is derived from non-belief. If they could but realise half the glory, even a fragment of the peace of this life I now experience. Oh! If I could only make them accept it, there might at last be some rationality. Rationalists are irrational, and it makes such a confusion, creates so much fear, when death, that deliverer approaches.

'Dear Death (9)

Yours,

'Win.'

Astor, they have faded away. I cannot get anything more. I took down from dictation the message from W.

(1) H.T.: 'This conventional picture is in fact the kind of impression my Mother sought to make on strangers.' He adds, 'It is by no means incorrect as far as it goes, but it is largely superficial—-just how superficial is shown by a later passage in the script.'

(Ed.) An early diary, 1902, shows her as decidedly in the London society of the period. Travelling, racing, fashionable dinners and doings were part of her life. She disliked the country in winter. From the same diary: 'How can anyone wilfully pass one day in the country in England in winter! It is the abomination of desolation . . . Tomorrow I go to London, thank Heaven!'

(2) H.T.: 'My mother's need for solitude was a marked feature of her personality. She shrank at times not only from strangers but also from old acquaintances. She never explained the reason, at least not to me.'

Astor's comment, 'She would and often did live in two worlds,' is agreed to by H.T. 'My mother often said as much. I think she used this expression. But she never mentioned her psychic-powers.'

Astor states: 'When she was a child she began to get automatic writing.' H.T. does not know if this is correct. In a later script it mentions that 'Winifred's' psychic experiences did begin in her childhood. They were rudely trampled on, and went underground.

H.T. comments: 'I thought it [automatic writing] first developed after the death of my sister Daphne in 1908. I find it very interesting that neither in this passage nor anywhere else in the G.C. scripts, so far, is there any mention of Daphne, whose death was the causal ancestor of the whole series of Willett scripts. I do not know if any reference to Daphne exists in the published material about Mrs. Willett. If G. C.'s knowledge about my mother is derived from the book *Christopher*, where the death of Daphne is naturally given less prominence than the death of Christopher, it is hardly surprising that Daphne is not mentioned in the scripts. But even if the scripts are the result of direct contact between Astor and my mother, it still does not surprise me that Daphne is not mentioned.'

'My mother's diaries,' continues H.T., 'which neither my brother nor I had seen until after her death, show clearly that the death of Daphne was a shattering blow, under which my mother's character virtually disintegrated and became reconstructed in quite a new form. From a gay young woman, fond of people and Ascot and parties, she became, at any rate in her private life almost a recluse. Now if Astor had really been allowed to look into my mother's mind and memories, he could hardly have failed to notice this watershed in her life; but a later passage in the script suggests that my mother was not laying herself open to inspection, and if this is so, I think it very likely that she would not have admitted Astor to her memories of Daphne. My reason for saying this is that she never mentioned this crisis in her life to my brother or myself. She often spoke of Daphne and we knew that her loss was one of the sorrows of her life, but we never guessed how profound an effect it had on her. In considering why it was that my mother had never mentioned her automatic writing to either of us, my brother and I came to the conclusion that that part of her life was, to use the words of the script, "too intimate, too private a matter" to be discussed even with her own children. While, therefore, it is natural that in this experiment in communication she should be obliged to refer to her powers of automatic writing in order to introduce what follows, I think it not surprising that she should have said as little as possible about the circumstances in which they developed.'

(Ed.) These comments were not given to the automatist until the series of scripts was nearly at an end.

Miss Cummins adds a note that in a much later script 'Winifred' wrote movingly of her grief at the death of her baby girl, here called 'Daff'. This abbreviation was never used, but automatists often get only part of a name. By that time, one presumes, she had acquired confidence in her secretary. G.C. also adds: 'I was very moved by the emotion of grief when this later script was being written.'

Miss Cummins states that she had never even heard of the book *Christopher*, which H.T. mentions as a possible source, but here of course one is in the presence of the argument that the subconscious of a medium can draw on any recorded source in the world, be it in books or in living minds.

(3) H.T.: 'I think this is psychologically accurate. My father always leaned heavily on my mother, and in a shared sorrow she would have been more support to him than he to her.'

(4) H.T. notes that his mother's extravagant praise of him to strangers is like her.

(5) 'Gerald' is later revealed to be Gerald, Lord Balfour. It is correct that he was partly Scottish, that his mother was English, that his ancestors were distinguished and of great ability, that he was on the verge of ninety, a scholar by nature, died during the war. Possibly he tried to get war work.

(6) Gerald Balfour was an old friend of 'Winifred'. The young man named 'Francis' is later on identified as Francis Balfour, who was killed young by a fall while mountain-climbing abroad. 'Win' recognises him, as he was a communicator in the Cross-Correspondences (page 4), in which she took part. This was not known to Miss Cummins, as yet unaware of the identity of 'Winifred'. Astor seems only to know that the two met and talked 'in some odd' circumstances.

(7) 'She was a very determined lady,' agreed to by H.T. Later on it is revealed in a script that there is a question of 'a memoir to be published', urged by 'Gerald', objected to by 'Winifred'. (This refers to the *Palm Sunday* case, not published till 1960.)

(8) The passage in which 'Winifred' lifts the ban on publication is regarded by H.T. as 'so true to my mother's style of expression that as I see it I seem to see the words in her handwriting'.

(9) H.T.: 'Less characteristic, especially the latter part. But my mother often used stock phrases in speaking about the afterlife.

"Dear Death" would be quite characteristic.'

13 September 10, 1957. Script 3.

Astor, I think that your other case must wait, as there is a small group here today. They are brought by that Lady Win. She is very persistent, and she has persuaded these two men to come and reinforce her power. I get the names Fred and Win. No, she says, they are not the names of a man and a woman. Put these two names together and you will get mine—Fredwin—she shakes her head. Yes, I see, it is Winifred. Winifred wants to write herself. She is nervous about it, but most anxious to try, so I will help her (1).

'Winifred.

'What shall I call you? I can't remember (word illegible).' (I said, Geraldine Cummins.) 'Geraldine Cummins. G.C.

'Dear G.C. Pray forgive my intrusion. I can only excuse myself by saying that I was, like you, an automatist during my past life.—Oh, a mere amateur. But it was an engrossing interest at one time. I was eager to investigate from this side, and now I perceive how very difficult it is for us poor souls to do so. I received an impression from Mrs. W.H. to set out on a search for you. It was with real pleasure that I responded. But our first meeting was unfortunate. This I write to explain, and if you will be so kind please send my explanation to our mutual investigator (2).'

(I said I would. G.C.)

'Thank you.

'Please tell W.H. that Mutual Selection, (3), is the explanation that solves the problem. The confusion in my first message through you was in a curious way due to my being in a sense compelled to select from your memories while you were selecting from mine. I am expressing what I mean very inadequately. It was as if I dived into a very deep pool—a dark memory of yours. Your sorrow for a loss in battle of a Henry or Harry of yours. That old memory of yours stirred up what my friend G. here calls a repressed complex of mine.

'Your Harry or Henry memory led me to see again my little son playing—my Henry or Harry soon after the news came of my eldest son being killed in action. It was the same war. But my Harry still lives on earth. When he grew up he went into the Army. You lost your Harry and that memory stirred up the awful pain I suffered when I lost my George (4). Our two memories blended. It has been explained to me by G., my friend here, that when I suffered that pain of loss, I did, as the years passed, forget it, so that was why I did not prevent my Harry from going into the Army. He fought in that hateful Second World War, and again I experienced the old fear and anxiety for a son at the front. But that is beside the point.

'What I wish W.H. to realise [is] that seeing and, well, feeling your memory of sorrow for your Harry, it opened the floodgates, as it were. I experienced the memory I had buried alive for many, many years, and is what is called a complex, so this explains the confusion and no doubt failure of that first message (5).

'I see now how we can wander and get lost in the memories of the automatist when we so-called dead try to communicate. This kind of mutual selection is bound to be what my friend Gerald calls a "mixed grill". But in the communication of the second message to W.H., whose letter is beside you, I meant what I said. I was clear and collected, as clear as if I was a magistrate sitting on the Bench giving his (Note: might be "her") verdict. I was one, you know, who sat on that hard bench (6).

'Now I am getting confused again.

'Must end,

(signed) 'Winifred.'

'Tell W.H. I can't succeed from here. It gets so confused and I forget everything when I try. I only remember bits.'

(1) The communicator's first name is mentioned correctly for the first time. Note the device of putting two other names together to make the one. As an automatist herself in this life Winifred had knowledge of the difficulty in transmitting names.

(2) 'Mrs. W.H.' is Mrs. W. H. Salter, the former Helen Verrall.

The 'mutual investigator' is of course Mr. W. H. Salter, who, together with H.T., initiated these scripts. 'Winifred' now communicates directly and not through the control, Astor. She mentions that she was an automatist herself, though an amateur, both facts unknown to G.C.

(3) 'Mutual Selection.' The phrase and the phenomenon are discussed in the Balfour 'Study of the Psychological Aspects of Mrs. Willett's Mediumship', (*Proceedings of the S.P.R.*, May, 1935, p. 200). In 1955 G.C. had read extracts from this great work in two books—Tyrrell's *The Personality of Man*, and Saltmarsh on the Cross-Correspondences— which is all she ever read of the Balfour Study. In neither of these extracts does the topic of Mutual Selection come in. This is relevant here, as the communicator is worrying because the automatist has hesitated between Henry and Harry as the correct name of her living son. Miss Cummins's brother, always called Harry, was killed in the First World

War. That memory having been aroused in her, 'offsets' one might say on the communicator's mind, and the wrong form of the name is given. A 'mutual', if involuntary, selection, has taken place.

(4) One of the names of Winifred's dead son was 'George', but it was never used. He was known as 'Christopher'. Quite frequently in mediumistic sittings a person's less used name is selected, for whatever reason.

(5) H.T. writes that his mother did not repress her grief, she in fact frequently commented on the loss of her son.

(6) H.T.: 'The mention of my mother's work as a magistrate and the way it is introduced are both characteristic. She was extremely proud of this work, and remained so till the end of her life ... I was often present when my mother met strangers for the first time, and I noticed she almost always took an early opportunity to refer to her work on the Bench. She often introduced the subject rather abruptly, but quite logically, as in the script.' This important bit of evidence was unknown to G.C.

Woodville, September 22, 1957. Script 4.

Astor is here. This very determined soul Gerald has been conversing with me. He is the leader of a Group and wishes to seize this opportunity to use, he says, Winifred, as a kind of liaison officer (1) in several brief communications. EBG (2) has been consulted and has agreed to this experiment if you can find the time. She says you can trust Mr. Salter to be intelligent in this matter. Here is Gerald.

(Handwriting changes; much smaller).

'Gerald:

'Dear W.H.

'I have taken the liberty to organise or try to organise Mrs. T. [Winifred]. She is very willing but is extremely nervous. I have suggested that today she tries to establish herself by writing of her origins. On another occasion she can write or endeavour to write a personal message to her son. The wheel makes full circle. As in the case of very old people still in the physical body, those who have experienced the full span of life on earth when they come here recall most easily fragmentary memories of the distant past and fail to recollect near events. As Mrs. T. says quite correctly, we seem to swim in the sea of the automatist's subliminal mind, and any strong current may sweep us away from the memory objectives we have in view, before we attempt to communicate. So neither of us can guarantee what, if any, identification she may write today or any other day. At any rate, the automatist is more isolated in this country-quiet from other human beings than in a town, so Mrs. T. is less likely helplessly to drift in the strong pull of tide or current, and thereby fail in his [her?] object-identification.'

Script 4a, same day. (Handwriting changes again.)

'Astor. Now this other communicator who is still very near to the earth level, as she is a newcomer, will write. I shall endeavour to help her in the writing.'

(Another change of handwriting.)

'Winifred:

'Dear G. C.

'Listen—please listen—Ah! the word leaps up to me. It is Morgan. Hold on to Morgan. Now there is a famous cricketer, W. G. Grace (3). Cut off Grace. It's W.G. I want. If you add on W.G. to Morgan, you have a name that may not appear to make sense, but it does make sense to me. I spent many happy years of my life loving, living in Morganwg. My mother too came from there (4). This has to do with origin of the species. My husband and [last three words between the lines] my species or race. The most important events in my life took place in Morganwg. I mean those that relate to origins, the birth of what we are, the mould of our creation as regards influences. I found my husband in Morganwg (5).

'There are memories of other births there. I think of my family, of my babies who grew into little boys and were often naughty, mischievous little boys. How often they played about in the pretty woodland country of Morganwg. By birth, I mean for my little boys all the early years, formative influences, not merely the incident of birth itself. That may take place anywhere. But the soul is only gradually born into the body. It creeps in during those first seven years. But I myself lived those seven years of my life mostly elsewhere (6). That did not signify overmuch because, through my mother, who was my principal influence in those seven years, I belonged to Morgan W.G. Yes, I was brought up in England. Morganwg which is (pencil note by G.C. "broke off script, returned later", new page begins) not English was the country of my adoption. It is different from England in many ways. The people who live in it are very independent. They are wilder in temperament and more imaginative than the English, perhaps less stable. It is the land they belong to that makes the difference. There are ranges of mountains and gloomy valleys in parts of the principality, and a long sea coast. My husband and his family belonged to it. My sons and my husband were of it, so that land became a part of me. My mother also belonged to it and brought me there (pencil note by G. C. "I, G. C., produced handwriting of Winifred").

'What is this paper you show me? (7). Oh, yes, the Memorial Day and the Lodge (8). The Lodge, of course, wakes up memory. The many years flowing by. But how can I grasp these many memories? They are like heavy showers of rain. You cannot separate the raindrops, pick them out one by one.

A Lodge may be anything from a three-roomed cottage to a mansion. I would suggest that a mansion is more descriptive than a cottage in this case (9).

'When I was young and visited that Lodge, the people living in it rather alarmed me (10). I felt so shy and nervous. That was how it began with the Lodge. I little thought then how much it would become a part of me. Generations had lived there of one family. How pretty the girls were that belonged to that family, and oh! how attractive. What was I in comparison—a very cramped, unattractive I, a very small I that diminished and diminished in my own view. Oh these false shames of youth and even mature years. But I must not ramble.

'No, Cad, No, now I am trying to get something Cadre, French for frame. No, please, listen. Cadre and O for Ox, put them together, Cadre Ox. It is not right. Do listen. Yes, that was my husband's frame, frame of a photograph—my husband-to-be, Cadox, Cadox Lodge. It was my husband's family home, he was central there. He was the link. He was the link. How kind he was to me when I was shy and nervous. Later the link bound me to Cadox. How happy we were there, living there husband and wife, how the memories are all about me like resounding echoes in a mountain pass—all the years, dear, sweet years, so much happiness and also as in every life times of grief, hours of pain. Illness, good health, parties, joy of quiet and calm solitary hours when one seeks and finds one's soul, things to manage, household duties—my boys' social duties. How crammed is one's life with detail! How difficult to pick out from the mass what signifies in memory. Cadox Lodge presents all that mass to me.

'There was Dorothy, there was Eveleen and there was Fred. Now I hear the ringing of wedding bells, honeymoon, but later the return to Cadox.

'Everything then pivots round Cadox, where the generations had lived and died of my husband's family. I mean that it was at least a permanent home for my generation, a past generation, and for my son

(11). *Confusion, can't hold on. But Swan rests on a black sea, a symbol, not a crest, connect it with Cadox Winifred.'*
  (Underlined in script.) (12)

(1) H.T.: 'This expresses very well what I had in mind when the experiment was conceived.' (Ed.) Very interesting in the light of the scripts dealing with the work of the 'group' that were to follow. But G.C. had only been given to suppose that a son wanted a message from his mother, in whose continued existence, however, he did not really believe.
  (2) E.B.G. is Miss E. B. Gibbes, also known as 'Bea', whose devoted and scholarly work in connection with Miss Cummins's automatic writings is well known. She died suddenly on December 18, 1951.
  (3) H.T. comments that his mother was ignorant of sport. The point, also mentioned by him, is, however, that the name W. G. Grace is used to transmit a difficult Welsh name.
  (Ed.) In an early diary Mrs. Willett mentions going to cricket matches as part of country life. And G.C. was fond of sport, had played cricket with her brothers.
  (4) Morganwg (Welsh for Glamorganshire) was a place where the communicator did spend many years. It is correct that her mother came from Wales.
  (5) H.T. comments that this might be true in a figurative sense, though she met her husband first in Austria, but in Morganwg she would have 'found' him better than in fashionable London.
  (6) H.T.: 'My mother was born in Gloucestershire in a house which my grandfather sold soon afterwards. We are not certain where she spent the first seven years of her life, but we do not think it was in Wales.' (7) G.C. brings out a paper with the communicator's handwriting on it. It mentions a 'Lodge' and a 'memorial'.
  (8) H.T.: 'The Lodge referred to in the paper was the Provost's Lodge at Eton. It had not occurred to me how appropriate the word would be to call up memories of my mother's early married life.
  (Cadoxton Lodge and Oliver Lodge.)'
  (9) H.T.: 'Cadoxton Lodge was quite a big house.'
  (10) H.T.: 'None of my father's family lived at Cadoxton.'
  (11) Near the end of this script Winifred tries to correct the misstatement that her husband's family lived at Cadoxton, after first in a very ingenious way having conveyed the main part of the odd name—Cadre-Ox. She explains that she and her husband lived there, from her present point of view a 'past generation'.

H.T. comments her remark that her husband's family rather alarmed her: 'I suppose that mother might have found the faded society beauties like Dolly and Evie pretty formidable, but I always understood that she had a great deal of self-confidence.'

She mentions, correctly, the names of her two sisters-in-law and that of her brother-in-law, 'Fred', who is F. W. H. Myers.

H.T. states that his parents spent most of their early-married life in London and did not move permanently to Cadoxton until 1908.

(12) H.T.: 'Presumably Swansea which was about ten miles from Cadoxton. "Black" is not understood. There seems no particular reason why Swansea should be mentioned here. It would be associated with my grandmother, who came from Derwen Fawr Manor near Swansea, and with my mother's work as a prison visitor which meant much to her.'

(Ed.) There was also a Swansea Canal that the family had much to do with.

General remarks on script 4. H.T. states that although his brother A.T. does not feel that these scripts convey his mother's style, 'nor is their content at all what I would have said was typical,' he himself does not entirely agree, adding: 'There are uncharacteristic features, but a lot of it seems to me fairly typical, though nowhere vividly so.'

(Ed.) It must be remembered that 'Mrs. Willett' did not let her sons share in her secret life. A.T. tells that when, after his mother's death, someone mentioned 'Mrs. Willett' to him he asked 'who is Mrs. Willett?' H.T. was informed of Mrs. Willett's identity in 1944, though his mother never knew this.

These are, of course, only the beginning scripts. After the series was finished, A.T. said of one particular long script, 'That is one hundred per cent my mother!'

G.C. adds: 'The names of Morganwg, Derwen Fawr, Cadoxton Lodge, as well as the family names and relationships are unknown to me. As for my acquaintance with Wales, some years ago I stayed one night at Swansea with a lady I had not met previously; we discussed psychical research and my books as far as my recollection goes. Her name I've found in an old address book, it was Lady Edwards, Hendre-foilav, Sketty, Swansea. Many years ago I stayed two nights with an uncle in Monmouthshire.'

September 24, 1957. Script 5.

Astor comes. I bring with me the lady with the darting mind. She tells me she is Mrs. Wills, and she smiles. She is prepared to write today, so I shall give her the pen (1).

'Winifred,

(G.C. presents a paper with Winifred's handwriting.)

'This paper, my handwriting again,—memorials—memorials to death, so stupid (2). Thoughts of death about this writing. But how ignorant, how foolish, when everything is life, rather relentless life sometimes. George, my son (3) is alive. Why brood about decay and death? Perishing, perishing, when it is all being recreated, reborn immediately. That is what is happening. We shall all be changed in the twinkling of an eye. Didn't St. Paul say that? But we shall still be We I must add. I know that as an experience now.

'Cambridge, yes Cambridge. This writing brings me childhood's memories of Cambridge, my life there in that country.

Cherry, Cherries. Yes, Cherry. Try and listen, please. Oh, stupid. My father, how big he seemed to me when I was so small.'

(G.C. had to break off.)

'Winifred,

Yes, I understand, a break. You could not help that. Now I want to try and concentrate. It is important what I give you today. I am directed by a Group here—people who once lived at Cambridge, or were connected with it (4). Ah, good, you have caught that. They say, give a general outline of yourself, origin, origins of species (5) first, then the significance of your life. Well, I must finish with my origins and write of sig—significance, then the—the epilogue. Morganwg gave me power (6)—power to do this automatic writing, to listen, to pick up. It was a kind of recharging, if you know what I mean, then it was mostly elsewhere the power was used. But I must get back to Cambridge. I loved it in a different way from Morganwg. After all, in one's childhood there is experience of beauty, joy and sharp pain, too—all the memories that crowd from this paper to me. But I often was back in Cambridge in adult life. I stayed there with good friends (7). I lived in London too. There was the social life of that time. You can't believe how different it was from today—Roman Empire at its zenith! How proud they all were, how small! Cambridge was far better. There they looked ahead. Deep thinkers come (might be came) from there. Dear Alma Mater (8).

'Now, please listen—I have been bidden by the Group to give this one reminiscence of childhood to follow. It has been a long time hidden away, but, like some little treasure, must be taken out and dusted, examined—in this case though it may hurt the owner who is reminded by it of the child's pain. There is a succession of me's throughout my life—psychic units all building up. The outward semblance, the personality varying, as each psychic unit acts its part upon the stage, then passes on. But behind it is one's real self, fundamental, greater than its personality. That is what the Group here say. It is what is permanent (9).

'Now. This small child Winifred whose part I shall now represent was a dream—day-dreamer. I loved my dreams, and when I was struggling with pot-hooks and hangers I would forget myself on occasions and would slip out to my dreams (10). Then it happened that when I was walking in celestial places I would be brought back by my teacher. I remember still the ruler's rap on the knuckles and my own shock of pain. (Note, last sentence written very wildly.) After that, reproof, scolding, and I was in a daze, vacant, I couldn't explain. I couldn't speak of my dreams—so clear to me. I must remain silent.' (Note: Last words wildly written.) (Note by G. C.: 'Please write less wildly.')

'I shall try. Yes. One moment while I collect myself.

'I was punished and scolded. I remained unrepentant. Apparently I wouldn't, couldn't, speak of it. Then the teacher reported me as being in one of my sulky moods, and that made my mother sad. Her sadness hurt me (11). I was afraid of what she might say about my dreams.— Walking in celestial places! It sounded blasphemous or very odd, and to have had my dreams trampled on would have deeply wounded me. How true was what the poet wrote: "Tread softly, you tread on my dreams," Yeats, yes, he wrote that. A strange man, but he understood the psychic world (12).

'But I must continue. Later in my childhood, I mean when I was a girl, I used to get scribbles of automatic writing (13). Because my day-dreaming was so ill-treated, I did not tell anyone about it. I was doubtful too, as I had grown to be critical as to its source. I tell you all this because it had its influence all through my life. It sowed in my soul a deep fear, and in my adult life I harvested its grain. When in my married life I began again to get automatic writing, my childhood's fear of disgrace through day-dreaming led me not to talk about it to people. Oh! There were other reasons too—the conventions of the time. But I would like W.H. to know the real fundamental reason, the source of my reluctance to sit with people, and later to permit publications about my writings, and I only permitted it in a limited sense, and I insisted on being called Mrs. Wills in anything that was printed about my work.

'I used to get my writing alone, of course. Frequently my dear husband asked to be present at it and I always refused. It was, as I realise now, that fear created in childhood that caused me to shrink from this ordeal. When I did at last let Charles witness the writing, I think the fear was so repressed, as Gerald tells me, it created a storm in my mind. Probably, G.C., you won't believe me. But I passed right out during that sitting with my husband. Did you ever go unconscious when you wrote? No, you say. Oh, you have been fortunate. I felt so cheap, so drained after it. But Charles was very kind and understanding about it (14).

'Now I must continue and tell of how it developed. My communicators, the Cam group, were pressing me to write for others. I resisted for a time, because of that fear, which was like a little ghost seated at the back of my brain—a spectre haunting me. Of course I wasn't aware of all this. It was a buried alive fear that oppressed me. But eventually I consulted a very clever woman about the writings. Oh, how understanding she was too. She gave me wise advice and exactly what I needed, courage. The quality of mercy is not strained. It droppeth as the gentle rain from heaven. Portia, you know. I shall always be grateful to Portia, my clever friend, for my encouragement. You, G.C., must know how we need that merciful encouragement! W. H. Give Portia's daughter my love. But she has heard from me already (15).

'Later in my life, or rather very soon after I was with Portia, the communicators got their wish. I gave writings to a scientist (16)—sat with him—I mean sometimes speaking, sometimes taking down what the communicator was dictating to me. It came sometimes just in bits and scraps (17). Gerald, my friend over here, became very interested. He was alive on earth then, and I think I did my best work for him. He used to talk to me quite a lot about it. It was all rather over my head. Oh such analysing! So I must confess I pretended I wasn't much interested in the research for which he had such a passion.

But I really was very interested. Only all such talk was like pulling to pieces my other-world dreams, and anyhow he couldn't simplify and used such long words (18). I sometimes didn't know whether I was on my head or my heels when I listened to him. But his wife, Betty, was a delight and rather a relief, so bright, so charming, and such a believer. I could tell of my visions of other worlds to her safely and she believed them all (19). I told them in confidence to her, and she respected my confidence and kept my precious secrets even from her Gerald, to whom she was and is devoted. She made indeed gentle fun of him, but she wasn't in the least jealous of his passion for searching, searching and re-searching. It made him so happy, she said, and so she encouraged him in it. Oh! What a wise wife she was. Gerald said to tell you this. He likes to laugh at his past serious self and as you are a searcher too, he says, warn her of its dangers—loss of a sense of humour.

'Now I must not hold you any longer. I will only say this: that I am pressing you on and have been hanging about you, because soon these things will become known and therefore only what I say now is of value. I have ignored any suggestions I was given from the earth level as to what I might write if I could through you. The group here still hold together, and I have tried to follow their instructions as to what you might be capable of receiving. The group consists of those of Cambridge who were my communicators and to them have been added others interested. Among them my friend, Gerald, the friend I called Portia. I am Mrs. Wills. That is not quite right. Never mind, press on—listen, O, the scientist is of the group too.

'I hope I may be spared the experience of slipping into the River of Forgetfulness. But there is another kind of forgetfulness. When we converse through a medium and with a medium or automatist we become, as it were, dependent on her thoughts, words and images, and we go wrong, we stray in that tide. It can be a River of Forgetfulness temporarily too, for the struggling communicator in many cases, and it can be a mixture; part the automatist, part the communicator, or it can come in flashes and be almost true. I say this for your encouragement, as I see how much you doubt and want to be done with it all. I know those moods. I had them at times. But what was always sure, true and wonderful to me were my other world visions, and these were not my imagination. I have since my passing rediscovered them, found they are what the S.P.R. call veridical! (20).

Astor: Winifred is the Mrs Coombe (sic) Tennant invited by W.H.S. (Mr. W. H. Salter) in his letter to you. She was directed by this group as to what she was to try and communicate.

She did not wish to be too personal, as she is a reticent person in regard to her family. But I think that later (she) would like to write a personal note to her son. That is, of course, if she trusts herself and trusts the automatist.

'Winifred'

(1) G.C.: 'There is here an attempt to convey her pseudonym, "Mrs. Willett", used in all her psychic research experiments. Revelation of her identity was first made in the *Journal of the Society for Psychical Research* for December, 1957, of which I was not told till January, 1958, but this script made me suspect it.'

(2) The paper contains something about a memorial. A.T. comments: 'I have come upon lists of the many memorials to Christopher, in mother's handwriting and typed. I think she has placed memorials to him in all the places where in his life he passed any material time.' H.T. adds: 'My brother mentions that the restoration of one of these memorials was one of her most earnest wishes at the end of her life, and that when she was very ill, she struggled to dictate letters about it to the nurses.'

(3) Another reference to her son killed in the First World War, to whom these memorials were put up, now deplored by the communicator. The use of the name 'George', her sons feel, tends to show that Lodge's book *Christopher* was not drawn on.

H.T.: 'My mother would certainly not have used the name "George". Nevertheless it is factually correct. I can suggest no explanation, assuming G.C.'s honesty, except a possible confusion with George Pearce Serocold, my mother's father.' G.C. adds: 'In December, 1959, at my first meeting with H.T., he spoke of a book called *Christopher*, by Sir Oliver Lodge. I had never heard of it.'

(4) A.T.: 'Mother always had great love for Cambridge, and took a keen interest in Cherry Hinton church, to which she subscribed for the general upkeep and repairs done in recent years. She had, of course, stayed at Leckhampton House, Cambridge, with F. W. H. Myers and her sister-in-law (her husband's sister, Eveleen), and there for the first time she met the academic world, for which she had such a life-long respect.' A.T. adds that later again she stayed at Cambridge. Her father was born there. As a young man, exploring in Queensland, Australia, he called a number of places there Cherryhinton.

(Ed.) In her diary for 1899, Winifred mentions that 'We spent a week at Cambridge in April ... went over to Cherryhinton, where I did due honour to the graves of my forefathers.'

The communicator also states that she is 'directed by a group here, people who once lived at Cambridge'. Given this clue, plus the names 'Gerald' and 'Betty' (see page 3), the automatist surmised that Mrs. Wills was Mrs. Willett, the pseudonym of a lady who took part in the Cross-Correspondences, an experiment in which several automatists, independently of each other, received from alleged communicators details of literary puzzles, which only made sense when put together by the experimenter in charge. (See 'Zoar', by W. H. Salter, for best account of this most significant experiment.) This deduction by Miss Cummins did not of course tell her anything about the life of Major

Tennant's mother.

(5) She uses a well-known phrase to make sure medium gets the word 'origin' as she wants it used.

(6) A.T. comments: 'This I think is very true. I once asked mother how she had learned the art of public speaking. She told me she had suddenly discovered the power—in Wales, during World War I. She had had to speak on some subjects and had suddenly found she could do it without strain.'

(7) See note 4.

(8) A.T.: 'My mother and father lived mainly in London for the first years of their marriage. My mother always said that London society was "proud", "small", compared with the thinkers she had known— G.W.B. (Balfour), Lodge, Sidgwick, A.J.B. (Balfour), etc.

"Dear Alma Mater" is particularly characteristic.'

(9) On page 149 of the Balfour Study, the entranced Mrs. Willett is cited as speaking of a 'chain of me's', and in Gerald Balfour's comments he speaks of 'psychic units' and considers their co-operating to form a primary or 'true self'. In the Cummins-Willett script these ideas are expressed in a few sentences, as an intelligent but non-academic lady might have mentioned them, and as it allegedly is Gerald Balfour, who (later) admits he is conducting this experiment from 'the other side', it is probable that his preoccupations would come through, especially as these remarks are relevant to what follows about Mrs. Willett's 'psychic unit' in childhood.

A.T. comments: 'Gospel truth—very typical—really the key to mother's character.'

(10) 'Walking in celestial places', a phrase used in the Balfour Study by Mrs. Willett to describe her personal experience when entranced.

(11) A.T.: 'The small-child experience—absolutely true, I think,—confirmed by some of the things Mabel told me years ago.' (Mabel, an aunt of Mrs. Willett's, daughter of George Serocold in his first marriage.)

(12) H.T.: 'My mother had a particular interest in W. B. Yeats, and studied and pondered his poetry very much. This particular quotation was one of her favourites.'

(13) H.T.: 'We know of nothing to confirm this.' In the Balfour Study (p. 49), he states that 'in early girlhood Mrs. Willett discovered that she possessed the power of automatic writing . . .'

(14) H.T.: 'This story strikes my brother as likely to be true, and I have a feeling that I have read or been told about it.' (Ed.) On page 75 of the Balfour Study, Mrs. Willett notes that she passed almost into unconsciousness when she tried for script in her husband's presence.

(15) (Ed.) 'Portia.' Here Mrs. Willett seems to be carrying over the habit from the Cross-Correspondence cases of using symbolic names to disguise identity. Nine months later G.C. guesses correctly that Portia is Mrs. Verrall, the mother of Mrs. Salter. This lady's 'judicial' power has been mentioned by Mrs. Willett elsewhere in these scripts, and is possibly the reason for the name.

(16) Later identified by G.C. as Sir Oliver Lodge. Correct.

(17) The Balfour Study (pp. 230-1), mentions the 'disjointed scripts' that Mrs. Willett began to produce (part of the scheme of the Cross-Correspondences) and about which Sir Oliver Lodge questioned the communicators. 'Bits and scraps' as Mrs. Willett calls them in the Cummins scripts would probably be a more natural expression for her.

(18) In the Balfour Study Mrs. Willett complained of the long obscure words often used by the communicators. A. T. comments that he remembers his mother as 'complaining to me of the long obscure words which Balfour was wont to use'. So she was badgered both by communicator and sitter.

(19) A.T.: 'I think mother was closest to G.W.B. and was trusting with him, but did in fact have just the relationship described with Betty. All this strikes me as absolutely true.' H.T.: 'My brother considers this very characteristic and typical in every way. "This bears the ring of truth— and is truly remarkable." —I myself should not have picked on this as especially characteristic.

(Ed.) At this point in the scripts G.C. strongly suspected that Mrs. Willett was communicating facts about Gerald Balfour and his wife Betty, because in June 1939 G.C. had given a sitting to Lord Balfour and his wife. (See chapter entitled 'The Beginning of the Cummins-Willett scripts', page 3, and also pages 83-4 in G. Cummins' *Unseen Adventures*, where this is described in detail.)

(20) H.T.: 'My mother often used this word in conversations I had with her (veridical), about the evidence of the survival of personality. She used it, so to speak, in inverted commas, and my impression is that she regarded it as a technical S.P.R. word (Society for Psychical

Research). I remember an argument over how the word should be spelled, I maintaining it should be "viridical".'

In general, H.T. sums up: 'My brother has been considerably impressed by this script. He feels that it has the ring of truth and is accurate in many ways, and over details which he does not see how G.C. could have known from other sources. He writes: "Reading and studying this last script has caused me to change my views very considerably. I feel that this script really has carried us a great way. I tried the scripts on J. (his wife) with little comment, and she is entirely of my way of thinking. I agree with her in feeling that it is a great pity to wish to bring these communications to an end, just at the time they are becoming really interesting. I doubt whether G.C. will want to shut off material which may come her way, for she refers to Winifred as a strong influence. G.C., tuned in now, is really getting something —and I am now very much impressed by her 'concert pitch sensitivity', which has made this possible." '

H.T. continues: 'In general I agree, though I think there are a number of uncharacteristic things in the script. The description of the incident when my father is supposed to have been present at a sitting strikes several false notes, though I have no reason to doubt that it happened. The reference to Winifred as being nervous and not trusting herself (which also occurs in some of the other scripts) seems to me inappropriate. My mother was physically timid, but she was completely self-confident in all matters primarily requiring mental effort and the taking of decisions. I do not recognise my mother in "the lady with the darting mind". Nor do I feel that she is likely to be "not sure" whether she can trust G.C. with a personal message to me. However, I entirely agree that the experiment ought to be continued, and I shall be very interested to see what G.C. does produce in the way of a personal message for me, for here if anywhere one might expect to find evidential material.'

G.C.: 'The communicator could have been self-confident in all matters primarily requiring mental effort, but not at all confident in the role of the automatist Mrs. Willett, as in that role a suspension of mental effort was required. That is my own psychological attitude.

I am usually nervous before a guaranteed sitting. But I am self-confident in matters requiring conscious mental effort and the taking of decisions.'

(Ed.) In the Balfour Study, Mrs. Willett is often shown as timid in her mediumship.

September 26, 1957. Script 6.

Astor is here. Winifred has asked to be allowed to write to her son one more letter. She tells me that she endeavoured to communicate through other mediums since her passing, that she knocked at Mrs. L.'s door, and sought also Mrs. W.H. She says that she finds it very difficult through not always knowing what has been picked up and what has been missed. How far the medium has picked up what might be likened to radar signals.

(Writing changes.)

'Winifred T.

'My dearest H.

'I want this to be a personal note and to make in it my little confession to you. I long more than anything to convince you that I am alive and no longer the tiresome old lady, but Winifred in her prime. To do this my friend Gerald B. advised me to give general facts about the family and myself in this way. But today I shall write more intimately.

'Three sons were mine and I ask myself did I fail them when they were growing up. I am rather worried about that. There was my eldest, George. My pride was mingled with my love for him. Pride was, I think, a fault in my character. Perhaps that was why his loss in the war was such a blow. My pride as well as my love was abominably hurt by it. Then, being older than you, Alex was more self-sufficient. But you were so small, so completely mine, my creation. The sight of you playing somehow helped me back to life. But I must not dwell on that time as I want to make my confession.

'I feel that during the times you three were growing up in those important early years of your early life I was not enough with you, and when I was with my children I expressed too little of that deep love I felt for them. If I failed, for this failure forgive me. I see now my weakness. I was the victim of several fears. I will write of one fear in particular. When you were children I had a fear of being too possessive in my love for you. A mother's possessive love can do more injury to a son's character than anything else she can do to him. I had the example before me of certain members of your father's family. One was your aunt Eveleen. She had inherited from an ancestor, the financier, a terribly possessive instinct. He satisfied it by acquiring possessions, making a great deal of money. But Eveleen satisfied the same instinct by loving possessively. She used to be so jealous if her husband paid any attention to any particular woman. He was a saint, and she failed to injure him through her possessive love. But it was different in the case of her son, L., when he was a boy.

'She has now in this life slowly and painfully realised how much she injured L. in his early years through her possessive love for him. It has indeed been her purgatory to see how much she contributed to the ruin of his life on earth, and how unhappy were the consequences for him after his death. His suicide led to his being plunged into darkness and isolation here for a very long time. L. had as well inherited the instability of abnormal possessiveness from his mother. It was not expressed in the desire for property, money, but in other ways and in a self-centredness. But I cannot go into those details now. It is sufficient to say that your aunt Eveleen's possessive love even led her subtly to antagonise the boy L. against his father. His father was idealistic, devoted to spiritual things, so L., disliking his father largely through his mother's jealous influence, became a materialist when he was a man. Later in life he developed a passion for a very beautiful married woman, who also was spiritually minded and of course rejected his passionate possessive love. All this—her spirituality, his father's spirituality, failure to possess this woman, drove him to unbelief and gave him a tortured mind. Eventually he took to drugs and, as you know, killed himself. That is a mortal sin. He took into this life his crude ego that hated and hated, and denied love. So he suffered much. Poor Eveleen some time after coming here had to perceive, as we all have to, the consequences resulting from her life on earth. She saw how much she was responsible for her son's ruined life on earth. She has been very brave about it and, though her reception by L. was grim, she sought him out and tried to help him out of his hell of her and his creation. She has done much to improve things for him.

'But now you may ask, why do I tell you all this about Eveleen and L. her son? It is to explain things in connection with myself. Long ago, quite soon I perceived intuitively more than by reason the harm that Eveleen was doing through her possessive love. So when you were all children I tried to avoid possessing you, tried to make you three independent little mortals. But I may have gone to the other extreme and not showed you enough of the deep love I felt for you. So forgive me please if I failed you in loving when you were a small boy.

'I am thankful that your father did not inherit from that ancestor as unfortunate Eveleen did. But bear in mind always that the danger in the T. family is this possessive instinct. If it is there, it is a force that can be used for good as well as for evil.

'St. Paul was so right when he said "We are members one of another." We cannot live a day on earth without affecting in some way some person in our circle. The little builds into the great as time goes by, and our influence may precipitate some other soul's downfall, through the accumulation of the little, through the building up of the bricks of time.

'And indeed there can be much jerry building, bad workmanship, thin walls that crash into ruins.

'Now I have preached enough, my dearest to you. But I may not have another opportunity to write of these things and they are important.

'Gerald B. has been so good to me, helping me to make all this out so that you may understand.

'I need not send my love as it is with you always.

'Winifred T.

'G.C. Pray give this to W.H. for my son.'

(Note: Script is endorsed as follows: 'This script was written at Woodville, Glanmire, Co. Cork, on 26.9.57.

Iris A. Cummins.')

(1) 'Mrs. L.' is Mrs. Gladys Leonard, one of the best known and most highly esteemed professional mediums. After the death of her son in the First World War, Mrs. Willett had a number of sittings with Mrs. Leonard. (The editor has seen the reports.) The note-taker was Sir Oliver Lodge.

'Mrs. W.H.' is Mrs. Salter, the former Helen Verrall. She was, of course, known to Mrs. Willett.

(Ed.) It will be remembered that in his annotation of script 5, H.T. wondered what G.C. could produce by way of a personal message. Script 6 is indeed personal. It is also correct. It does not seem right to mention the full names of the persons, but their first names are the real ones and the situation described as well as the tragedy resulting from it are factual, and unknown to the automatist.

Here is one of the main themes of these scripts: the wish to make amends for what the communicator considers an inadequacy on her part in her relationship with her children, joined with her fervent desire to convince these children of her continued existence.

February 14, 1958. Script 7.

Astor is here. I think that if you hold W.H.'s letter, I may find her. Wait. Here is Winifred. She is pleased to be called, but doubtful of your capacity to take down what she has to say, as she says you only get things from her in patches. It is like a patchwork quilt. Bits are hers and other patches yours. Hold that letter in your left hand or keep it beside you, and I will help her to write, then we may do better.

'Winifred, T.

'Thank you, G.C., for calling me.

'Pray listen intently.

'Dear Mr. and Mrs. W.H.

'You remain dear relics of our age. I am happy to write to you. So much to tell, so little opportunity.

'In this life I have been fortunate in being welcomed by so many. Apart from my son, George, Charles, relatives, friends, there was dear Mrs. V., Gurney, Fred, and your professors, who worked so hard to make us stupid women listen to them. I call them yours as you and Helen (1) alone have any real appreciation of them now. But neither G.C., as I call this automatist, nor I, are skilled enough to weave the old pattern, to attempt cross-correspondence as they would wish (2). Besides, I am sorting memories as one sorts out the contents of old cupboards —enjoyment of flowers, pictures, the wonder of a young girl who goes abroad for the first time. (Word illegible.) Also annoyances, small quarrels, people being petty. What a heap of little pleasures, little occasional triumphs, vexations, mistakes, make up the detail of life!

'Many of the memories have lost their shape—are like old clothes in shreds. But here is one episode that came out recently quite clearly. I tell it to you because this letter contact with W.H. rouses it up. W.H., at any rate, would like to hear of my posthumous view of it.

THE MEMORY

'Many years ago I spent a strange hour in a room being one of a trio. We were listening to great music. All was peaceful. But the music did not carry me away. It peopled the room with the invisible dead. But at first I felt rather than perceived their presences. As I know now I became linked with the third in the trio, the deeper mind of a living man, who was resting and relaxed and appeared to be half asleep. And suddenly the presences of the dead I sensed became one visible presence from another life. I saw nothing ghostly. It was as real to me as my hand—simply a woman wearing an old-fashioned costume.

She was of another period. But I want you to realise that it was the third of the trio—this old man of eighty years or so—who gave me the power in some curious way to see this young woman, so attractive, the embodiment of youth, who literally shone down upon him as she stood beside him—rays of a hidden sun, as it were, emanating from her body, as she stood looking down at him.

'To me the effect was utterly strange, non-human, yet in appearance she was wholly human, with hair thick and beautiful. In that period women cherished their long hair, of course, she was so dated by that dress she wore. But the old man was old enough to be her grandfather, yet he was her contemporary and I felt from this illumination she cast upon him she loved him not as one loves a grandfather, but as a woman loves a man greatly of her own generation. He so ancient and she so young, yet they had been young once together. There's a riddle for you! But I later learnt that I had seen and described to my companion, the second in the trio, one dead many years. That this vision of mine meant much to this old man who was lying down resting, oblivious of this visitor. She was of his early manhood, and there had been no other in his long life! Incredible, you will say. But when I met him, he was cold and austere, and I was in awe of his admirable intellect. He had schooled himself, punished himself, like a flagellating saint, and so had kept himself immaculate for her.

'That scene I have described took its toll of me. As she you will call the ghost appeared beside the aged man, I felt myself slipping, fading, passing into the sleep of trance. Oh! I was always afraid of losing control, of being banished. It meant I might unfit myself for my work in life, which was dear to me.

So I struggled frantically to keep my hold on my self. I got back, but that meant the ghost disappeared.

'My companion learnt from me what had happened, and imparted my experience to the old man. For me, then, it removed their masks. I looked into their souls and perceived behind the aloof manner there was within warmth and a fine humanity; they were not by any means merely intellect and courteous manners.

'So that memory I drew out from the cupboard was still informed with life, because of the emotions roused by the coming of the lady into my perceptive life. Oh! How strong their emotions were! The younger man was devoted to the elder man and was moved because he was moved by my presentation of the presence.

'Brothers are seldom so linked. But they were.' (3)

(Ed.) This is the first script after Miss Cummins, on January 19, 1958, had had her attention directed by Mr. W. H. Salter to a notice in the *Journal for the Society of Psychical Research*, December, 1957, which repeated his information that the automatist of the cross correspondence cases, Mrs. Willett, and 'Winifred' and 'Mrs. Wills' were one and the same person.

(1) 'Charles' is her husband, 'Mrs. V.' is Mrs. Verrall, 'Fred' is F. W. H. Myers. 'Helen' is Mrs. W. H. Salter.

(2) It had been suggested by the experimenters that information about the cross correspondences might be given.

(3) On page 85 of the Balfour Study there is an account by Gerald Balfour of a visit from Mrs. Willett, which turned into a spontaneous sitting. It is dated October 16, 1929. She describes seeing 'a phantasm', 'a lady in an old-fashioned dress, young and with thick, beautiful hair. She was standing beside the couch, a brilliant light streaming round and from her whole figure . . .' Mrs. Willett adds that she barely escaped going into trance. It is also mentioned that 'another person was in the room, lying on a couch, also listening to the music and paying no attention to us'.

The above is all the information given. Even this was not known to Miss Cummins. Not till the publication in February, 1960, of 'The Palm Sunday Case' (*Proceedings of the S.P.R.*, vol. 52, part 189) were the same facts revealed as those stated in 'The Memory' of the present Cummins-Willett script, namely that 'the phantasm' was that of a young woman with whom A. J. Balfour had been in love and who had died young. He never married. In the Cummins script it was correctly stated that the two men present were brothers. They were Gerald Balfour and A. J. Balfour.

G.C.: 'About a year later I met H.T., and he told me that about the time script 7 was written Mr. and Mrs. Salter were reading an account of "The Memory".'

February 15, 1958. Script 8.

Astor. Yes, she is at hand and would like to finish her letter.

'Winifred T.

'I am still as a child in this life (1), and I am learning all the time. You two—Helen and W.H.—who have made such a study of ghosts and apparitions, of their sudden appearances, regard them, I think, as projections of the individual man or woman's mind. I can assure you now that human souls born into this world after death in many cases pass on to a different level, where their appearance is of a kind not known to any human being on earth.

'They are not merely moving at a different rate; they travel on a different scale. On that scale and changed key, they are cut off from earth. Only when these souls drop back into the scale and slower rhythm and sequence [frequence?] near the physical, can they project or put on the likeness of themselves as they were on earth, so that she or he who has the inner eye perceives them or their projected images. Or they, in that minor scale and key convey fragmentary communications to the subliminal mind of a skilled medium. But medium is an incorrect term. They should be called interpreters, and bad ones at that! So often there is mistranslation. They catch perhaps what the communicator emphasises and then fill in their own subconscious material.

'Oh, the woeful mistranslations! And these after a good beginning— a correct few words. Some only read stray memories and there is no communicating intelligence expressing himself.

In this I speak of proxy sittings at their best, and of some excellent evidence with a sitter, too often said to be telepathy from an incarnate mind. In my public life, I had at one time much experience of interpreters, and I know how they miss the idiom, how they can damage the essential sense, the shape of the speaker's remarks in another language, or if they give the sense, it is the views, the idiom of personality that is lost. So there are no mediums, there are only interpreters, and most are extremely inefficient ones. If the communication passes through the sieve of the interpreter's subliminal mind, the brain may play havoc with it. So please abolish the word medium, and employ the word interpreter instead. These are facts I have gleaned from Fred and others (2).

'A quite early experience of mine, after I had left behind me my ancient bones and become a risen mind, was to meet and be greeted by the gracious youth of the lady with the old-fashioned dress. She deliberately adopted the cast-off shell, put on the ancient costume and appearance in order to re-introduce herself, and thank me for imparting faith in her resurrected self to that wearied, bored, apprehensive man I described in the earthly scene of the trio listening to the music thirty or more years ago.

'Words commonly used have such different meanings for people. There is the ancient definition of man—spirit, soul and body. I prefer to call what spiritually influences composite man for evil or for good the anti-self, for it is not egocentric, it is not literally incarnate. It is outside the human being and reveals itself to him only in flashes. It can be inspiration, intuition, prophecy, even wisdom, and these flashes are used for evil or good by the receiving human being.

'There is, you may not know, gossip in this life. I shall gossip now.

'I have encountered A. J. B's friend. I am free to tell you of their intrinsic inviolable unity. They shared the one anti-self, while consciously separated by her early death.

'So many years parted after her passing. An emptiness, a dissatisfaction continually then for him. No joy. He merely put in time with hard and varied mental work. Such faithfulness, such patient waiting. Then at last, after sixty years or fifty by the clock, the meeting at the other side of death when his old age dropped from him like a ragged garment. But oh! It was well worthwhile to wait so long for that event. If they had not been parted by her death, he would never have worked with that industry, that brilliance that made a name for him. Work was his escape from intolerable memory. Oh! He was so idle before she passed.

'If she had lived, she would have been his all-absorbing playmate, life brilliant in the sunshine of just being, instead of doing, instead of a rough path each followed solitarily of struggle, and in his case of fine achievement.

'But hers was also fine; they tell me that she remained waiting, waiting at the border for him, returned from the higher level, at what sacrifice! A world so tempting beckoning, but she ignored it. She put all that away from her so as to meet an old man's soul. Therefore it need hardly be said that she was the first to greet A.J.B. when he came home to her. A lonely man throughout his life until then. They have gone to that other level together. Happiness incomparable for them, they now and then, I am told, they come back, as he feels still a responsibility for Britain (3).

'Now I can't hold on.

'Winifred T.'

(1) In mediumistic messages from the newly dead they often refer to themselves as children in their development.

(2) On page 182 of Miss Cummins's *The Road to Immortality*, which consists of scripts transmitted to her by F. W. H. Myers, a medium is described by Myers as 'an interpreter. It is an interpretation not a literal statement that is conveyed through him . . . You should study the medium, and if you perceive any very strong prejudice expressed, you will know it comes from the subconscious overflow and not from the poor shade who has the greatest difficulty in contending with any fixed ideas in the medium's deeper mind.' Note how Mrs. Willett elaborates a similar idea in her own style, illustrating it from her own experiences with interpreters at the League of Nations.

(3) The love story of A. J. Balfour is again referred to, and now his initials are given. It is correct, but the story was not made public, as mentioned, until a couple of years later in 'The Palm Sunday Case'.

February 16, 1958. Script 9.

(G.C. has received her first letter from Winifred's son, Henry. He writes that he and his mother always disagreed on the question of survival. He believes in extinction at death.)

Astor comes. Yes, hold Henry's letter. She will want to scan it, read it. There is force in the writer of that letter, a man with a strong will and an independent character. He would never flatter. His frankness might make him enemies. Honest speech does not assist ambition. But I think he is learning or has learnt to be silent when it is unwise to speak.

Here now is this quicksilver lady. She is still developing, emerging, and has become more unified than when first she wrote.

'Winifred T.

'Ah! My son Henry's letter. It stirs up so much. How good to see and feel his presence once more. Steady, steady. Let me sense its contents. (Violently large scrawling writing.)

'Oh dear, oh dear, a Daniel come to judgment!

'I am confused—must collect myself. What does this dear letter tell me? The magistrate is the prisoner in the dock, and her son is Judge and Jury. He has to give a verdict in an unusual law case. There is, I think, no precedent. At any rate no magistrate was ever tried before in a law court with her son as Judge to decide the issue. Briefly, What is the issue, my Lord?

'Does the prisoner exist or does she not?

'That is the question—a grave question.

When there are so many graves, such entire interments. It deserves much consideration. But will the Judge put on the Black Cap and decide for entire annihilation? Or will he show mercy to the criminal, taking into consideration her entire incompetence to plead, her total inexperience, her lack of preparation? Pray, my Lord, adjourn the Court and at least give the prisoner time to prepare her case against decapitation and annihilation! '

G.C.—A pause. Call me in half an hour. I am so touched, so pleased by this letter I must compose myself before I reply to it.'

(The pause.)

'Winifred T.

'Dear my Lord, 'I should like to try and tell you something about my early experiences in this other life. I don't intend to be a missionary. Far be it from me to convert you to a belief that a vestige of your mother still lives on quite comfortably, without ache or pain. Later I may explain why it is probably far better for you to keep your belief in my annihilation. But it is happiness to me to get your letter, to write to you again, and tell travellers' tales.

'After I woke up from the sleep of death, and following its uneasy dreams, some pleasant, some nightmares, my father and mother appeared to welcome me. Then your father and my sisters came. But my end was my beginning. I was too overjoyed perhaps at getting a glimpse of George, your brother, so father and mother soothed me, calmed me, took charge of me and gave me my first sense of locality and environment.

Here now is this quick-silver lady
She is still developing emerging and has
become more emified than when first he
wrote

Winfred

at my south way — A letter
I love — I do so much
How good to see and feel —
his presence once more
Teddy & lady — not more sensed —
contents
Dear oh dear, it amis icome
to judgment

I am confused — must collect myself
What does this dear letter tell me
The magistrate is the prisoner in the Dock
and her son is Judge and Jury.
He has to give a verdict in an unusual
law case. There is I think no precedent.
Anyway no magistrate was ever tried before
in a law court with her son as Judge to decide
the issue — briefly What is the issue my
Lord ?

which does not resemble the normal writing of
their mother, in the opinion of the sons
(*facsimile from Script 9*).

A sample of Geraldine Cummins's normal writing.

'It was all rather gradual—time of oblivion and unawareness, then these two were there beside me—my parents almost like doctor and nurse, and they guided me back into real consciousness.

'Over here we have freer movement in space-time. For we have our own kind of space and succession of events. It was not strange to me to go back to a time before my marriage, reliving familiar scenes in memory, through perhaps my hearing my father calling my mother "Mary" and she calling him "dear George" (1). Understand that the present Mary and George customarily live on a higher level than I am in at present. On that level, if I could attain to it, they would be almost unrecognisable to me. But after my passing they came down to my level, put on their mortal semblance as I remembered them, in order to greet me.

'To give me confidence in my beginning, to reassemble my bits of mind, as it were, my mother took me through some of the earliest of my memories that had made an impact on me and are all pictured here. I saw again a visit to her home, Derwen House (2). There was I, a small naughty child. This film was a little dim, but a touching one. This was [word illegible] home. When she was a tiny girl and I heard again the sound of Welsh voices and I felt again the excitement of the child I once was on a visit to a new country, Wales. I know I was told it was a different country from England. My first instruction in Welsh nationalism. Then the pictures moving back in time.

'I perceived Cambridge and Cherryhinting [Cherryhinton] (3) surroundings—my earliest life—even the baby in the pram, my nanny, the queer, old-fashioned dresses of the ladies when the little girl that I was went for walks, and accepted all that millinery, those sweeping dresses, as a matter of course.

'Then at home, I, the youngest, at play with my elder sisters (4). Our doll's house, my cherished doll. My father, so big, so great to me. There was I, the very old woman, a spectator of my small child self, entering into her emotions, throbbing to her tears, uplifted by her small joys. Those little dramas enacted by my past child-self were all reassuring to me, the spectator, after the lonely passage of death. Somehow I felt that what should have been the experience of everything being dead, breaking up, nothing was dead, nothing lost. There was the moving spectacle of childhood in this unrolling film—more, of course, learning my letters, lessons, youth, the social training of my period, my sisters being launched. Then my coming out, the hair being put up, long dresses, shyness, gawkiness, grotesque, historical costumes—a costume play!

'*My ambitions.* At one time I dreamt of becoming an artist. I loved colour and form (5). I drew, I tried to paint. But there [were] too many other attractions and I had no real talent. I read much poetry and secretly tried to write what was bad verse, that long dead, romantic self that was me made me laugh.

It was just as well [that] people as people interested me, and I became snared in the social life of the time.'

H.T.: 'General: Apart from one or two discordant notes, this script strikes both my brother and me as true. I think it is not uncharacteristic of my mother to present the material in this and the next two scripts in dramatic form, as a defence in a court of law, and the bantering tone of some of the contents is also characteristic of her reaction when she thought I was being ponderous and severe.'

(1) The names of Mary and George are correct, unknown to G.C.

(2) A.T. writes: 'Mother often spoke to me of Derwen Fawr, which I think was her grandfather's house. She told me of the pans of milk with rising cream in the dairy attached to the house, and of the old coachman who had been so kind to her. I know that she was very happy there.'

(3) Should be Cherryhinton.

(4) It is a fact, unknown to G.C., that Mrs. Willett had sisters, half-sisters, as her father had been married before.

(5) A.T. writes: 'I know that mother longed to paint and told me that she had as a girl tried to draw and paint but had no real talent.

February 17, 1958. Script 10.

Astor. Yes, here she comes.

'Here comes the incredible Winifred! Or would it not be better to call her Margaret, a more credible name, less suggestive of impersonation as she faces her stern judge? (1)

"What's in a name?" says Shakespeare. Everything when one falls in love. Mine was not a sudden, swift fall. It was a slow-motion picture in this film of memory. When Charles came to figure in my life how shy I was of him! He seemed much too old for me (2). I had experience of undergraduates who were far too young. I was very flattered by his attentions, but did not believe that they were more than kindness to the rather "out-of-it" girl. Strangely they persisted, but they were oblique. In other words, he was cautious, and, as I later realised, he was apprehensive of the criticisms of his women-folk. Poor Charles, he was family-ridden then; I think I'm glad, H., that you are free in that sense. What is called a united family is an unnatural phenomenon. An Englishman who quarrels with his family is following a natural healthy instinct. It does not matter who or what started the quarrel, they are obeying nature's law in casting each other off.

'I was very nervous too, and therefore rather elusive during that courtship. But it became amusing to me and gave me self-confidence. When Charles began to arrange for us to meet by subterfuge, while he would ignore me almost to rudeness while we were in the company of others, at first I took it all lightly.

Then he became serious, ardent. He could not conceal from me his deep feelings any longer and suddenly love woke up. He swept the young girl off her feet. The old, old woman can only write of it now because she has been watching it scene by scene, living again its varied emotions, its keen anxieties, its palpitating wonder, its fears, its hopes, and yet remaining detached, the spectator in the stalls. Oh my dear, you do not know your mother (3), or rather you only know one aspect of her, the role she played as mother in your life, and a very busy mother too.

'The family didn't like the choice of their Charles. Eveleen and Dorothy were distinctly disdainful, patronising (4). They were fashionable married women. I was the young nobody. My prospective M. in L. alarmed me absurdly at first. I, the sophisticated old Dame, surveyed this comedy of memory re-enacted, saw how his women-folks' attitude spurred on Charles, when they tried so hard to put him off. I was dazzled, enchanted, uplifted by his increasing devotion. And though very hurt, I was determined to show the family I was not a nobody by any means.

'It all seems so small now in these days of a Welfare or Illfare State. Yet their attitude was quite understandable in that period. And I was really rather crude, as I see myself now.

Dorothy was much admired, and her husband famous for his African exploits (5). Eveleen was the belle of London and Cambridge society. But Dorothy was a really enchanting person, when I came to know her better.

'For some time my mother-in-law made me feel very nervous. Her very name, Gertrude, meant dignity. As the years passed my alarm of course disappeared, and she changed too. But I think I remained a little in awe of her, as I see my memory now, until the day of her death. Just before the bells of Victory rang in the War, she went, and the curtain was pulled down on sorrow, in the relief from massacre of youth. Gertrude slipped away quietly, reposefully, the old following the young— following my George hardly a year between their exits, his violent, hers peaceful. That phase in my life was like the tragic climax at the end of an act in a play. As I viewed it again, I was deeply caught by its conflicting emotions. But I, the spectator, could perceive the change it and the war wrought in my personality. There had been one change before that in 1908, in my first grave loss through death (6). But actually I became sensible of the great change in myself in 1918 (7). Then such losses through death to nearly everyone I knew became cumulative, drove me back from the dust and ashes into public life, eager to make a better world. My soul yearned for contact with workers for the people. How great was my ambition to work for the living and their preservation, how little, if any, my achievement (8).

'Did I neglect my husband and my two boys then, in that eager pursuit of life, of work on committees? (9) I, the spectator of that turning point in 1918, saw that I was in such busy occupation instinctively hiding from the massed death of millions, seeking life, more life, by working for the public weal, and, as I believe, serving it.

'Dear H., before that change in my personality you were a baby and then a small boy, indeed you were so young you did not know my pre-war personality. I was sentimental, softer, more retiring then. My new self was harder, more satirical, toughened by the war. I make this point, my Lord, so as to show how in our terrene life human personality can and does often die several times in a lifetime and a new or much changed human personality is born, continuing in many respects differently. A part of ourselves is buried, rots away, and there is re-creation, an adding to the self or a lessening or hardening or coarsening or otherwise. As we or our human personality can thus die several times while our physical body continues in one life, so death makes a great change in the personality, and, my Lord, I can see from your letter that you regard me as already a disintegrating mother, heading swiftly for final dissolution.

'One number I always remember—8—. Turning points or deaths of my human personality seemed to come in eights for me—study them— 1908—1918—1928—1938 (10).

'1938—another turning point, the beginning of a new human personality of an elderly disillusioned woman that saw another war inevitably coming and quite soon. Of course I tried to play hide-and-seek with it. No one knew, I think, of the war of regrets in my soul. I had worked so hard for the gracious arts of peace—the arts in Wales (11). I had in my time talked so much in that talking shop in Geneva. All was in vain. And the personal. You would be going off to the war, just in the way my George had gone. Gas masks, defence training, Red Cross classes. What a change from the lovely arts of peace! Was it surprising that I grew a new human personality—one concealed as far as possible, but becoming evident at least to myself as the months went by.

'1928—that other turning point. I cannot continue now. I shall continue my pleading, my Lord. No, perhaps I should say Your Worship tomorrow?

'W.T.'

H.T.: 'General: This script strikes both my brother and me as remarkably accurate. It contains a good deal that has already appeared in previous scripts.'

(1) 'Margaret' was Mrs. Willett's second name.

(2) Her husband was twenty-two years older than she.

(3) Phrase often used by Mrs. Willett. A.T.

(4) The family names are correct as mentioned previously. Their patronising attitude is referred to in Mrs. Willett's diaries.

(5) African exploits correct. It was Henry M. Stanley.

(6) The loss of her baby daughter was in 1908.

(7) A.T. believes the great change following the death of Christopher in September, 1917, might not have been felt by his mother till 1918.

(8) This refers to her work as delegate to the League of Nations.

(9) A.T. told G.C. that when he and Henry were schoolboys and small children their father was decidedly more with them than their busy mother, often engaged in public work.

(10) Correct. In 1928 her husband died. Her change of personality in 1938 cannot be confirmed, but the script claims that she concealed it as far as possible.

(11) A.T. says that his mother bought French pictures and sent them on loan exhibits through Wales. She bought pictures on behalf of Swansea Art Gallery and other Welsh galleries. In the half-time breaks in concerts, she often spoke in chapels on the life of Bach and well-known musicians.

February 18, 1958. Script 11.

Astor. The quicksilver lady is very imperious at moments and then at others persuasive. I think that in life she liked to get her own way. She was subtle and so intuitive. She could enter sympathetically into people's hearts and was at times all softness, kindness, fascinating people she met. But she could be satirical and was impatient of stupidity. There was a deep reserve, and she was by nature secretive. She got on better with men than with women. One thing she possessed and that was persistence. She is very persistent now, but still finds it difficult to manage the writing. I will try and help her so far as she will permit. Too loosely bound, owing to her acute psychic sensitivity. She is not a skilled communicator (1).

(Writing changes.)

' "Alas poor Yorick!" Alas, poor Winifred! She appears again before her Judge of the High Court on the issue of everlasting death or a frail continued life.

'Old people and things that pass. Have they passed forever? No, my Lord, I dispute that point.

'Where was I in my pleading? Ah yes, I was discussing the eights.

'I became a widow in 1928. What a weary year it was! How filled I was with fears. Death terminates more than the life of the one who has departed this life. It means for she [her] who was intimate a death for herself. It means a blank, a void, a travail of birth for her into another life that has to be organised, arranged in all its painful details. If she is mentally to survive adequately, so many memories of past years have to be locked out, doors closed. For Winifred, the adoption of another human personality. For now she is the widow instead of the wife. For Winifred her saddest, most anxious concern was a son called Henry, a schoolboy at Eton (2). Eton, Windsor, is all associated with that year. How will he fare? He is her sole charge now. What about Alex? Oh, he was older, different and had not Henry's sensitivity nor that special link with his mother.

'My Lord, I am prepared to admit that as the human personality perishes—in my case it did so—every ten years during a long lifetime, so human personality perishes sometimes only gradually after the great change of death.

'But of Winifred there remains the inner being, the core of self, with a few of the characteristics, just trimmings of the past personality. They continue permanently in a discarnate state.

The trimmings will eventually wither away. [Note: Last two words crossed out and "be parted with" written above.] But she, Winifred, is undying, as for one thing she goes on loving the changing personalities of the small son.

' "Augustus was a chubby lad", you know the nursery rhyme, the schoolboy at Eton. "On wintry days too thinly clad." You mustn't wear overcoats. It is not done.

'Third personality, the young man at Cambridge. Alma Mater, the Varsity (3). He is taking an independent line. No ancestor in the male succession was ever a soldier. After all they came from the heart of Yorkshire. Trade, business, finance was their metier. But away from commerce is the decision of this original young man. Winifred is pleased, approves of this new emerging personality. Love is reinforced for her. Here is the independent young lieutenant serving in his country's Guards and there follows the older soldier who has won his cross. Need I go on enumerating my son's changing personalities? I did not abandon him because chubby Augustus died, the Eton schoolboy replacing him, a stranger at first but inwardly the same. Similarly there followed the undergraduate, the Lieutenant in his first uniform. The War. Veteran, older, changed again, back home at last (4).

'All had different human personalities, different appearances. Outwardly and in conversation different. But in their deep roots of the self I knew them to be one, and gathered them into memory's heart.

'As he informs you in his letter, G.C., my son and I never agreed on one issue. He did not and does not believe in survival.

But now I plead, my Lord, that we may compromise. Human personality does not survive death, but the soul or real mind survives. However changing the mask of human personality, whatever have been the misunderstandings at times between the son's and mother's personalities, there is unity deep down and behind their masks.

'Memories persist like the leaves of the tree, from the consciousness *the living self or person discards them.* But all that is deepest and best or worst continues after and before death.

'In this other state the human soul continues living, expanding or contracting. Describe the soul, you say. It is something essential, rarely recognisably expressed, save in the highly developed, through the outer trappings during the span of existence on earth.

'Here that core of self laughs at the episode of mortal death and seeks and finds life, more life.

'My Lord, you may sentence the mother to annihilation, but for the son somewhere is buried the uneasy suspicion that a fragment of her goes on living and loving him. He cannot annihilate her quite, however often he affirms that he does, however long through the decades of his present life he banishes her from memory and conscious life (5).

'Yes, Henry, my dear, I survive, and I have not survived death. My human personality has certainly shrivelled! So at last, through compromise, I think we can agree on this issue of life or extinction. Thank

God, my last old crone personality is extinct! My Lord, the case for the Defence is now closed.

'Does the prisoner in the dock exist or does she not? I, Winifred Margaret, await your verdict with calm.'

H.T.: 'General: The style is quite characteristic. A.T. is particularly impressed by this script.

(1) H.T.: 'Astor's analysis is, as far as it goes, entirely accurate.'

(2) H.T.: 'My mother was, with some reason, anxious about my development at Eton, especially in 1929 and 1930.'

(3) H.T.: ' "Alma Mater" was a favourite expression, but I have never heard my mother refer to "the Varsity".'

(4) H.T.: 'It is true that I was the first soldier in the family and that the Tennants came from Yorkshire. The biographical details in the rest of the paragraph are correct.'

(5) H.T.: The paragraph beginning, "My Lord you may sentence the mother to annihilation" strikes me as highly characteristic.'

March 1, 1958. Script 12.

Astor. Yes, Winifred is like a bird perched upon a bough, inquisitively watching a human being. I think she will approach in a moment or two. She loved birds, flowers, colour and life.

But she told me that she refused to sentimentalise about them, as so many English people do.

With regard to human beings, she was occasionally inclined to be too impulsive if they won her sympathy. This was also the case with causes, so she had her disappointments in life.

She is appraising us now, having learnt to be cautious. Ah! she approaches and has decided to give a message. You can take up her son's letter in a moment.

'Winifred Tennant.

'Dear G.C., I think that I may now sign my full name to you. My work on the magisterial bench taught me to be cautious about the writing of surnames. So I have been careful and left them out when dictating to you. Surnames commit. Christian names do not to the same degree in handwriting.

[Editor: The son's letter is produced, in which his mother is asked for advice on the choice of careers, oddly enough as it is from the son who does not believe in survival. The mother discusses, correctly, certain changes in the family surnames, and shows a correct knowledge of events in her son's life. Two names unknown to the automatist are mentioned, names relevant to the problem of a career, and correct knowledge is shown about property owned in Africa by a member of the family. Various possible careers are coolly and sensibly discussed, not far-fetched suggestions by any means.]

In this script there are various indications of anti-Labour Party bias. H.T. comments: These are not characteristic of my mother's political views, as she used to express them in later life. In fact Bevan ("dear Nye") was one of her heroes.' A.T.: 'Mother was a true Liberal. She was fanatically anti-dictator, whether the dictatorship was from the left or the right.' (Ed.) As the automatist's political views verge on the Conservative, this may be a case of the communicator being unable to swim against the currents in the medium's mind, a fact of which Winifred sometimes complains. She stayed at Chequers as a guest of Lloyd George in 1922, and she has written a brilliant account of it, apparently only for her own satisfaction. At that time she seems to have seen a rising dictator in Winston Churchill, of whom she says: 'A bully and militarist. He is a heavy, ill-built, old young man, pasty-faced, bulldog jowled, bald-headed; he looks puffy and unhealthy, muscularly poor ... he spoke for an hour—his speech was clever, satirical, not moving.'

March 2, 1958. Script 13.

Astor. Yes. Here is the lady anxious to continue.
'Winifred Tennant.
'Dear H.,
(The mother continues discussing possible careers, still with relevance to actuality.)
(Later.) 'Now as to the human and personal element in your life, I am not perhaps one to advise you. At any rate I look back rather pessimistically on my failures at times to link up in close friendship with women. I ought to have been able to get on in that respect with both sexes. But I did not understand women sufficiently. I could get on well with women acquaintances, but I certainly recall that I failed in the intimacy of a close companionship, a sharing of daily life, with one woman.
'You remember Mrs. R., and how, through my knowing the L's so well, I went to live with Mrs. R. at Y.

I recall that at the outset I discussed with her the problem of quarrels and quoted Pope's lines:

"Forgiveness to the injured doth belong
For he ne'er pardons who hath done the wrong."

'Mrs. R. said reverently, "How beautiful! How true! How right! We must remember that, and it will put an end to any disagreement we may have."'

'"Oh no," I replied, I think that Pope gave very bad advice in that rhyme. In any quarrel, if the injured party decides in the end to forgive, she must take quite a long time about it.

It is essential that the injured party remains unyielding until and unless the offender has made a concession and an approach already. Then she should, if she is a Christian, give generous terms.

'Well, as you know, I lived with Mrs. R. for a time at Y. But it ended disastrously. We parted company. In fact I was dismissed and had to leave her.

'But the point is that now I realise that Mrs. R. was the injured party in the quarrel. That is at least the obvious view which is not always the correct view to be taken of it. I am not particularly intelligent, but I had a higher level of intelligence than Mrs. R's. I became somewhat satirical about her stupidities.

They exasperated me. She reacted far too sharply to my criticisms. I admitted later, when we had a showdown, that I had been too outspoken, but it was all very well intentioned.

'Fortunately for me, Mrs. R. did not recall Pope's lines, which she had described as "so beautiful, so true, so right". Though I became abject, promised to reform, never to be critical and suggested a further trial of me, she rejected the trial, insisted on my departure. So I went.

'Now, though Mrs. R. was stupid, her instinct in this respect was wise. I would have curbed my tongue if she had forgiven me and I had stayed on. But that would have been going against my own nature and was no satisfactory solution of the problem. The fact was that Mrs. R. and I were wholly unsuited for the intimate companionship of sharing the same residence. We were on different levels of intelligence or imagination, and she could not stand frequent criticism. She curled up and got hurt (1).

'My dear H., when you share your life with anyone, it is most important that there should be give and take, freedom for both partners to criticise each other. A life completely single, when one is growing very old, is lonely, unless one is very fully occupied. Partnership in living can give extraordinary happiness if it is based on democratic principles. There must be no totalitarianism. The exercise of free speech is essential. Mrs. R. was totalitarian in outlook, though she was always so exasperatingly polite to me before the quarrel. She would not allow me free expression of my no doubt unkind opinions.

'Dear H. In life, whatever you do, be sure that the right of free speech is respected, [it] is the law in any collaboration in business or personality. With that right recognised, must go the capacity to take it, if unjust criticism or seemingly unjust is hurled at one. In a collaboration there should be no summary breaking off of all relationships because of criticism when one is in perhaps a bad mood, or one is feeling out of sorts.

'What are words after all? They never express adequately, except perhaps in great poetry, the feelings of faithful enduring affection, that is not totalitarian.

'In the years to come in any partnership with man or woman insist on the rights of free speech and add that there must be recognition that either our vile bodies or our minds are sick, when unjust hurtful criticism is made in the give and take of daily life.

'Oh, the need for allowances on both sides! Above all, there is the need for the two to be on the same level of intelligence and to have the capacity for sharing the same interests. Sexual passion is deceitful, lying, cannot last long, must stale between a man and a woman. But the mental or passion of imagination between a man and a woman can permanently preserve unity, can produce the devotion of a lifetime and the happiest of lives. So, far more important than the choice of a career, is the choice of a partner who can fully realise in imagination the other's needs. But encouragement is necessary too when criticism is made.

'The worst of it is that so often dissembling cruel nature prohibits a wise choice. So it may seem best, especially in these days, for a man to remain a bachelor (2). But I totally deny that it is best. And even if he makes a mistaken choice of a partner, he can rectify it later. There is always a second chance.

'In this fundamentally Mind World in which I am now, I see how unimportant is the transient sexual attraction and passion on earth among human beings, how vitally important is a rich imagination in which two minds are on the same level. So the partnership here endures even as the two journey to wider horizons, if there is sufficient imagination.

'No doubt you will say I have been sentimental in what has just been written about the personal relationship. But I see it now so clearly as more important than any worldly success or fame.

'Please do not think that any blame should be attached to Mrs. R. for our quarrel. She was essentially feminine, and of course I could be rather trying. But men like that in moderation, enjoyed it even, if displayed by me. It keeps them interested in a woman, when her meek docility fails. Above all it reminds their unconscious of their mother when, in their earliest days, she began their training. Thus the mother remains the basic subterranean influence in most men's lives.

'I hope, dear son, that does not give you the creeps!

'As always yours (3),

'Winifred T.'

(1) H.T.: 'By far the most impressive part of this script is that relating to the quarrel with "Mrs. R." In April, 1942, my mother went to live as a paying guest with a Mrs. R. in Y. . . . and my mother lived there for nearly four years.

'My mother was by temperament incapable of making a success of prolonged intimate companionship with a woman. Such associations always came to grief sooner or later, and life with Mrs. R. was no exception, being marked, however, by an unusual degree of bitterness. The quarrel was of course no secret in the place, where, according to my mother, Mrs. R. used to refer to her as the "Paying Pest". I cannot say whether the incidents described in the script actually occurred, and Mrs. R. died recently, so she cannot be consulted. We may find confirmation of the poetry episode in the diaries.

[Ed., I haven't found it.] At all events, this part of the script is completely convincing to my brother and me. In the front of my mother's diary for 1945 is a cutting from the *Daily Telegraph* of 12.1.45, in which a psychiatrist describes some patient as "suffering from a constitutional psychopathic condition, emotional instability and an exploding primitive sadistic aggressiveness". Underneath the cutting my mother has written: "After over two and a half years of observation I know this as a full and accurate diagnosis of the mental condition of Mrs. R." (cf. page 53 of script: "She was a totalitarian in outlook".)

'Also we came on a letter from Mrs. R. among my mother's papers after her death, which was an attempt to make up the quarrel. The writer pointed out that they were neither of them getting any younger and suggested they should make their peace while there was still time.

My mother had endorsed the envelope of this letter with the following or similar words: "Ridiculous letter from Mrs. R. pleading for forgiveness." I think there was also a note to the effect that she did not intend to reply. This also bears out the bit on page 52 of the script.

A.T. comments that my mother's diaries are full of references to her quarrel with Mrs. R., and I know that it made a deep impression on her.' 'The term "Mrs. R." covers reference to the lady in question, both by her correct Christian name and by the correct initial letter of her surname. The place-name is also correct.'

(2) H.T. was a bachelor, unknown to G.C.

(3) H.T.: 'The bit at the end of the script about men liking to be teased is characteristic, so is the sentence beginning, "I hope dear son . . ." "As always yours" is not.

March 22, 1958. Script 14.

(G.C. to Astor: Please ask Winifred, if you can find her, to write about the Process of Communication (1).) Astor: Wait a few minutes, please. I shall inform her of your question.

'Winifred Tennant.

'Oh, dear! Process of Communication! In that case this letter should follow the previous one written to Mr. and Mrs. Salter, who are herewith appointed judges of the High Court in conjunction with Henry Tennant, owing to the fact that ramifications of a conspiracy have to be revealed. A second charge of a serious character now enters into the case of Winifred, the prisoner who is on trial for her very existence.

'At the instigation of one Gurney and his accomplice, Gerald B., she became once more their intermediary—a woefully indifferent interpreter of their general conception of what constitutes Homo Sapiens. To the best of her ability she presented their present view, illustrated by her stray memories, in her last pleading, but her ability was admittedly not adequate.

'Why, then, it may be asked, was she allowed to plead; why were Gurney and Gerald B. not appointed as Counsel engaged for her defence? It is because they were not invited, not desired as communicators.

PROCESS OF COMMUNICATION

The realisation of the self of a communicator depends largely on the recognition of his reality by the automatist and by the assumption of recognition of him on the part of the investigator.

'There has to be co-operation on your side. Mr. Salter is a skilled investigator, and he anticipated with such histrionic skill messages from Winifred T. She picked up his call, and through Mr. Salter's desire she obtained the necessary directive power that not merely led her to find this automatist but to continue the writing. Should Mr. Salter's desire fail—and Ecclesiastes tells us that desire frequently does—then Winifred will fail in further communication written by this pen.

'As regards the success of an experiment, the investigator is frequently of more importance than the medium. The surviving souls, whom I shall call "the living-dead", must also desire to communicate. Reciprocity or reciprocal desire between the investigator and the living-dead, an assumption if only temporary of the two conversationalists' reality, induces evidential results at sittings (2).

'Needless to say, I longed to let my sceptical judge, my son, know that I was not merely dead, I was also alive. He may as a result of these my communications bury the whole of me in a neat little coffin but at least my desire has not failed so far. And anyhow, as the poet wrote: "A beaten man is a story forever"—poetic licence here necessary. Even if I am defeated and my son does not believe in the reality of my continued existence, someone else who reads my report may find a fragment of reality in this "story".

'*Reciprocal.* That is the word needed. When the soul of one newly dead seeks to come back, she has a sense of paralyzing isolation. She fails, if no living human being invites her and extends a welcome. In my first timid attempts the automatist G.C. and Mr. Salter did this for me, welcomed their guest.

Strangely enough, though my son held very firmly the belief that I no longer continued to exist, he sent me a whiff of desire.

His affection for me temporarily, naughtily, overcame his intellectual powers. What joy for me when I realised that he was prepared to be my judge and consider the evidence if any! Oh, it stimulated the half paralysed prisoner in the dock.

CROSS CORRESPONDENCE
PROCESS OF COMMUNICATION

In very rare cases, highly intelligent communicators, exceptional people who have a purpose, some warning to be given to a human being, some wrong to be rectified, or something mistaken put right, may, even if there is no human desire, no invitation extended to them, break out from the fastness of the dead, and convey a communication quite unsought to a medium or automatist or sensitive. The numerous apparitions of the newly dead, announcing by their appearance to friend or relative their departure from earth, often come from people not gifted. That is because, with the sudden realisation of their own death, they are consumed with the desire to announce they are alive.

'Very often it is their one and only communication, as they cannot maintain that white heat of desire, also they are incapable of making a further communication once their being is coordinated on a higher level, especially if no radar signal of desire is made to them from kith or kin still resident in the physical body.

'When I use the word desire, I mean, as Fred tells me, the wishful emotion, the longing, that has imagination as its source, and he says that imagination is the mental and emotional faculty that forms ideal images or combinations of images. Attaining the ideal means reaching one's standard of perfection. Springing from the imagination is the explorer's desire to know even a fragment of an unknown land, or state of being, if it pertains to a supernal realm [the words that follow were apparently added later] or simply is exploration of the unconscious mind of man in the view of the seeking human being.

'The cross correspondence case went on for about thirty years. I was a participant in it as an automatist. My death, I surmise, roused the imaginative curiosity of the explorer W.H.S. and his desire that I Winifred, known as Mrs. Willett, should send a signal, came as a call to me, giving me the opportunity I desired and was seeking. Thus there was reciprocity between me and W.H., mutual action which enabled me to write, through G.C. a stranger, that Mrs. Tennant was Mrs. Willett, or at least Mrs. Wills, the automatist who played her small part in that monumental correspondence edifice (3). Ours—G.C., W.H., and I, was a trio, not a duet, and each member of the trio was endowed with sufficient imagination to produce the conditions necessary for the recording of what is called evidence or ESP.

'The Group Cross-Correspondence Case might be likened to an orchestra's perfect performance. The several communicators were scholars, whose
intellects were married to imaginations that cherished an ideal image of
scholarly perfection in the evidence they conveyed. The investigators and
the mediums had sufficient imagination to envisage the ideal image, the
objective of perfection. Thus deep called to deep in a unified desire. An
orchestra must play as one if the performance is to reach towards perfection with any real success. All the performers were detached, seeking only
the ideal image. That is how the high standard of evidence was maintained
over a period of thirty years in the cross-correspondence case.

'Does that answer your question, namely, "How was the high standard of evidence maintained for such a long time, when in most other
single cases it seems to peter out after a while?"

'I must add, however, that in this unique case the group of deceased
scholars were principally responsible for the high standard of results.
They selected with shrewd wisdom the human performers, the investigators and automatists. These are not now to be found on earth, for
human desire springing from imagination has failed. So further group
evidence cannot be conveyed of this kind.

'Investigators. It is when imaginative desire fails on the part of human
beings otherwise fitted for the work that "cases peter out", as you describe
this process. At the present time imagination is too completely subservient
to the intellect among well-educated people. The over-riding intellect produces sterility of imagination. Such people are therefore wholly incompetent as investigators: they are bound, if they investigate, only to meet with
negative results. But atheists or agnostics who do not subdue the imaginative desire of the explorer will, granted other conditions, a skilled medium,
etc., obtain fruitful results. If the desire is there, the gift is there. There were
various other causes for the success of the cross-correspondence case. I
have only herewith given the primary and essential cause.

'Rest and dream now, then listen.

(A pause. Resumed later.) 'You are sleepy.

'Hold the pen now, G.C. and listen.

'You know the title of the greatest woman in religious history is the
Virgin Mary. No, the Virgin Mary isn't present but her namesake is.
Then there is another, our West Country King Arthur. Again remove
the title, thus we have Arthur and Mary.

'That's right. You have caught it. Add to this the faithful Gerald. My
three companions, three of the living dead. Must people on earth live
without hope? No. Surely the reply is No.

'A ring, owing to his caution and his dilatoriness, was not present-ed. Oh, what infinite regret! She was not there. She had gone when he arrived. Bury it, bury it with her in the earth and say Goodbye forever. That is what he did. But only his reason said "Goodbye for ever", his heart, his imagination did not.

Once a year he returned and wondered, pondered, as he stood by the grave. Was it earth to earth, dust to dust, solely?

'King Arthur and his knights. Did they ever find the Holy Grail? There's a mystery for you, with a query for all mankind. 'But my tab-leau here, previously mentioned, represents this twentieth-century soul, Arthur. His human personality, his appearance, are that of the nineteenth-century man he was, at the age of thirty or so. In the pres-ence of Gerald this Arthur presents the girl Mary with a ring he was too late to offer her when he lived on earth. This tableau was objective, or is objective, an event that actually occurred in a supernal realm of recent years by your clock (4).

(A pause here.)

'Oh, Oh, Miss G.C. I peep into your mind. I see that you think that what I have just written is a sentimental fiction or a myth. Yes, I can see that verdict in your mind (5). But even a spinster such as you are can un-derstand that a myth is sometimes the bearer of an ultimate truth.

'You would most appreciate of all the legends told of The Quest of the Holy Grail, the original and very ancient story that was the ances-tor of every Arthurian legend.

'It is the Welsh tale of Perdue. In this tale there is no grail at all, but only the Quest!'

(1) G.C. has been asked by the investigators to put a question to Win-ifred about 'the process of communication'. This topic had been amply dealt with in the Balfour Study, when she herself was the medium. Some of her present comments, through G.C., find their counterparts in this study, which, as mentioned, G.C. had not read, except in the fragments cited by Tyrrell, and by Saltmarsh. It is not a case of literal quotation. The Cummins-Willett script brings forward some of the same ideas, but in a style that is often more colloquial, as well as adapted to the situation, i.e., the incredulity of her son as to her continued existence.

(2) cf. Balfour Study, p. 182: '. . . belief in the personality of the commu-nicators "is an absolutely vital part of the conditions which make it easy for us to work". idem, p. 183: ' "There is a paralysing sense of isolation in the experience of coming back . . . one needs something reciprocal." '

(3) In G.C.'s autobiography, *Unseen Adventures* (1951) it is mentioned on page 133 that for good evidence a medium requires not only a communicator who knows how to communicate, but one who has an emotional longing to do so, and a sympathetic sitter. See also the 'Palm Sunday Case', pp. 108, 109, the description of the three groups of co-operators needed for good evidence.

(4) Not till the publication of 'The Palm Sunday Case', about two years later than this script, did any but three or four people know the true story here reported, the love story of A. J. Balfour and Mary Lyttelton. On page 115, King Arthur of *The Idylls of the King* is a symbol for Arthur Balfour. On page 93, at A. J. Balfour's wish, it is described how 'the ring was placed upon her finger and buried with her'.

(5) That G.C. did doubt the story is proved by a letter to the editor in which she told her that she had just written a script with a romantic tale that probably was unconscious fiction. But the ring was buried in the grave, and A.J.B. did return once a year.

(Ed.) This script was obtained on March 22, but not at once sent to Major Tennant for annotation, as Miss Cummins was interested in 'the process of communication' part, wanted to copy it and didn't have time. So she put it away.

On March 30 she went to tea with Mrs. S., and they talked of her friend the Irish poet AE, also about Yeats. Miss Cummins said that in her opinion Yeats's head always ruled his heart for all his lyrical poetry about Maud Gonne. Mrs. S. capped this with a story to show the heart may rule the head, even in the case of an intellectual. She said Arthur Balfour had been in love with a girl who died while he was abroad. He rushed home to offer her an engagement ring, but it was too late. Mrs. S. did not mention her name. That was all that was said about it. Miss Cummins continues; 'On my way home her story struck me as being similar to the one in script on March 22. But I couldn't find it till April 4. I then told Mrs. Gay (member of the S.P.R. Council) about it and wondered should I destroy the script because of the similarity. She told me not to. I visited her and brought her the script to read, also showed her my engagement book which contained date of "Winifred" sitting and my visit to Mrs. S.'

Mrs. Gay having told Mr. Salter about this, he wrote to Miss Cummins on May 9, 1958, urging her most strongly not to destroy the script. 'Nobody would doubt your word that it was written before your Palm Sunday meeting with Mrs. S., and, therefore, it was not in any way influenced by anything she then told you ... I feel sure that Major T.

would be interested in seeing this script, as I should be myself. Your scripts are among the most interesting developments in psychical research for many years.'

April 12, 1958. Script 15.

Astor. Yes, I will inform her of the letter.

'Winifred, T.

'I am very interested to hear of a message to me in Mr. Salter's letter. Please read it.'

(Message read: 'I see Winifred writes: "Should Mr. Salter's desire fail—and Ecclesiastes tells us that it frequently does ..." When you next meet her, tell her how gratified I am to know that I am mentioned by name in Holy Writ!'

'I am pleased to hear of Mr. Salter's gratification. But I fear that he does not know Ecclesiastes as well as I do! Of course, his Sunday School days are somewhat distant in time. In my case, owing to the beauty of Ecclesiastes, I learnt for pleasure much of it off by heart. It was suitable for the sombre mood on the rainy days of youth.

'Now my comment. There is no mere mention of Mr. Salter's name in Ecclesiastes. Ecclesiastes is actually addressed to him. Pray note a statement in an early verse in which the Preacher says he is seeing what is good for the sons of men and what they should do all the days of their life. At the close of this lovely and instructive poem, the poet reverts from the general to the particular, i.e. Mr. Salter. He wrote, "My son, be admonished." I hope Mr. Salter is fittingly admonished! He is everyman or in the Preacher's words, "my son".

'It may certainly be gratifying that this masterpiece among sermons is solely addressed to the male members of the human race. Noticeably women are left out of it, as if they did not exist! But here for our reassurance, I may mention that Ecclesiastes is bracketed with the Song of Solomon, at any rate by King James's inspired translators of the Bible.

'In the years of my adolescence, I was impressed that this twin poem is obviously intended as instruction for the daughters of women. But to me when I was a girl, the Song of Solomon was informative rather than instructive. What is Helen's view? Are those two poems twins? One for the instruction of every man, and the other for the instruction of every woman?

"Meantime, W.H., go back to your Sunday School and seek instruction from the teacher concerning these two poems (1).

(1) The relevance, if any, of script 15 has not been discovered, but it is in 'Mrs. Willett's' style.
April 13, 1958. Script 16.

(A clear day—got following script.)
'Astor. Yes, she is here and very impatient.
'Winifred T.
'Now I must revert to serious matters.
'I had a vision of a scene on earth that slowly approached me.
It looked like an old manor. Then suddenly it seemed that I was wafted into its interior, and I perceived Mr. and Mrs. Salter looking at papers. I received the impression that they were studying past records in which I played a part. The whole thing steadied up in a picture of these two in a lovely old Elizabethan house, with shelves and shelves of books. Oh so many books!' (1).

'It gave me a little heartache to see Helen so like her mother when incarnate and also W.H., both studying. They were reminiscent of a swiftly vanishing adornment of English life—scholarship and a tradition of culture so different from their primitive ugly age of speed records, cars and planes and bombs.

'But I must not be sentimental. I only wish to repeat that they may publish what they consider suitable from the records in all that concerns me personally.

'One of the attractions of dying is the feeling of escape from earthly responsibilities. It is not that I am an entirely irresponsible being. But I see that I attached an exaggerated importance to the conventions.

'At any rate, fresh information from the records does not matter now, as the reaper has been so busy with his scythe.

'Through my fears I placed restrictions on the report of adventures of the soul, which, even if small in themselves, if known might help to convey the larger hope to some few thinking people. I am not alone in this belief. The Group, Fred; Professor V., Gerald (2), and others urge such publication as Helen and W.H. consider of value.

'We are all as dead as a Dodo to human beings, however much we are alive to ourselves in this hither state. Those related who come after us stand on their own merits. They are not responsible for their ancestors' performances on earth. If they are hurt by revelations, then it is only hurt vanity ... a reprehensible quality.

'I am not sure whether Helen caught impressions my other self sent her. They were despatched when I was not studying her and W.H. in their residence as one does a painting in a picture gallery.

'Their house is rich in memories. No doubt owing to its age and its inhabitants. This and my emotional tension on a matter about which I have thought much made my perception of what may or may not have been received confusing.

'Gerald was right in believing that a human being consists of a number of selves or aspects with a primary self, the total of a sum in arithmetic. From this hither state, one aspect of me seeks a contact with Helen, another aspect seeks to make a contact with G.C.

'We only become unified in spirit or the other self on the higher level.

'When I communicate, I blend with the automatist in the sense that I depend partly on her memory and her standard of intelligence for words in which to express my thoughts.

Occasionally her subliminal mind enters my mind, plunders an idea or memory. It is not all a one-way traffic.

'Then, of course, her mind may insert in patches its own mistaken interpretation. Supernal and infernal juggling can occur (3).

'Losing hold now.

'Winifred'

(1) In a letter to G.C. (23.4.58), W. H. Salter writes: 'Her (Winifred's) references to the house are of interest. She speaks of it as Elizabethan, which may be right, as the house is certainly a good deal older than the date on the porch, which is 1692. That was when considerable alterations were made and the present ornamented front was added. The Crown and roses that figure in the decorations are traditionally supposed to commemorate a visit from Elizabeth. We have a good number of books but not, I fancy, as many as Winifred had in her own home.' G.C. adds: 'For all I knew the house might have been a modern villa.'

(2) (Ed.) She probably refers to the proposed publication of 'The Palm Sunday Case'.

(3) The Balfour Study, pp. 299-300, contains the same idea in subtle detail, and with many technicalities, supposedly transmitted by Edmund Gurney to G. W. Balfour. The latter says, page 300, 'If the scripts in question are the product not of inspiration from an external intelligence, but of subliminal mentation, I am driven to the conclusion that the subliminal in this instance has exhibited a subtlety of speculative thought very decidedly beyond anything I believe the Mrs. Willett with whom I am intimately acquainted to be capable of. Mrs. Willet

herself, to whom the trance productions have now been shown for the first time, assures me that they are "so much Greek" to her, and leave her utterly bewildered and *bored*.'

April 19, 1958. Script 17.

Astor is here. Yes, this soul says she is anxious to continue her memoirs today. She expresses the hope that you will be all attention and not misinterpret what she wishes to convey.

'Winifred Tennant.

'Oh, what am I going to commit myself to today through signing this document? 'Now, my Lords, my judges, I shall speak of the influences that shaped a portion of my long life. These may show that Winifred still exists, despite the fact that she has discarded her ancient bag of bones.

'Fragments of memories flutter by me as do the leaves in the fall of the year. It was not solely the First World War that gradually altered my outlook and inspired in me a conceited missionary zeal to reform mankind. I call it conceited because it is rarely possible to reform anyone. Only bitter experiences may do that.

'There was an influence that at one time in my life helped to leaven the lump called Winifred. I had the privilege of acquaintanceship with a remarkable family. I shall endow them with the surname Lob, so that I may write the more freely about them.

—G.C., you must know where that word comes from—yes, cricket (1).

'Lob is a very suitable pseudonym as the men of that clan were brilliant in performance in the serious game of cricket.

In the more trifling pursuit of politics, a couple of them held high positions. But in that field their performance was average, they made no boundary hits. Lob best describes their political play.

'Another of the family of Lob attained to what was regarded in that era as one of the highest educational positions in the land. After all, he deserved it, as he was a very fine cricketer in the estimate of what was called the ruling class of that day. I was in awe of him but did not like him on the occasion my husband and I deposited our son in the educational establishment over which he reigned for a time. George was a nervous boy.

'Then there was another brother. A Lob married to Edith. He had an attractive personality. Edith with her seriousness, I suspect, tempered his brightness somewhat, but gave him drive, purpose. She was a steadying influence in respect of his concentration on one pursuit instead of several. He was a versatile man. He came to work in the political field, and gained an important position (2) in it, dealing with our far-flung lands—our greater Britain. How proud Edith was of him!

'The Lob family was largely male—a number of sons. One Bob married another Edith. Two sisters-in-law called Edith were awkward, so Mrs. Bob was generally known as D. What a contrast were these two sisters-in-law! Edith was cultured, had great practical ability, was a managing woman redeemed by a capacity for deep and loyal affection, very reliable, but, Oh, she was so serious! D. was lively, a musician and not at all serious, attractive. She was an excellent pianist, a good accompanist, and on the piano she improvised beautifully.

'D's father, of course, sang divinely, sang to so many hers . . .er. Do you get it . . . sang . . . er.

'Music gives permanence to passing memories. I shall not easily forget Mrs. Bob. But music is, as I have recently discovered, more of an other-world art than any other art" (3).

(1) G.C.: 'Did Mrs. Willett try to conceal from me who the Lytteltons were by the name of "Lob"? But in my youth I had heard of the Lyttelton brothers, their cricket exploits and political success, so I soon guessed who the Lytteltons were. The "Edith" mentioned on page 65 is obviously Dame Edith Lyttelton. George went to Winchester College, not Eton. Mrs. Willett corrects this mistake in script 26, page 100. A.T. and H.T. went to Eton. A "Lob" was headmaster of Eton.

(2) G.C.: 'A Lob married to Edith. This is clearly Dame Edith Lyttelton. Her husband was a Cabinet Minister.'

(3) G.C.: Two sisters-in-law called Edith were awkward, so Mrs. Bob was generally known as "D". I learned from Mrs. Heywood that Dame Edith was known as "D.D.", so this looks like a mistake of the communicator's. On the other hand all the information about "Mrs. Bob" on page 66 is correct. This I learned when, after the termination of the scripts, I met a lady, Mrs. Willis, on the island of Jersey. She said that Mrs. Bob was attractive, very lively, also an excellent pianist who could improvise. Her father was a singer called Sanger or Sangster.'

April 20, 1958. Script 18.

Astor. Yes, here is Winifred.

'Winifred Tennant. What did I say last? Ah, yes.

'Now Edith and D. disagreed on a number of topics but they were at one in their interest in psychical research. D. might be more correctly described as being intermittently interested in the marvellous and the supernatural. Oh, she had a mind that flashed and did not stay—except perhaps in music—in groove of any one pursuit. In that we were akin. My interests were multiple.

'Of course any psychic experiments were all a very private affair. Inviolable secrecy about them was emphasised when I was invited to join the circle. It was agreed that no word of them should be let slip to anyone. Careers had to be protected (1).

'A certain statesman of no mean repute who had been a frequent visitor to the clan of Lobs was a friend. He became interested in the sittings held by them. A loss through death had drawn his attention to the question of whether there was or was not a supernatural world.

'I may say now that I was the recipient of certain messages that impressed this intellectual and metaphysical Scotsman.

Racially he was half-English, and that made him at first very critical. His personality intrigued and impressed me. I was curious and wanted to plumb the depths and get behind the mask.

'Charming and aloof by nature and inclination, a scholar and a metaphysician, he yet controlled himself to work in humdrum politics. But heredity and family influence on the distaff side drove him to become an M.P. and a fine speaker. It has to be remembered he was a leading figure in the political world.

'I did not care for his charm when he exerted it. All that repelled me, as it was not his true self. But once in early days of our acquaintance he made to me a remark I never forgot: "The ways of clear thinking lead straight into the valley of mysticism." It was contrary to my small mystical experience in the sense that I likened it to a soaring into the empyrean.

'But no doubt that notion of mine was, as I see now, rooted in the belief of the small child that heaven was somewhere behind the blue summer sky. Anyhow his remark for the first time linked me to his real self, unveiled it to me. Behind his mask, behind the ambition of the English part of him, was the potential Scottish mystic. One cause of the unhappiness of this man was because his ambition to serve his country, the influence on him of relatives, led him to be a hard-working politician. Such a life compelled him to crush down his mystical nature, banish his real self. The woman he loved had understood and drawn out that anti self, as I have previously described it. But she had gone.

'Of course my meetings with him were comparatively rare—I mean at the Lobs' house. But later I saw more of him when he was old (2).

'However the point I wish to make is that the Lobs and this statesman all influenced me. They helped to encourage in me an ideal of service in some capacity in public life. Oh, I heard such good conversation in the Lob household. How quick their men folk were! How pettily feminine I felt myself to be as I listened! 'As to my career.

'In the political sense I was, as I quickly learnt, an abject failure, and also that through political work it is rarely possible to reform anyone, such as in that talking shop, the League of Nations. But for one of my type, with more ardour than intelligence, it is possible in a small way, to ameliorate people's humdrum lives, brighten them, give them interest and provide a little beauty, and in Wales I worked on that line of welfare.

'The Welsh have never been properly understood. They are a very independently minded people. Early Puritanism flourished in Wales, and the Methodist revival there in the eighteenth century indicated their independent outlook. Behind a somewhat rough manner, their working people have a warmth and kindness and religious feeling.

'The Presbyterian Churches preserved the Welsh language organised under Cumana Gyfredinol. All the same, there was a certain grimness, bareness, I might say ugliness in the religious services and churches of the majority. I, who had lived in Italy, and loved it, wanted to bring a little of its beauty into the lives of the people. I. tried to encourage art, whether painting or music. Oh, I worked hard on committees with that object in view. I attended and helped at musical festivals and picture exhibitions (s).

'You will say that I have a bad conscience and so I am trying to justify my terrestrial existence with such boasting. But such activities as I have mentioned gave me very real pleasure. I should have loved to be an artist, but had no real talent (4). So I sought to encourage potential Welsh talent of an artistic kind.

Also practical details in public work helped to keep me balanced.

I was rather afraid of the psychic or dream side of my nature.

It might tip down too much the seesaw, for mine was a dual nature. Like the statesman I so much admired, whose inclination was towards mysticism and metaphysics and who is only remembered as a politician, I too suppressed and I think with advantage the desire to dream, to seek other supernal worlds. Only occasionally I became Mrs. Wills.

'All this about myself may seem very dull. But if I am to seem real to my judges it is necessary to show motives for my actions, and how I was moulded into a definite personality. Of course what was fundamental was bestowed on me as a small child.

'Mary Richardson created the fundamental aspect. To her I think I owed the Celtic Welsh power that enabled me to travel in worlds unseen (5). From her side, not his side, it came, though neither had it. Can't hold on.

'W.T.'

(1) G.C.: 'Mrs. Willis told me that Mrs. Bob first roused her interest in psychic research. Also that Mrs. Bob had a quick mind, flitting to a number of things, but especially music. Mrs. Willis likewise told me that the psychic experiments made by the Lytteltons were kept secret, as the men were in politics.'

(2) G.C.: 'Winifred in script 18 mentions A. J. Balfour as "the metaphysical Scotsman" attending such sittings. Correct. A.J.B. had sittings with Mrs. Willett at the Lytteltons, after the death of May Lyttelton. See the "Palm Sunday Case".'

(3) See script 10, note 11.

(4) See script 9, note 5.

(5) (Ed.) Here she attributes her psychic gifts to her Welsh mother, Mary Richardson, saying it came from her side not from her father's, George Serocold's, side. From her diaries it is clear that she confided her psychic experiences to her mother, but she is wrong about her father, or at least the 'script-personality' remembers incorrectly. Her Father wrote a memoir of his life, in which on page 82 he mentions that as a child he had a vision of an aunt the night she died, and as a young man on board a ship at Hong Kong, he had in broad daylight a vision of his father coming into the cabin on the very day his father died in England. On page 103 of the (MS. memoir) he describes how on a punitive expedition in Australia he saw bushmen being shot and saw them fall, then saw them rise/and run on, but with their bodies still remaining dead on the ground. He says he thinks it was their 'psychical bodies' that ran on.

So it is evident, as seems often the case, that Winifred had inherited her remarkable psychic gift.

May 3, 1958. Script 19.

Astor is here. Yes. Winifred is eager to write and presses in today.

'Winifred Tennant.

'I am still seeking the motives and influences that shaped my life. So, G.C., pray be all attention and do not misinterpret what I shall try to convey to you.

'Last time I wrote I mentioned the statesman A.B. His political opinions were not mine in the old days. I have told you, I think, that his superficial personality, his perfect manners, his cool, exasperating detachment in speaking about world disasters and cruelties (1) I greatly disliked. Actually he was like a player at a chessboard, who exhibits extreme calm when his pawns are hard pressed, his Queen threatened.

'It was only when at last I penetrated behind the facade and briefly was illuminated by his real Scottish self that I was affected and influenced by him and moved by the conflict in his nature. But L.G. was my political hero in the far days when the Liberals deposed A.B. and then L.G. became prominent and some time before that too. He represented my loved Wales for me, you see.

'Then in those, to me, wonderful years of Liberal reforms in the H. of C., before the outbreak of war, it was this Welshman's Celtic eloquence, the imaginative quality of his oratory, his pleading the cause of the poor, that carried me away.

Looking back on my earlier personality, I feel that what the foe called "lime-housing" in his speeches led me more than anything else to go in for public work and made me a fervent Radical. I was rather crude in those days. My hero tumbled off his pedestal later (2).

'It is strange how I forget so much and then I meet some old friend here, and it prys [prizes] a hole in the earth-time past, and one digs out some nugget of memory. I have met dear friends—Pry-Pryse. Stupid. Listen. I used to stay with them in their lovely country house, long, long ago (3). Such happy days.

They reminded me of our one disagreement, politics, and of how disturbed they were because of my extreme Radical views and worship of the Welsh wizard (3). I agree with them that no man is fit to be placed on a pedestal and how little the political *strum und drung* [drang] of that period matters now! But, oh, it was good to meet these dear friends and play the game of memory-tracing. But I had another meeting. I have been too sore about it to mention it previously. It was a kind of disintegrating disappointment. You, H., wouldn't realise what that loss meant to me, but when my daughter died, I wept and wept (4). Soon after my exit from the earth I was with her again. The long separation should not have made such a difference. But she has much changed, and she behaved like a stranger to me. Your father is all in all to her (5). Perhaps after all my connection with her was only through the physical maternal link, but how powerful that can be. I deeply mourned her death. Oh, I was beside myself at the time she left me. I see of course that it is not the maternal physical link but the permanent soul link that is of account when we meet in this supernal world. Of course I may not be ready yet. I may link up with her later.

'What did you say? A letter from my son. Please hold it so that I may perceive its contents.'

(A pause. G.C. held letter from H. Tennant.)

'It was my loss through the sudden highwayman robbery of death that led me to start my automatic writing again.

'So I am to write about "the inception of my work as Mrs. Willett".

' "Inception"? Oh, my dear H., what a clumsy word to use about those hours of grief, when I had lost what was then most precious to me! Plundered by cruel death, and I so longed for news. Oh, the loneliness!

'Forgive me. Recollection for the moment has made me relive the emotion of that poignant time.

'Eventually I was rescued from it. Eventually I found one I have in a previous script called Portia (6). In my despair I wrote to her, and received the kindest of letters from her in reply. It was steadying, calming, made me rational again. We exchanged further letters. V. Portia was wisely judicial. She got me to read a printed record or review of evidence of survival received by a stranger. If I remember rightly, the lady was the wife of a judge in India and an automatist (7). It does not signify who it was. The record discussing her writing was encouraging to me and gave me confidence. In fear and still emotionally overwrought, I tried to listen in and obtain automatic writing for myself.

'At first I was distrustful or perhaps too anxious. There were a few scribbles only. Then I made a great effort, managed to keep calm, to dissolve into the hush of one lovely still autumn day. Its peace gave peace to me. I took up my pen, and the writing came swiftly, coherently. Oh, I was overjoyed at first when I read it through, and later two or three other scripts came with the same speed. I sensed my communicator—my brother-in-law. He gave me such good news. All was well, all was happiness for my beloved dead. But one morning cool reflection came to me after waking. I read again Portia's advice. She had told me to be critical, to weigh and measure any script I might obtain. I reviewed the circumstances of the writing. I noted that the words seemed to shape in my brain before they were written, but not the sense of the sentences that were written. Still the words coming just beforehand to me seemed not at all as it should be, if it was a communication from Fred or anyone else.

The hand was different from my own handwriting, but then I knew the character of my brother-in-law's writing and the other (illegible) hand.

'Was it then, all invention, the invention of a hidden part of my mind? Yes, it seemed that the news in these scripts was too good to be true, though here and there I found a something unexpected, unlike any wish of mine, unlike me. 'Words were written that had no meaning for me, though they might have meaning for others. I was urged by Fred, the alleged source, to continue with these scripts. But my critical faculty, now on the alert, led me to feel that Fred was not dictating. So in a fit of disappointment I tore all those scripts up and burnt them. We forget much, but we do not easily forget the emotions engendered by sorrowing disappointment and frustration. That was a bad morning for me. I became extremely depressed.

'The approach of winter was gloomy, shadowed by that loss, shadowed by my doubts as to whether there was any future, if so what future, for my darling. I did not ask for news of the Blessed casting down their golden crowns before the glassy sea. I only wanted one light whisper, one sure sign from over the border. It had so far been denied me.

'That Christmas was certainly not a festive time for me personally. I tried to be cheerful for my son George's sake. The poor little fellow would be going back to school so soon. Then he fell ill and really was ill most of that time. If death snatches away out of what has been a happy home life one dear, suddenly, awfully, it is impossible not to be apprehensive. I was in a tension of nerves. Absurdly in dark moods I imagined that death would come and snatch my George too. There was one day when he really seemed so ill I could believe only the worst would happen, and I was compelled to hide my dread from everyone. Then as I sat down to dinner that cloud lifted strangely through an active irritant. I felt someone unseen very disapproving close to me talking, lecturing me. Soon I knew for a certainty that it was Fred scolding me for my crazy fear for my George. Oh, he was so pressing in his urging me to have faith and not be gloomy and anxious any more. I was to try for script if I had the least doubt about it.

Well, I very nearly left the dinner table then and there, but I pulled myself together and even made a show of eating, but for a few minutes I couldn't speak. Oh! I didn't give myself away. But the impression was strong. No doctor could have been to me so emphatic as was Fred then.

It was the first time, apart from my automatic writing attempts, I had the direct sense of the presence of the so-called dead and of urgent speech from one I knew well.

'After dinner when I was alone, I got a line of writing from F.M., assuring me that there was no need for anxiety and that George could go back to school. As it turned out, he was quite right. Oh, the relief I obtained from that experience.

'You may, G.C., think I was a foolish, believing person, who imagined it all. But you cannot understand the feelings of a mother and the hopeless mood that then possessed me. It changed to such complete reassurance and hope. I only tell you of this episode in my life because it happened to be the turning point for me. After that I had confidence in my automatic writing and in certain impressions conveyed to me mentally and sometimes unexpectedly. So if when later a sitter was present I sometimes spoke and sometimes wrote the messages.

'Alex was not born in the year of my loss. He came the next year, in 1909. He was my second son, and the little baby was a joy to me. I wonder why it is, G.C., you draw me on, and make me draw up from memory all forgotten things so pent up with emotional wishes and fears, and the sense of life after death.

In 1909 I gave birth to Alex and rebirth to my psychic faculty (8).
'What a year!'

(1) From a MS. account by Winifred of a visit to Whittingehame to the Balfours in 1923: 'Arthur is a typical *Grand Seigneur* who has been sheltered from friction and offence—his circumstances have brought him great prizes at the cost of far less effort of most men—the thoughts of "The common herd" are not only hid from him, but—all unguessed as they are—brushed aside as trivially unimportant. Arthur has no capacity for moral indignation and none of that imaginative sympathy which makes the tragedy of human life as it is and must be in a world like this, a pain personal and real to oneself... he just misses being a great man by reason of his lack of humanity and imagination.

In fact I believe it is a lack in the capacity for imagination that is at the bottom of his emptiness.'

(2) Lloyd George is described by Winifred in notes made by her during a stay in his house at Churt, December, 1922, as 'Certainly the most vivid, vital, dynamic creature I ever met.' It was of course he who had made her a delegate to the League of Nations. He told her, in October, 1922, 'Balfour says you did extraordinarily well.' She admired him greatly but in these very remarkable series of notes on her various visits at his house she also saw him with critical eyes.

When the script says 'My hero tumbles off his pedestal later,' this decidedly borne out by an entry for March 1, 1946 in her diary: Listened to broadcast on L.G. . . . at end I asked myself—How could he—how could he have abandoned everything he stood for and died in the degradation of a Renegade . . . and becoming a peer!!' She seems to have forgotten a note she made while staying at Churt in February, 1925. Lloyd George asked her: 'If you could meet one character in history who would you meet?' Winifred said 'Socrates'. Ll.G. said, 'Morgan the buccaneer before them all.'

(3) G.C. 'Since these scripts were written I have learned from Mrs. Douglas Fawcett that Winifred used to stay at her parents' house in Wales, when she herself was a young girl and Winifred newly married. Extract from Mrs. Fawcett's letter, June 30, 1964: 'My maiden name was Pryce . . . the original form was Prys (son of Rys) . . . Winifred Tennant periodically came to stay at Gumley and invariably had battles (fierce) with my father, an out and out Conservative and one who politically disliked Lloyd George, because he had just brought in Form 4, a measure which greatly affected landed proprietors adversely financially".'

(4) After the death of her baby daughter Daphne, Winifred writes in her diary that she is 'finished with life' and 'each day brings me nearer Home'.

(5) In the (MS.) Daphne memoir, written by Winifred, she mentions Daphne's father's great love for her, his playing with her, and how she was always by his chair at Margate.

(6) H.T. now asks to be told of 'the inception of her work as Mrs. Willett'. In moving words she retells what is told in the Balfour Study, pp. 49-53. The two accounts complement each other although dealing with the same subject matter and in places using identical words.

(7) Winifred refers to 'Mrs. Holland', a sister of Rudyard Kipling, the name is a pseudonym; she was the wife of an officer in the British Army in India.

(8) Correct. Her son, A.T., was born in November, 1909.

May 4, 1958. Script 20.

Astor. Here is this obstinate and charming person.

'Winifred Tennant.

'I note with amusement that in my son's letter to you, G.C., he puts "Winifred" and my pseudonym, "Mrs. Willett", thus in inverted commas. Dear "Henry Augustus", I return the compliment (1).

'Your curious punctuation suggests doubt, continued doubt, so I also register doubt of your real existence with retaliatory punctuation. Is "Henry Augustus" myth or legend, or is he a dream I dreamt in my infancy long ago? Dream or reality, I love him still—so much so I shall now continue my reply to his request that I write of the "inception" of "Winifred's" work as "Mrs. Willett".'

Pray give me all your attention, G.C. I must now return to a comparatively early period in my life, considering the length of its duration.

'I used, when I was young, to think that the prayer in our prayer book to deliver us from sudden death an odd and mistaken supplication. It was one in which I never joined (2). For it seemed to me a healthy death to slip out of the body in a moment or in a very brief time. Healthy because, beyond perhaps a few moments of disintegrating pain, the consciousness was not tortured by long degrading illness before the transit from one level of existence to another. But the sudden death of my darling in 1908 gave me such mental pain, such a shock, I always afterwards joined in that supplication to deliver us from sudden death.

'Yet the loss of my treasure then was also my great gain. It led me for the first time to become a thinking person, seriously to ponder, and I had time, to read about the mystery of life and death. My reading led me nowhere, but V. Portia led me somewhere. She made me an eager explorer, as eager as was any participant in the ancient Greek mysteries. But I did not go in for any elaborate practices or preparations. How could I? I had various duties, a husband, a son, a household to look after. I was carrying a child in 1909 (3).

'And now I am going to write something that you "Henry" won't accept or in any way believe. From the date in January your uncle Fred relieved my mind about George, I was convinced that he and another wanted me to write at their dictation. Oh, they coerced, coaxed, and bullied me later. But at first I now and then became sensible of their presences. In that time I obtained scripts from Fred, I did not even tell Portia about. They were too private. But I may say that Fred and

Gurney became very pressing, urging me not to be afraid of my subliminal "mind's" interference in the writing. They could achieve much, they believed, with me, if I would only give them opportunities for communication. What you, "Henry", will not believe is that Fred and Gurney were living in 1909, and when communicating Fred was the same as ever, exhibiting his characteristic impatience and eagerness. He got so annoyed with me, and then so sad and earnest when, out of mischief, I threatened not to go on with the writing.' (4)

(G.C. Emotional explosion sensed by me.)

"After that I certainly did not put his name in inverted commas. He was real, he was beside me, in spite of being invisible to my eyes. Though my memories are fragmentary, I have never forgotten that peak point in my life. The pressure from the other side of the invisible presences was more continuous than I ever dared to admit to anyone. You see, when Fred really wanted a thing he had great persistence. And on this occasion he was very much his earthly personality in his eagerness to do his kind of missionary work to convert a worldly world.

In that year I also received private and personal statements that were connected with his family problems that explained much to me. Such messages are not of any interest to the public. But to me they were utterly convincing and saturated with his personality. Fred had lived his life before he was married.

In earlier years there was a woman he deeply loved. But she was taken away from him. Unfortunately for him and Eveleen the allegiance of his heart was irrevocably given to her. Though he was kind and good to Eveleen and showed her, I believe, a passionate love at times, that was largely of the physical, therefore the superficial. She could not help but know that hers was a secondary place in his life. Poor soul! At first great was her suffering. But she seemed to overcome that for a while. At any rate she took pride and joy in the fact that brilliant F.W.H.M., so much admired, was her possession. She fenced him round with her jealousy and her fear of living women led her to be always on the alert and at times very suspicious. Oh, there were occasions when Eveleen made him very unhappy. He was true to her, but though a faithful husband he was not hers.

She might suggest that he paid too much attention to some living woman. But with all her instincts she knew that he was married in his soul to that first love. This woman was the more formidable in being dead, and incidentally years later she caused much annoyance and trouble.

'Now Eveleen was the belle of Society in the London of her day. She had everything that the world could give her, yet she had nothing. For she who was so possessive, did not possess her husband's soul, his permanent love. Pity Eveleen, though it was Fred who suffered most from her tantrums.

'In that time of the inception of my work as Mrs. Willett, Fred made references to the situation in his married life (5).

His own death had not altered Eveleen. She was still jealous (6). He remained her prized possession. So Fred advised a pseudonym for me. He urged it, or at least secrecy, if, as he prophesied, I was to carry out important work for him.

'So here was the primary reason for my secretiveness about my supernal experiences during my work in the passing years with Gerald and others. Of course there were other reasons also for my anonymity. But this warning in that early time deeply impressed me. An automatist is usually over sensitive and has to guard herself against other people's angry, passionate-driven thoughts. The thoughts are more dangerous than any row face to face, as you will no doubt understand, G.C.

'Naturally I did not inform Mrs. V. Portia about what I called the family scripts, which mainly related to Fred and Eveleen. Even now I cannot bring myself to tell you all about them.'

(1) H.T.'s first name, not second, is Augustus.

(2) A.T. remembers that his mother told him she used to omit this prayer.

(3) Correct. She was pregnant with A.T.

(4) In her diary, November 1, 1904, Winifred writes: 'Fred's new book out... he was a strange man with a brusqueness and irritability of temper that disconcerted one . . .' (5) A correct account of Myer's secret love. Not made public till five months later than this script. See paper by W. H. Salter in *S.P.R. 'Proceedings'*, vol. 52.

(6) 'Eveleen was still jealous.' G.C. cites letter from W. H. Salter (25.1.58) that 'When she [Winifred] began to get communications from Myers, Eveleen behaved very badly to her, as to other automatists of the S.P.R. group'. When Mrs. Verrall, Mr. Salter's mother-in-law got communications from Myers soon after his death, and thought to please Eveleen by showing them to her, quite the contrary was the case.

May 5, 1958. Script 21.

Astor. Yes, she is eager to continue while conditions are favourable.

'Winifred Tennant.

'Of course the ordinary citizen will dismiss the statement I wrote on the last occasion about "the inception" of my work. He will say that bereavement led "Winifred" to become temporarily insane. But unlike the mad I heard no voice or voices with my ears when Fred, at the awkward moment when I was dining, addressed me with such compelling vehemence. 'But I have even more scandalous news to relate about Winifred T., the magistrate.

'Such impressional conversations with Gurney, Fred and occasionally two or three others singly occurred at intervals over the years that followed. Yet during that period I behaved with normal mediocre sanity in my public and private work. My remarks made when I sat on the Magistrate's Bench later were treated with respect as the utterances of a mature, experienced woman (1).

'But I had to protect myself against the allegation of insanity, and this was another reason for my adopting the pseudonym of Willett.

'But, to be precise, dear mythical "Henry", some little time after the startling break-through of Fred, Gurney stole into the field of my attention. Here was another impressional approach. His was the same method as that adopted by Fred, but, oh! so different! There was for me no sense of impatience, of urgency. All was calm. Yet I felt Gurney's nearness, though I had no visible sense of him.

'He was as completely real as he would be to a blind woman on whom he was paying an afternoon call (2).

'However he informed me that he was always very close to me, in touch with me (3). It was somewhat surprising to me to learn that the unseen visitor was no visitor but a permanent companion. Later, thinking it over, it seemed to me a completely false statement. For I had no sense of his nearness, of his presence during the day or night as a rule. For some time the impressional visits were rare.

'I now know that his statement was true. The me Gurney referred to was not the conscious Winifred, who was going about following the daily routine of her life. It was her subliminal mind. Both Gurney and Fred haunted that unconscious part of my mind, preparing it, training it for the inception of scholarly words not in my conscious memory (4). It might be likened to training a retriever to sit and to fetch game when their masters are out shooting.

'As a rule the communicator depends to a great extent on the automatist's memory centre for words and sentences. Words not in it can only be registered so as to create familiarity with them in her subliminal or submerged mind. Gurney and Fred trained it to take at certain moments complete possession of my conscious mind. A great strain to me and to them (5). Then on certain occasions they conveyed unknown words either spoken or recorded by me. The greater number my subliminal mind failed to retrieve from the depths and push up to the surface.

'To put it simply and crudely, the word or words unknown, the unknown surname of Christian name come in the form of sound images to a medium's inner hearing.

'She is like a reporter for a newspaper. It is extremely difficult for a reporter to take down words in a foreign language unknown to him. It is even more so for a medium.

'But let us return to Gurney's message conversationally on that first occasion. This Gurney invited me to take up the pen and write what came into my mind. Doubtful and questioning I obeyed. Hardly anything was written. I put down the pen. Then I got that afternoon-visitor impression. A lively conversation between us went on in mind. I swear to you, "Henry", I was my ordinary self, not in the least excited and I was fully awake.

'Later on Fred in automatic writing informed me that I should have more of these unexpected impressions. It would be preparatory and some of it might appear later in my automatic writing. G.C., this is the method I have adopted with you.

'Indeed I have been in close touch with you whenever you were alone. I can't hold on properly when you are with people on your own level. I tried to impart to your subliminal beforehand what I intended to write. That was difficult.

'I wonder did you now and then get a flash or rather a sense of words a few of which afterwards appeared in our blended automatic writing.

(G.C., Yes, and I wondered then if most of it was my subconscious invention. My story-telling faculty at work.)

'Well, human beings are all story-tellers and produce some excreable [execrable] fiction about themselves at times, and in all sincerity I should like you to be less silent, to make replies to me.

(G.C., I was so interested in you, I did not wish to talk.)

'Stuff and nonsense! There must be give and take, if there is to be good conversation. I had many talks never recorded with the select few who singly honoured me with their presence in the house of my mind. I, after the first nervousness had worn away, made the visitor listen to me, and I had control of the situation.

'When intelligent human beings are less primitive, they will acquire my method and frequently have telepathised talks either with distantly placed human beings or, in more rarified conditions, with their dead. In the latter case it requires solitude and ease of mind for the deep concentration that is needed to pick up accurately what the visitor is saying.

'There is more I could tell, G.C., about my work on different strata's or grades of mind. I have endeavoured to reply today only to my son's question described as the inception of my work.

'Now you are tired, so I shall let go.

'W.T.'

(1) Genuine appreciation of her work as a magistrate was paid to her in a tribute when she resigned.

(2) In her diary for December 22, 1909, Winifred writes: 'Edmund Gurney—no one will ever know the constant help I have received from him.'—Gurney, born 1847, died 1888; together with F. W. H. Myers the chief founders of the S.P.R. In the Balfour Study, p. 52, Winifred is quoted as saying that (in her trance state) 'I don't feel a sense of "seeing" but an intense sense of personality, like a blind person perhaps might have

(3) Winifred in a script of January 29, 1909 (Balfour Study) writes: . . . Gurney ... I am always keeping in closest touch with you . . .'

(4) Balfour Study, p. 51, Myers in her script speaks of framing 'a psychic education' for her.

(5) 'A great strain' a sentiment frequently met with in the Balfour Study, as well as here.

May 27, 1958. Script 22.

Astor. Yes, Winifred has been asking for the pen. Wait a minute. Here she comes. I think that she would like today to present you with another of her backgrounds. She is still intent on her purpose, that of coming alive to her son. And she would like him to become acquainted with that fragment of herself he did not know, because he was not born in the time she describes.

She tells me—'Winifred Tennant.

'My dear G.C. When I received your welcome invitation to write, I was studying a past human personality of Winifred of a rather inchoate pastoral character—at any rate very different from that of the aged Winifred at the time of her passing. But how strong were her emotions. Oh, the innocent vanities, the raptures and the despondencies of the Victorian girl and the young woman! There are not, when the years have added up, any such experiences for the aged woman. Yet deep down I am the same young girl and young woman.

'In a long lifetime the permanent self is always in residence and is as the axle in a wheel round which revolve the spokes, each spoke that superficial thing, a different human personality, but all of them dependent on the axle (1). If a spoke is cracked or breaks, it may be likened either to a neurosis, an obsession, or, when there's a break, a form of lunacy that invades a man or woman. But the normal man or woman's permanent self is united, as is the axle to the spokes.

'So though I am sitting in judgment on my selves as I study the revolving film of memory, I respond again to the emotions of each past personality. Let me talk to you of one of them.

'Far off hills are green. I have just been looking at the moving pictures of my youth, and very moving they are to me. I see again the Cotswold hills. Seen through the eyes of the young, easily stirred Winifred, they seem quite lovely. Pray note that we were living in Gloucestershire for a while in those far off days of my life in a past century (2). G.C., have you stayed in that country?

(G.C., No, never.)

'It is a very pretty county, tame but quite charming. The Cotswold hills are not harsh, high and noble, like the Welsh mountains that at times bewitched me. The Cotswolds are gentle and sweet. I think of the prettiness of a Watteau picture as I survey again while I write that Gloucestershire range of hills. When I lived in that county, one drove in a carriage—how slow the tempo—or I walked in spring or early summer, and rich flowing pastures, wheat fields, perfume, scented and various, delicate honeysuckle twining the hedgerows, May white and pink, all the budding, thronging vegetation inspired me with gaiety and hope.

'Gloucestershire, with its picturesque market town—I saw again North Leach, Chipping Nailsworth and the great river Severn in that film of memory. Orchards, apples, pears, fold on fold or rich luscious land in sunshine. Then its larger towns, Bristol, Cirencester, filed before me. Shelley used that country for his writing. Dear Shelley, your poems nourished my youth with beauty (3).

'Lest this letter become a Baedeker guidebook, I now shall introduce the human element—a scene from my Gloucestershire life just witnessed by me.

'A friend telling me that I was very French in my manner and appearance. I took it as a pretty compliment—she meant it as the reverse of one—and warmly embraced her. Oh! she was so taken aback at what was intended as a depreciatory gibe being received with such a spontaneous expression of joy! But the intended gibe temporarily gave real reassurance, as I was painfully conscious of the disfigurement of being very stout! (4).

But Frenchwomen have an air, a *je ne sais de quoi*, that has always seemed to me admirable (5). This Englishwomen sadly lack, however slim and beautiful they may be.

'But for years my displeasing stoutness caused me grave concern. It quite possibly hurried on my courtship and marriage by increasing my wish to be married to a man much older than myself. Charles was safety and middle age. A safe and affable companion I sought. There is no safety in the too attractive, handsome young man.

'Yes, I have just seen the likeness of that stout young woman in the Portrait Gallery of Memory, and have felt again the old humiliations attendant on too solid flesh. If you would know me, G.C., you have to be introduced to this *vain* young lady, however trivial now seems to me her self-conscious concern about the redundancy of her figure, that, had I but known it then, would have been admired in France. Life is so much an affair of trivialities and one's life is so often moulded by them. It is necessary occasionally to descend to trivialities in what now appears to be becoming my autobiography. But I allude to this physical fact because for one who is an automatist or medium, it is useful to be comfortably covered. When journeying in supernal worlds one is less exhausted, there is less likelihood of injury or illness from exhaustion, the depletion of reserves attendant on the raising of oneself to another vibration.

'One stayed at or paid a weekend visit to country houses. I was so shy I talked too much or was aggressive (6). But such a pleasant life! Lounging in a hammock in a beautifully kept garden, a book and dreams on brilliant summer days. There are two kinds of dreaming, one the grotesque, ugly Freudian kingdom of dreams in sleep, the other the wideawake dreaming in a garden hammock. The latter kind of dreaming during my country-house hours in the hammock was training me, though I knew it not, for my subsequent sittings as an automatist. It meant suspension of one's conscious mind and the flow-in of fancy that maybe was other world life, so rich, so strange was it. But I was very ignorant in those days—only that dreaming was pleasure to me.

There was entertainment of course. I recall the slow crawl of a brougham taking one to a dance—Polka, Waltz, Cotillion, Lancers, winding up with Sir Roger de Coverlet, which ended in a romp. Other days in the glorious burst of decorative green life of early summer, when one went on pony trap saunters through the countryside. No hurry about anything. A life so delightfully leisurely. All this is gone now. People rush about the countryside in stuffy cars and see nothing.

'Why do I tell you all this? Because you cannot know a person unless you know something about their youth and background.

'Lest you should think me frivolous, G.C., I must tell you that in the course of my life I collected many books and eventually possessed quite a meritorious library of them.

'In the period of my life I am at present describing I favoured poetry, and more especially the poems of Tennyson, Shelley, Keats, Wordsworth, Browning, etc., and I am not ashamed to confess that I was an eager reader of the writings of such poets, and others whose works are now considered as out-of-date by authority or as sentimental rubbish, and, indeed are abolished from the memory of the general public (7).

'But the practice of reading poetry or in fact reading discriminately has now almost vanished, I believe; yet it is a far better education than that of listening to the modern vociferous machines, or more unfortunately staring for hours at the procession of ugly little photographs exhibited on television sets. But I am a back number. So it was high time my soul spread its wings and took flight. Indeed, I lived too long on our small planet. Now [that] I am in the course of reviewing my past, I am trying to find out why I was condemned to such a long term of imprisonment in such cramped surroundings (8).

'Vast is the extent of our universes invisible to man's senses.

Glorious the fields of vision I may some day be permitted to explore. Meantime I am doing what the schoolgirl calls her homework, reviewing my past minute life on earth.'

(1) A reference to Myers theory of the soul, see Balfour study, p. 268. As Myers and Balfour are 'in charge' of these Willett scripts, it seems natural that their ideas are occasionally brought in.

(2) According to the Serocold memoir Winifred lived in Gloucestershire during some of her early life.

(3) A.T. 'My mother loved Shelley.'

(4) After the scripts were terminated G.C. was shown a photograph of Winifred as a young woman in a group. She looked 'decidedly stout' in it. Mrs. C.S., also told G.C. that she had heard from an acquaintance of Winifred's that the latter was distressed by her stoutness.

(5) In her diary for April 13, 1898, Winifred writes: 'I think French women are the most elegant in the world.'

(6) See note 3 in script 19, page 71, where her tendency to argue is mentioned.

(7) She had just such a fine Victorian library.

(8) This attitude towards modern man is borne out by an entry in her diary for March 23, 1946. She had seen a play by O'Casey, *Red Roses for Me*, at the Embassy Theatre, and comments: 'A noble play, very unequal in parts, and three things struck me in the face as it were with a brutal fist: the horror of seeing fine drama through a haze of tobacco smoke, the hideous insensitivity of English audiences, the places where they laughed—those which they missed. Woolworth minds, incapable collectively of wonder, awe or stilled emotion—.'

June 7, 1958. Script 23.

Astor. Yes, Winifred is near. Wait for a few moments.

'Winifred Tennant.

'The serial continues.

'What a sharp contrast to Gloucestershire is Wales! Today Wales is my theme.

'I perceive again the hilly road leading to the mountains.

Not a tree breaks the barrenness of those hills, big and wild, short green grass clothing them and in their hollows graze sheep and black cattle.

'The road winds parapet above the ravines. The intense silence is impressive. It is broken gradually by a peasant singing in Welsh—a distant sound, then clear—down the wind comes drifting that wistful lilt of song.

'Now I am travelling a road beyond Dollygelly (l), up through wooded glens. One emerges from them into the warm sunlight. And here come the wide spaces; far below the climbing road lies a great sweep of lowland country, placid and silent.

In the distance the mountains stand massive and aloof, a blue wall stretching along the west.

'The Iris mountain unchanged since its history began. Iris blocks the end of a valley, is massive, indomitable, towering over all things.

'It was not till after my marriage and during more mature years (2), that I came to know Wales off by heart. Its many mountain landscapes were to me both dear, eerie, and occasionally frightening. I loved their heavenly silences in summer sunshine. But in storm they could look so fierce and cruel.

Then I likened Iris, or another greyer, darker, to some huge old Druid capable with his knife of making blood sacrifices, epitome of savage nature, but with a certain primitive noble air.

In contrast the Gloucestershire scene might be likened to a pretty very feminine woman, gentle and sweet. I have seen my Welsh mountains in all moods. I preferred their masculinity, their magnificent aloofness to a rather too sweet womanish Gloucestershire.

'But there were towns in Wales and more especially Swansea an ugliness of architecture! Little grey houses, rows of them, grey chapel, greyness and grimness. I see them still.

'During years of my married life I often felt, despite my own pretty residence, the need of escape to town.

'Charles, my husband, was very understanding.

'And I used especially when the need came over me to flit to town, live in a flat, plunge into the gaiety of London life (2).

Yes, I had a restless nature. Flats in London, its social life, and my country house in Wales. My nature required that contrast.

I was perhaps too much (word illegible) over easily tiring of the same place. Then trips abroad, visits to my beloved Italy.

'It was only in old age I became static, contented to reside through the years in Wales, my body anchoring me there (3).

'There are many things one can never tell about oneself or indeed about other people. I have in these last writings, G.C., committed no indiscretions about contrary human beings and have enjoyed myself in trying to describe the influences of life and nature on that flitting changing speck of mingled matter and mind called Winifred T., during the illusory and disillusioning span of her earthly existence.

'Illusion! Illusion!

'Oh, it is so difficult to be correct in one's statements, to be honest with one's self and others! All unconsciously misstatements slip out. In the Bible one of the most comforting and reassuring passages for me was contained in that episode in which St. Peter told lies before the cock crew. For even when innocent of intention, I used on occasion to talk too much and words ran away with me in decorative fancy.

'It was an American and not the Jew St. Peter, who told the most reprehensible lie in history. George Washington said: "I never tell a lie"! 'When I was a small child, my teacher repeated this Washington anecdote *ad nauseam* to me.

'Thus experience gave me an overstrained conscience—a deep fear of myself that came uppermost during the period I gave sittings to others and was examined or questioned about them by an investigator afterwards. One sometimes emerged from a sitting dazed and drowsy (4). The daze only gradually wore off. It was not a time in which to tell the exact truth, when indeed one wasn't collected enough to know it. Or a letter came later, questioning me about my impressions and my knowledge in connection with the content of a sitting.

'Again how difficult to tell the exact truth about a past, mist-robed experience. After all, Pontius Pilate wrote: "What is truth?" The wisest man on earth does not know it.'

(1) 'Dollygelly' is mentioned in a diary. A.T. says the view is marvellous beyond it.

(2 A.T. says this is correct.

(3) A.T. confirms that she did live in flats in London, that she did visit Italy. Her early diaries are sometimes decorated with Italian.

Until the death of her husband she did live in Wales.

(4) See Balfour Study, p. 57, where she is reported to be 'very dazed' by the communicator.

June 8, 1958. Script 24.

A question to put to Winifred: Your son has asked that you write what you can remember 'About your sittings with the scientist?' Astor comes. Very well. I shall at once ask her the question; she won't like it, as she says she wants to continue her serial.

'Winifred Tennant.

'Oh, dear! Oh dear! I wanted to amuse myself with my serial for a Woman's Journal, and lo! I find myself ordered again into the witness box by my Judge. Pray give me a few moments in which to shift the direction of my thoughts.

'Sittings with the Scientist.

'Now I must apply myself very seriously to the task of recalling that long gone time.

'Fred, my brother-in-law, wrote in that fateful year of 1909 that he was going to make me hear without my writing. Later I would receive these impressions without pencil or pen in my hand. I must speak them, or I could write them down in notes afterwards.

'I think I have told you in a previous letter that in that fate-filled year of 1909 I was very doubtful of this faculty of the soul that was being reborn in me then. It also alarmed me yet fascinated me. At the time I was in a highly nervous state so I came greatly to fear anyone, even such an understanding person as Mrs. Verrall being present and in charge of a sitting of mine.

But Fred pressed me to demonstrate to the scientist of all people.

I must now confess that such a prospect caused me extreme alarm. Mrs. V. or Portia was judicial and advocated it. But when she called on me one day ours was a talk of a general character. It was a wise attitude on her part. There was, as it were, no offensive, no gesture or motion to frighten the easily scared rabbit, so, owing to the encouraging and reassuring things she said I compromised and agreed to give her a sitting.

'It took place in the morning, a time when we would not be disturbed. I may say that my communicator, Fred, was as I knew him a very persistent person when he wanted something badly. And for my own peace's sake I could not let him go on any longer playing the role of the importunate beggar.

'During the morning before Mrs. V. came for the appointed sitting I was agitated, I might almost say stiff with fright; but eventually a sense of my communicator's nearness steadied me.

Such nearness is difficult to describe. But when two minds attempt to play upon one machine, the physical brain, the process may be described as "nearer than hands and feet", nearer than any physical nearness.

'Of course I now know that the owner of that physical machine the brain lends her semi-physical instrument to the communicator, and certainly did so in my case. For in everyday life the instrument the human mind uses is what I can only call the brain of her subtle body. The latter is, I believe, something that is semi-physical and is invisible to the physical senses. One's real mind works through the liaison officer and not directly on the brain machine. In numerous moments of conscious life but not by any means in all, there are physical body effects initiating the brain activities also, but of a lower character.

'But in the case of purely mental processes the brain is the machine and the mind works on it via the semi-physical organ, the instrument. There is in fact a subtle distinction between the subtle body, the instrument and the physical body, the machine. Their harmonious working together or collaboration is of extreme importance for an individual leading a normal civilized life. I may add that once a human being has acquired a habit, the physical brain can go on repeating it without any direction from the mind working through the vibratory instrument. This explains a number of cases of abnormality among human beings and certain character contradictions in the case of normal people.

'Now let us return to the sitting I gave Mrs. Verrall on that bright spring morning. I closed my eyes and then the communicator began to use my instrument, my organ, pulled out the stops, as it were, took control, and my lips spoke the message. I recollect I obtained no automatic writing on this occasion. The reactionary play on my brain of the previous nerve storm led it to go on feebly, owing to the repetition habit motif I have previously mentioned. So the message spoken was hesitant and it was not a good sitting. There was a cramping effect and a limitation of what the communicators desired to say. Yet Mrs. V. expressed pleasure and interest in the results.

'Bear in mind one cause of my nervous condition. Sir Oliver Lodge had been asked for and his presence proposed at a future sitting of mine. This request came not merely in a previous automatic script I had obtained, but in the involuntary impressions I had been receiving from Fred. As the prospect was in conflict with my wishes and had alarmed me, I had only disclosed the fact of Sir Oliver being mentioned in a script when I correspond with Mrs. Verrall. That, at any rate, is my recollection of the circumstances now.

'Oh! I have forgotten to say that on the day after the experiment with Mrs. Verrall, I received a message from Fred in writing, in which he said that he was pleased with the experiment, and he reassured me by saying that he would not repeat it or attempt to repeat it, until a very much later date. How relieved my poor nerves were! For what is postponed may never happen.

'I must add that I met Sir Oliver Lodge for the first time shortly before Mrs. V. called on me, and before our first sitting. It is possibly the impression he made on me when we met socially that led me to take the plunge and sit with Mrs. V.

'How may I describe that first meeting with Sir Oliver? Charm is not the word to apply to him. Kindliness is a more suitable noun with which to describe his gracious reception of me (1). We had only a short conversation. He spoke very appreciatively of my brother-in-law Fred, and of the greatness of his work, and of the need for people psychically gifted, who were of good standing and repute, to devote time to experiments in order to follow up and develop his pioneer work.

'I was deeply impressed. On this occasion Sir Oliver made me feel that it was my duty to keep the door open to my communicators and some time later—oh, I hoped much later, obey their request and give sittings to this great scientist.

'It was not fear of failure but rather another fear that dominated me at that time—that made me put experiments with a critical investigator on the long finger.

'This was the year Alex was born (2). But that is beside the point. This particular year I was also recovering from the shock of loss through death. This personal grief is also beside the point. I merely mention these facts so that you may the more easily understand my somewhat nervous condition and my heightened emotions.

'Today it has been an effort to rummage in the cupboard of memory, so, please, G.C., let me come soon again to write another script in response to my son's question.'

(Ed.) General: Mrs. Willett, who has been cheerfully reminiscing, and providing good evidential material, is now interrupted by a request from her son, H.T. He asks her to remember her 'sittings with the scientist' (Sir Oliver Lodge). This throws us again to the Balfour Study, that most fundamental document. Much of what is said by her in this script can be almost paralleled in the Study, yet never literally, because it is told from the medium's point of view and in her style, again the difference between the 'metaphysical Scotsman' and the lady who is intelligent but no scholar.

She makes it clear in both places that lending herself to the experiments is an immense and at times painful effort for her. What made her do it? We know that it was the death of her child Daphne in 1908 that made her turn to Mrs. Verrall, whom she hardly knew, for possible communication, through Mrs. Verrall's automatic writing, with the child. Being the sister-in-law of F. W. H. Myers, she knew of course about the Society for Psychical Research, was in fact a member of it, until 1905.

Until 1908, however, she was a passive member. Until 1908 her attitude towards death was vaguely pessimistic. During the Boer War, she writes in her diary about 'the dead who sleep a dreamless sleep'.

In May, 1904, at the deathbed of Henry M. Stanley, she writes: 'Oh this process of dying, how bitter it is! This dying by inches ... is there any spring for human beings ... is there a beyond . . . when the mechanism breaks up does anything survive?' At Gladstone's death, which she mourns bitterly, she wonders about 'the mystery of death'.

Then when through the aid of Mrs. Verrall she is started on her own automatic writing and feels that she has received proof of Daphne's survival, her gratitude is boundless. She writes in her diary for January, 1909: 'S.P.R. and cognate interests have of course become the chief thing in my life, the absorbing interest, the greatest source of hope and strength. The miracles wrought by them none will ever know, of succour and compassion and inspiration—nor any words of mine convey the passionate gratitude which reaches out to them from the inmost fibre of my being.

'If this work be not denied me, I feel I can go on, but I can wait . .

She had called her dead child The Darling, and in her diary she speaks of the S.P.R. experiments as 'The Darling's work'.

Sir Oliver Lodge ('the scientist') she seems to have met briefly on February 13, 1909, for the first time, and on the same date she writes in her diary about 'the great difficulty (of) Eveleen's attitude to the S.P.R. and the effect on the whole Tennant family. Mother alone knows all about it. I cannot think of the future or how it will all be—but I am clear to bear all things that the whole world may know the truth . . .

'All this must, I believe, profoundly influence modern thought for the evidence cannot be explained away or accounted for except by admitting the survival of human personality in its fullest and most vivid form. God willing, I will devote my life here and Beyond for this work.'

(1) Most of the facts mentioned in this script are verified in the Balfour Study as well as in Mrs. Willett's own diaries. But her feelings on her meeting with Sir Oliver are not recorded in the Study.

Compare, however, her entry in her diary for April 15, 1909: 'Of the S.P.R. the most surprising thing to me is Oliver Lodge. His *accueil* to me has been astonishing—so extraordinarily kind and gentle and understanding, so unlike my idea of a Professor. I have lost any sense of shrinking in that respect which I had and feel as if I knew him already.

(2) Correct. Her son, A.T., was born this year, 1909.

June 11, 1958. Script 25.

Astor. Yes, here is Winifred. She is anxious to write something, some memory, quickly.

'Winifred Tennant.

'I think I should first write about what Fred called . . .

(words not written.) 'Oh, Listen, can't you! Well, if you can't, I will try another way.

'I described how in 1909 I began the year by getting a mental impression from Fred. Later there were more of these to me at first strange experiences. Occasionally, when I was fully conscious, mentally alert, I received these impressions from communicators. If there was a pencil by me, I used to scribble them down. They came at odd times and sometimes at moments, when it was not possible to make a note of them. G.C., I have tried to adopt this method with you.'

(G.C. Yes, and I became aware of your personality at such times.)

'Of Winifred's mind or character, you should say, I hope (1).

'Now, pray, listen intently.

'Fred gave these mental impressions a name. You may, G.C., have heard of that event, D. Day. A surprise attack if ever there was one. The first mental impression from Fred was a surprise attack. When he gave me good news about my son George's health. Now, liken that to D.Day and you have the name D.Day impressions, or D.D.I., for these mental impressions received by me from communicators (2).

'From D.D.I, impressions there developed, I think, communicated messages spoken, not written, by me. I repeated aloud at sittings what for instance Fred and Gurney were in turn conveying to me. At the outset, I am afraid I was an incompetent interpreter of their words. But Fred wished me to speak and not always to record in automatic writing. I shall call what was spoken by me at sittings "Night Impressions", for at first, and indeed for some time, they were rather a night-mare to me, more particularly when I gave further sittings to Mrs. V., and I began my sittings with Sir Oliver.

'So, please note—

'D.Day Impressions. Communications I mentally received and later or at the time wrote down—all conveyed to me when I was alone—D.D.I, for short.

'Night Impressions. Those Communications I spoke when there was a sitter present—N.I. for short (3).

'I was very much less nervous in the year following my momentous year. The strain was over. My baby had arrived also. My communica-tors were persistent in their demand that I give a sitting to the scien-tist. But I first gave several to Mrs. V.

In my Portia's judgment I had the utmost confidence. Oh, she was so kind, so encouraging. She removed almost all my fears and also gave good advice, told me to let myself go more. I was still too much on the alert. If I would sink my ego more and not keep asserting myself, conversing too much with the communicators as they came along, she believed that I would get remarkable results. It wouldn't hurt me to suppress my ego.

After all, she had not injured herself by this practice, when she obtained automatic writing. This last statement of hers gave me the necessary reassurance. Oh! if it had not been for Mrs. V.

I should never have given a sitting to any scientist.

'As a result of her advice I not merely made three or four experiments with Sir Oliver present, I let go after the first, to me formidable, with him.

'In other words what I had begun to experience in my D.D.I.'s a kind of drowsiness crept over me. I became as it were so remote my ego did not register the words my communicators spoke through me. But what had been my dominant fear, that of going unconscious, did not occur. Perhaps my state was that of the sleeper who in the morning is awake and not awake. Words go through his mind but have little or no meaning for him. My sense of words uttered, but not connected meanings expressed by the sentences, was mine, very vaguely. Certainly in the last of these, I think four sittings I gave to Sir Oliver, that was the case near the close.

'At the end of this sitting I had a feeling of being shaken and was scolded by the communicator, and was told to pull myself together, so I made a great effort and found myself again.

'I have forgotten the details of many of my later sittings and their sitters, but these first attempts with Mrs. V. and Sir Oliver I cannot forget, because of the emotions—I might almost say of anguish—I experienced beforehand. For me emotional experiences cut deepest into memory. They stand out for me now. But these first experiences were like a bridge thrown across a chasm. For they alleviated my dominant fear—that of falling into the chasm—in other words of going unconscious, when the communicators were speaking through me.

'I never cared to confess this, my craven fear. But after all there was some justification for it. I had my duties to others. I was a wife and a mother; I had many other interests and I loved life. Also there were my experiences of D.D.I., impressions or conversations I had when alone with Gurney, Fred, also the Butcher.

But worst of all for me would have been a state of unconsciousness when I was giving N.I., Night Impressions—that is to say speaking communications with someone present.

Oh! it might have been reported of me. Can you ever quite trust anyone? Besides, once initiated, unconsciousness was likely to happen again (3).

'I used to begin an N.I. sitting with automatic writing (4).

I think I may confess now that this was deliberate, for I was more wide-awake holding a pencil or a pen. No danger then of possession. But my communicators preferred the spoken communications. This was doubtless because they found it easier to convey evidence in that way for of course I was less alert in that condition, so I was compelled by them to drop the pencil and speak in the latter part of the sitting in most cases.

General: Mrs. Willett once started on her recollections of the Lodge, Balfour experiments, (cf. Balfour Study), continues, but never literally copying the B.S. either in sequence or in words.

(1)   Balfour Study, p. 80, letter from Mrs. Willett to Mrs. Verrall, of September 27, 1909: '. . . it gives me no more sense of oddness to be talking to these invisible people than it does to be talking to my son, for instance. But ... it is as "minds" and "characters" that they are to me, and yet not at all intangible or not-solid realities.'

(2)   These 'mental impressions' are called in the Balfour Study 'D.I.'s', daylight impressions. Mrs. Willett, probably distrustful of G.C.'s ability to get this odd expression straight, links it up with 'D.Day' which G.C. has heard of, but the result seems to be that instead of 'D.I.' what sticks in G.C.'s mind is 'D.Day Impression' or 'D.D.I.'.

(3) The distinction is made in the Balfour Study, p. 51, between 'Daylight Impression', which are 'mentally received communications that are consciously apprehended and either noted down at the time or subsequently remembered and recorded', and what he calls 'Spoken D.I.'s', in which the 'messages as they come are repeated aloud in the presence of a sitter'.

In this script, Mrs. Willett calls 'Spoken D.I.'s' by another name, 'Night Impressions' since, she says, they were 'rather a nightmare to me.' It has not been possible to find this expression elsewhere in her normal writings. Perhaps she used it in the script as another device for helping the medium not to confuse the two expressions.

(4) Balfour Study, p. 64: 'The rule of "no D.I. without preliminary script" continued to be observed.'

June 13, 1958. Script 26.

Astor: Yes. She is eager to write.

'Winifred Tennant.

'Attention, please, G.C.

'I think that my son's question refers to a number of sittings I gave to Sir Oliver Lodge in 1910. I wrote scripts dictated to me at them, but I also repeated messages aloud.

'I must mention that I took part in my D.D.I, talks with my communicators. I continued to make remarks to my communicators at my first sittings with Sir Oliver, which took place when the Mayflower was out (1).

'I had to help to start things or keep them going—like winding up a gramophone, perhaps. Or let me put it in another way. I had the habit of an experienced hostess of greeting and talking to my guests. Englishmen especially have at first to be encouraged to talk. Can you imagine them filing into a drawing room and conversing with a dumb hostess?

'When they joined the ladies after dinner I never allowed the men to institute a Quaker meeting—in other words to cluster together and only talk to each other. To let them do that was to my mind an unpardonable error. So on these occasions in my ordinary life I developed the fixed habit of producing interaction between male and female in conversation. If I was the sole woman present and two or three men were to be entertained, it was my business to start them off and make intelligent comment on what they said. It paid in my sittings to carry on this hostess habit—drew my two or three communicators near to me and was productive of evidence.

'The difference between my supernal conversations and a conversation in which both parties are visible to each other on the material plane is that in my sittings I had to repeat their remarks to me aloud for the benefit of the sitter, as I did in those 1911 experiments with Sir Oliver. This kind of conversation I have called N.I., Night Impressions. It was somewhat tiring, so, as automatic writing came easiest, I often opened the sitting with it. Much depended also on the wishes of the communicators, as to whether it was to be writing or conversation. In fact I had to obey them.

'G.C., You will, I hope, pardon me for saying that you appear to have the mind of a typist secretary. When I try to give you D.D.I, messages, as you move about, you look attentive and sometimes, as I did, you make a note of a remark or two of mine, but you do not make a comment or in any way reply to me.' (G.C., I am so sorry.)

'Do not apologise. No doubt you have not the habit of being a hostess.

'I would now like you to note that my invisible guests—Gurney, Fred, Butcher, Sidgwick, were absolutely real to me—their minds and presences, I mean. I did not like Professor Sidgwick because I found him dull—too erudite. He did not seem to realise that I was not another University Don. He did try hard on occasions to converse with me, but often his remarks were too complex for me to grasp in order to repeat them to my sitter. So when in this difficult corner, my other self sought to engage another in my group of visitors, or turned away in protest from him. This fact Gurney has informed me of since my demise. Professor Sidgwick was disappointed. It led to Fred and Gurney being my principal communicators.

'There are grades of mind—ranges of varying depth. Though timid at first, I soon found it of intense interest to strive to reach the depths or heights of the mind conditions of these very intelligent men of an invisible company. Much I know I missed of what they sought to tell me, for after a sitting I occasionally felt their disappointment. But I may say that those early experiments with Sir Oliver Lodge made me feel the more assured of their reality, because he spoke of them as if they were present in the flesh. After that experience I knew how correct was my feeling that they were living, vibrating minds.

'My dominant fear of going unconscious was gradually allayed. But a part of that fear was lest people should learn of my N.I. conversations. Hearing of them, the average individual would, for a certainty, have regarded me as insane or most unpleasantly odd. Later on my public work would have become impossible, as I would have been regarded as a quite irresponsible person, incapable of sober judgment. I did not even dare to tell my son Alex about it. I could have trusted him to be discreet. But what would he have thought of me? Hence my secretiveness.

'I was at first appalled when I was told that Gerald Balfour would like to be present at a sitting of mine. Here was another individual who would be a witness of my supernal entertainments. Of course I realised that G.B. was of the strictest integrity. But I had hoped only to share my secret with Mrs. V., Sir Oliver and my husband Charles. How could I be sure that G.B. would not regard me as an oddity. I don't think that it was wholly my vanity, but a kind of shrinking sensitiveness that made me fear the verdict of this intellectual man. The unuttered thoughts of a stranger or friend in my case penetrated and were wounding. Part of my fear was the fact of my getting drowsy and sometimes completely stupefied in the course of a sitting. In such a dazed condition of which I began to have experience, I might make a complete fool of myself, and G.B. would possibly think it was all play-acting. I had learnt that he was a very sceptical person. But Sir Oliver answered this objection—said that I had appeared quite dazed in one of the sittings I gave him, but that he realised it was a natural condition, attendant on the supreme effort I was making. "After all," he jested, "when a champion makes a world record in a race, you do not think the worst of him for gasping, speechless condition after it." (2)

'All the same, I am glad that I made those first experiments with Sir Oliver. At the beginning G.B. was somewhat intimidating. He could not help it, for his was a cold, shy nature, and he had, I think, a fear of committing himself in words in any way. But he was so kind. 'But Sir Oliver's warm enthusiasm about those early sittings of mine gave me a confidence that G.B.'s manner, if he had been the first learned man as a witness in charge, would probably have shattered. You see, owing to the confidence the scientist gave me, I did better than I expected with Gerald, and I silently registered that he was pleased and took my odd entertainment and behaviour at it as normal and natural. Well, St. Teresa was, like myself, an automatist, and this did not deter, but in fact rather stimulated the Cardinals to canonise her! (3)

'It is strange to think that these experiences of mine—some in other worlds, for I had a number of wonderful mystical visions of them, would not have occurred, 'if it had not been for the most poignant grief of my life, caused by the loss of my darling. If my little girl Daff had not died in 1908, I would not have knocked at the Door. I would never have sought to develop my inner hearing, my psychic gift. But I was desperate, despairing. I had to know.

'That death turned a worldly woman into a questioning one—later a seeker for truth through scientific experiment, then at deepest in the various ranges I explored, a mystic . . .

'All self-delusion, it may be said. But it enriched my life more than I can tell you in words.

'I had to lose myself in order to find myself. It was a second birth for me, as it was for Daff in another world.

'But I must tell you that I had to lose myself in order to find myself. I cannot emphasise that enough for human beings.

'G.C. Attention—too dazed.

'Rouse up—attention, please.

'But I must tell you that I always longed for a little girl. Yes, from the time I played with dolls, I wanted one to cherish. What joy when Daff came. Oh! I had an entrancing year and a half with my baby girl. The first funny words a baby utters—the first staggering little steps, can give such happiness to a mother. Daff was just reaching the baby's delightful walking and talking time when she died (4).

'I did so crave for one little daughter and she was taken from me. I had no other later. Of course I was very fond of my boys and I gave much thought to their education and future. Charles and I had a talk with that schoolmaster Lob about George's education. But we decided against depositing George in his educational establishment, probably because I didn't like that schoolmaster. So we sent George to a more ancient smaller school of perhaps less standing (5). I was impressed by its motto, "Manners maketh Man". Perhaps it was the alleged French quality in me that led me to value good manners. In that I have observed that the educated young Frenchman scores off the Englishman. But my Henry did not need training in manners. His were naturally pleasant and easy.

'We sent him to the educational establishment over which Lob had presided for years, after the latter had left. He was the only Lob I didn't like among those I knew.

'Oh! Why do I ramble on like this? But these memories keep drifting by.'

(1) In her diary for May, 1910, she says, "... pink May out in blossom. Page 55 in the Balfour Study mentions that she gave three sittings to Lodge in May, 1910.

(2) A.T.: 'Once when Sir Oliver was visiting us he said he was going to walk to the village. I was a little boy but I asked if I could come. "Well," he said, "as a matter of fact, I was going to run." "All right," I said, and so he took me by the hand and we both ran to the village.'—So the simile of a champion runner in this script seems natural to Sir Oliver.

(3) This mention of St. Teresa seemed odd, but in Mrs. Tennant's diary for July, 1945, an entry was found recording that she has put up a memorial to her dead son which includes an ex-veto to St. Teresa of the Infant Jesus.

(4) Correct, as recorded in her diaries.

(5) Correct, George was sent to Winchester.

June 15, 1958. Glanmire. Script 27.

Astor is here. Yes. The lady waits for the pen.

'Winifred Tennant.

'It is very difficult for me now to be in any way exact in relating my experiences of sittings. Oh, how precarious is memory! I told you of the reassurances I received from the Biblical record of the lies that very human St. Peter told. But it was lying in ignorance, or rather through temporary faulty memory that worried me during my psychic career.

'I deliberately told white lies with a good conscience when I with much regret refused someone's unspeakably boring invitation. But it was quite another matter to comply with my own urgent desire to tell the exact truth when my mind was still very slowly functioning immediately after a sitting, and I was being questioned by the investigator about it. I will try and give an illustration of what I mean.

'At sittings, even in those early ones with Sir Oliver in charge, I would get very drowsy. Later, with G.B. present, (Gerald Balfour) I, at times, became completely stupefied and was not my conscious self for quite a little while after the sitting. No doubt my condition was due to what Mrs. V. called the suppression of the ego during the sitting. So I could not remember after the experiment what had been said or written at it (1). On numbers of occasions I knew I had myself joined in the conversations with my communicators, but I did not remember what my interjections or comments had been,, and what my communicators had said was a complete blank to me, totally forgotten.

So, when questioned by Sir O. or G.B., I replied that I did not remember anything that had been communicated. It was the truth at the time. But on several occasions, perhaps a day or so later, I would recall some fragmentary impression of the content of the sitting. It may have been a mistaken recollection. It came like an echo and soon left me. I should have written it down at once, even if it came to me when I was socially engaged. But I did not do so, as I was a very busy person. And it soon faded like a dream. It was a kind of lying not to have reported it to the investigator, for ours were scientifically conducted experiments —that is, a search for the exact truth, so far as it could be obtained.

'You must understand that the experience of these sittings was exciting for me. One might describe it as a heightened life. The emotional memory of the experience remained with me, but so very often the details, the words, vanished from my memory—were not with me when

I passed out of a dazed condition after sittings. But not all were so. On occasions I was not drowsy.

'The communicators arranged the whole procedure. I now know that they led me to begin with automatic writing in order to quieten me down—to suspend my conscious critical self. It was followed by my spoken communications, when I had as it were been turned [tuned?] into their higher vibratory level. It was those conversations that mostly provided what was evidentially valuable, as they have told me since I met them after my death. With my conscious critical self-suspended, it did not of course remember the evidence given, so could not spoil or interfere by building upon it in further sittings. But my hostess habit had sunk deeper into my subliminal and my secondary self used the habit and talked in these higher-level conversations with my unseen guests. That is now Gerald's view.

'That secondary self, that different unit of my soul, had no place in my conscious self. And so the memory for words which resides in or is attached to my critical ordinary self did not function in an abnormal state, as the latter was not functioning during those conversations with my unseen guests. I do not know if secondary self is an apt term for that emotional part of my subliminal mind. But I can find no other words for it.

I think that though my critical self was not in abeyance and had to be suppressed by my preliminary writing from communicators, this was not always the case. For it comes back to me now that at one sitting with Sir Oliver I only wrote automatically. Nothing was uttered by my lips. But I was so stupefied that when I woke up after the sitting, I was sure that I had spoken a message and said so (2). But Sir Oliver assured me that there had only been script writing. This happened in my first year with a sitter present, and I was quite dismayed at this complete blank, when I reflected on it afterwards.

However, later, at a time I was by myself Fred came to me and assured me that they were going to take the greatest care of me that I would never be allowed to become unconscious (3).

In my conversations with them alone, I, the critical Winifred, was alert and not banished or suspended usually. I think I was very near banishment in that sitting for writing only with Sir Oliver. Fred's assurance comforted me, and led me to continue to give sittings with someone present later. Perhaps because I scolded Fred and insisted that it must never occur again, he did not allow it to happen later.

'What, G.C., do you make of it all?'

(G.C., I can make nothing of it. I just know it isn't me that produces the writing, but I think I remained more alert than you did. But I do get stupefied at times.)

'Ah, you are different from me. I mean that you are a reporter—a typist secretary—if I may say so, without offence.'

(G.C., A very incompetent reporter at times.)

'The newspapers quite often demonstrate that fact of gross incompetence. Do not be discouraged. And now farewell and thank you for the pen, little reporter.'

'W.T.'

(1) Compare Balfour Study, p. 215, extract from D.I. of March 13, 1912, Oliver Lodge present: 'Lodge, that's Edmund who speaks now, did you notice just now she was so completely over the border that, though in those instants things swept into her consciousness, she couldn't pass them back?'

(2) Balfour Study, p. 57, where this or a similar incident is described.

(3) This must hinge on what is meant by 'unconscious', for it seems that she gave many trance sittings after this one.

July 7, 1958. Script 28.

Astor is here. Winifred asks for the pen.

'Winifred Tennant.

'I wish to continue to write of my secret life.

As a sitter Gerald B. was remarkable, because he was all walled-in, as it were. Never by word or manner did he give anything away that might be informative to me. He occasionally used that debased adjective "interesting" as applied to a script or N.I., my spoken interpretative impressions later in the day after a sitting. Then I knew that we had not wasted our time. For of course some sittings were failures or of no interest.

'But the point I wish to make is that, owing to Gerald's Iron Curtain, he would probably appear to a medium to be what is called, I think, "a difficult sitter".

'I did not find it so in my case. Indeed to work for Gerald became fascinating. It seemed that in some strange way he was complementary to me as a participant. Perhaps it was a case of negative and the positive fitting into each other. But the fact I have recently realised is that O.L. and

Gerald's subliminal minds were in the same mental worlds as that of the communicators—a fact of more importance than is generally recognised. Thus during an experiment in each case their subliminal mind [minds?] helped to uphold me as one swimmer will uphold another in the sea of what is called the Unconscious Mind or Mind at large. Yet they knew nothing of this. Nor did I, consciously. Yet it gave me confidence. So, as time went on, I let myself go into a deep trance when working with G.B. and O.L., in spite of the fact that I was terrified of becoming unconscious and possessed like Mrs. Piper (1). But with either of these two men present I intuitively came to know that could not happen.

'When I obtained D.D.I, impressions—scripts alone at home—distance did not seem to break this once established connection with O.L. or Gerald. I was of course almost wholly conscious when receiving D.D.I, impressions. Neither was I always, in my sittings with Gerald and O.L., in trance. There were occasions when I was my normal self. Then the emotional yearnings of the communicators to prove their existence were sufficiently forceful to lead them to penetrate the denser level and make a contact with me there.

'Even temporary belief on the part of the sitter and automatist in the personality of the communicators is a vital part of the conditions. It makes it so much easier for them to work. I held more than a belief in them. I knew them better than many human beings, acquaintances of mine.

'Gerald's intellect happened to be wholly sceptical, but his imagination was not. It could clearly conceive a situation his intellect did not admit, for imagination has its roots in the subliminal mind. His subliminal mind, as well as his deeper emotional being could wholly believe in the communicator's reality. Yet in ordinary life his cold, impersonal intellect governed all his actions. So though as an investigator entirely dispassionate and revealing nothing by word or sign, he was in fact an excellent and for me ideal investigator. During a sitting both he and I and O.L. were as one in accepting the reality of Fred, Gurney, Butcher, Sidgwick, Mary and Francis, etc. All this I clearly perceive now.

'Of course I know that Gerald, Pid and Mrs. [Sidgwick] rejected much of the scripts afterwards. The subliminal mind of the automatist might be likened to the earth in which here and there are sown the seeds of real evidence. That subliminal produces many weeds that have to be discarded. But at a sitting, by temporarily accepting the reality of the communicators, the best conditions were obtained for both communicators and automatist, in my case, at any rate.

'The opposite to Gerald and O.L. is the egocentric sitter who has a deep-seated complex, such as a repressed horror of death, or inordinate vanity that derives from an insecurity fear. How dreadful to the egocentric is the thought that others might deem him credulous! Another quite useless investigator is very much a creature of his physiological brain patterns. Communicators are cut off through his being cut off from his subliminal, and through a paralysing emanation from him. G.B. and O.L. were fortunately free from any of these crippling hindrances which prevent any results of value being transmitted in most cases.

'To sum up, the Mrs. V.'s, G.B.'s and O.L.'s concentrated subliminal power became allied with the communicators. Or, I should rather say, held the nice balance of successful sittings much as an efficient chairman holds a meeting together. It steadied, helped me to control the mechanism of utterance, of emission or conveyance by speech or writing. If I had lost that control through becoming unconscious, I should have lost the power to record.

'But when all went well and I was deeply in trance, I became partly identified with the communicator. It seemed as if somebody else was me, as if a stranger was occupying my body, as if another's mind was in me (2). I recall one occasion uniquely intense. You may, G.C., mock at me as being abnormal, hysterical, when I say that it seemed as if, lifted up on wings, I was in a state in which I understood all things. All were summed up in one and brought to a point. Bliss in such union was mine.

'There are many ranges of different depths for the mind or soul. That brief experience, when all was summed up as one, was the effect of Fred's mind flowing into mine. My held suspended mind, or dominant self, mirrored and absorbed his mystical experience. But this was not sharing. It was more than that.

'Fred has explained this experience to me. I can only put it into my own words now, so it will be crudely expressed.

'The human being's soul belongs to, or is derived from, a Group Soul, which is inspired by one spirit (3). If we make progress in the after-death, we become more and more aware of this Group Soul. It is more than a brotherhood, it is organic, an organised psychic or spiritual structure. Its spirit is the bond that holds together a number of souls. The spirit might be described as a thought of God, or the Light from Above—the Creative Light from Above. It has an apartness from God, as is the created thing from the One who gave it life. At first an embryo innocent, it has to gather a harvest. There are uncountable spirits, each one connected with a Group Soul.

'As we evolve in the Hereafter, we individual units enter into the memories and experiences of other lives that are derived from the earthly and other existences of the souls that preceded and are of our Group. It is not, therefore, necessary to reincarnate, as Buddhists and Theosophists—I believe—claim, hundreds of times on earth.

'Fred is a member of my Group Soul. When I had what I have called that "unique" experience at a sitting, it was for me union with the spirit of my Group. Fred was the agent, as it were, who brought it about.

'A number of human beings who have mystical experiences assert that in those ecstatic moments, they have obtained union with, or absorption into, Deity. Actually it has been usually union with the spirit of their Group Soul. But now I only want to explain that "unique experience" for me at that sitting. For I think that there has been a misunderstanding of it, and I should like therefore to clarify the position so far as is possible in words.

'During that "unique experience" I surmise that the sitter's supporting force held the nice balance, so that my dominant self was not swept away into unconsciousness. The communicators claimed the direction and training of me, but it is only fair to mention a lower sustaining force from the sitter.

'If psychical research is to make progress, more attention should be paid to the selection of a qualified sitter and to the idea of qualified communicators. Oh! the incompetence of some communicators!

An automatist can obtain interesting results—even striking ones—from making contact with an effective and qualified communicator. But for really impressive results maintained over a long period, a trio is needed—the third in the trio is the sitter.'

(1) Winifred had had a sitting with Mrs. Piper, as recorded in her diary for June 26, 1910. She says that she thought it 'unpleasantly uncanny'. Also on September 28, the same year.

(2) Compare with the Balfour Study, pp. 219-20, 'from waking stage' following trance-script of April 19, 1918, present Sir Oliver Lodge: 'Oh—(pause)—Fred. Fred. So strange to be somebody else.

To feel somebody's heart beating inside you and somebody else's mind inside your mind. And there isn't any time or place, and either you're loosed or they're entered, and you all of a sudden know everything that ever was. You understand everything. It's like every single thing and time and thought and everything brought down to one point.' Quoted in G. N. M. Tyrrell's *The Personality of Man*, p. 160, which G.C. had read.

(3) *The Group Soul* is a concept in communication said to be from F. W. H. Myers to G.C. See pp. 62-5 in *The Road to Immortality* by G.C. (1955), and pp. 68-72 in *Beyond Human Personality* by G.C. (1935), where the ideas found in this script appear to have their origin, F. W. H. Myers of course being their supposed originator in either case.

July 11, 1958. Script 29.

Astor: Here comes Winifred.

'Winifred Tennant.

'What I have written so far about my experiments might be described as a posthumous survey of my memories of them, in the light of my increased knowledge. But I have endeavoured to review them in my role as magistrate.

' "All the world's a stage and men and women merely players." Though this is our revered Shakespeare's statement, I feel it needs revision. One man or one woman is a company of players, their life a tragedy or tragic comedy, or even a farce. But it is a play in which one human being acts all the parts in one sense. Supposing a cast of seven players. The central character is the primary or dominant self. The other six characters are aspects or units of the primary self. I do not agree with Gerald that they are anything as definite as different selves in the normal man or woman—even if the cast is twenty or thirty in number. The minor characters might be called units (1).

'I do not know how many were the players in my drama. I merely wish to point out, Mr. W.H., that neither my son nor any human being has witnessed the whole drama of my life, perceived all the players in their minor roles acting on the stage of my life. So how can my son or anyone else know me, when they review these scripts which I am communicating? For it is not always the primary or dominant self that expresses itself. It was a minor character, sometimes an aspect, who played out her part even before my son Henry was born, that communicated part of a script. If I am immersed in an early memory, such a minor actor may make his speech then through G.C.

'As you know, Mr. W.H., I was a magistrate for a number of years. When my legal personality expressed itself from the Bench, it was quite different from what many would regard dubiously as an illegal personality, that aspect of myself that played out its part in my secret life—Mrs. T. making experiments with O.L. and G.B. on the quiet, or as I should call the character—Mrs. Willett.

'I have yet to tell about that practical prosaic magistrate, who was created principally out of the woman's movement that sprang into life during the first years of this century. Now I must inform you of some of her origins.

'My youthful enthusiasm for Lloyd George to a certain degree waned. My shock at Asquith coming out as a declared enemy of women, refusing them the vote, and proposing to give adult suffrage to all men, however half-witted, as were some of them, caused me considerably to revise my ideas about the Liberals. There was the odd difference between the two—G. and A. Balfour coming out as Liberals, or liberally minded, in favour of Votes for Women, and Asquith playing the role of a hostile, diehard Conservative, disgracefully trying to put down the Women's Movement in the rough treatment he caused to be meted out to women who committed militant acts. I was no militant, but his decadent view of women stimulated me to overcome my nervousness in regard to work in public life.

'My desire to do public work, owing to the unfortunate position of women in regard to the law, which was largely due to their disfranchisement, grew up in me during the early years of the century. Consciously I was not then influenced by the increasing agitation for Votes for Women. But during those first years of the century this militant movement began, through a lighting up here and there among women all over the country, even in remote isolated places, far from halls and speakers.

As my friend, Lady Betty B., said to me or wrote to me in later years—"It was a spiritual movement and had fire' It released great stores of unconscious energy." I had no doubt in the after years that my own unconscious mind was, as it were, ignited and its own little flame lit from the fire, producing zeal for public work.

'You may ask why do I write of this forgotten history of the Women's Movement and the W.S.P.U.

'In the first place, it helped to mould me, all unconsciously giving me the urgent desire to serve in some public capacity, and I want Mr. and Mrs. W.H. to know this aspect of Winifred.

Oh! I had to overcome considerable timidity in order to become a woman magistrate. In the second place, memory of that long gone time has been roused in me through my recent meeting in this life with a dear lady, called Con by her friends.

'On earth I only talked to her once. She was a sister of my friend, Lady Betty Balfour, and her book *Prisons and Prisoners*, which I read, I think, three or four months before the outbreak of the First World War, was one of the important books in my life, because it moved me so deeply, with its grim truths about the harsh, utterly stupid treatment meted out to women prisoners. As I read I reacted poignantly and then wrathfully to Con's suffering, to her martyrdom when, as a militant suffragette, she served her prison sentences. For making a protest against gross injustice, she was gaoled, and the cruel treatment she received in the prison brought about her early death.

'But in her books she made little of her personal experiences.

It was her presentation of the law as it applied to women, and her account of their prison conditions, that made it so revealing to me and to many readers. It roused me to furious thinking and the material in it illuminated my road later in my public work for women.

'Apart from that, Lady Constance represented the spiritual history of numerous women of her own class, including myself, which led to the breaking of our many shackles.

'If she had not gone down into hell and been martyred in her prison cell, I think there is much in my life that I would have left undone. Her actions and her thoughts lived on. This fragile lady, sister of my kind friend Betty, had a share in altering the world and shaping thought among women.

'Her heroism cannot of course be realised by your generation, G.C. What it cost her in pain and fortitude to break out from the sheltered life of a late Victorian lady, belonging to an exclusive class near the throne, and go to prison for her spiritual beliefs can only be realised by women who lived that life in her class, and now all such women are among the living dead.

'It was a notable experience for me recently to meet Lady Constance and be warmed again in the flame of her intense spirituality. Hence my need now to pay this brief tribute to the continued influence on twentieth-century Britain for a forgotten great lady (2).

'Today another unit or character in Winifred's company of players has been expressing itself. But you may ask why I have not, in these memoirs of mine, written of the last phase of my life on earth. There are several cogent reasons for my ignoring it.

'In the first place, any evidence of my identity, and memories of my last years conveyed, would by learned men be attributed to telaesthesia, or by the general public to telepathy between the minds of my son

Henry and the automatist. Alleged telepathy between two human be-ings' minds would not in any way establish my surviving identity or demonstrate to Henry that at least some fragment of his mother still exists. Thus, my principal object in dictating to my reporter, G.C., the automatist, would be defeated. So I must write of events that moulded me and took place before Henry was born, so firm in his belief in his and the automatist's telepathic powers! (3)

'Secondly, the action—the drama of a life—do not take place dur-ing an individual's old age, when happenings of a routine character are circumscribed to one's family and circle, who are all living people on earth, and therefore taboo as material for recording. Also in the dra-ma of one's earlier life come highly emotional memories that cut deep grooves in the psychic substance. All passion spent, the memories of old age make very little impression, are faint, and less easy is it for the extramundane self to record the ancient's trivial round.

'Oh! I am determined as far as possible to exclude all people still living in the body from these memoirs. In this respect my secret life continues. For I might wound or hurt someone on earth by describ-ing a family quarrel, or by writing of an indiscretion on the part of a friend or relative, and thus stir up trouble and appear treacherous. It might not be possible for me to prevent some unpleasant revelation. For in the process of communication there can be what is called mu-tual selection.

In other words, an automatist's subliminal can and has occasional-ly selected facts from the memory of a deceased person and recorded them, and the communicator cannot always prevent such thefts.

'On occasions it is a two-way traffic, the communicator selects and tries to press the evidence through, and the automatist picks up more rarely facts from a discarnate memory via her subliminal mind.

'So in these writings I have kept the automatist, G.C. within the web of my early life.

'You see that generally speaking I may write or rather dictate to my reporter any memory of the earth-lives of the living-dead, without fear of appearing dishonourable and fomenting resentment or causing an-noyance to them. For the living-dead, those in my circle here, are no longer personally concerned about that fading episode, their life on earth and their past peccadilloes.

'So, for the reasons I have mentioned, I gave permission to Mr. W.H. in one of my first messages to publish what he deemed suitable for the evidence I insisted should be kept secret, which I produced as the reporting automatist, during my sessions with O.L., the Balfours, etc. Only the group of scholarly men who were communicators are still concerned that their work should be completed for the benefit of students on earth, through publication there. No human being should be distressed or annoyed now through the embargo being lifted.

And the same can be said for the souls concerned who pursue other lives in the Hereafter.

'It is time to close. Oh, I nearly forgot—

'I have an odd message to give from Fred. I don't know what he means by it, but he was very pleased when he entrusted it to me.

'The message runs: "I dropped the seed of my disregarded wishes into Peter's unconscious mind, and it seemed at last to grow. So what has too long been kept in darkness will now come into the light. At any rate, I feel I can trust Salter to act." (4).

'Then Fred closed his mind to me and passed from my sphere.

'All very enigmatic! But men love mysteries and are never happier than when ostentatiously concealing something from women. This character trait appears to persist here.

'I certainly had experience of it in the course of my sittings with O.L. and Gerald. I always avoided pandering to their weakness by showing a complete lack of interest, though I was far from feeling uninterested in the results of my sittings.

'*Mrs. Willett.*'

(1) In these remarks Winifred again mentions a theory of the soul, more or less as it has been expounded by F. W. H. Myers and by Gerald Balfour.

(2) Lady Constance Lytton was the sister of Lady Betty Balfour, the wife of Gerald Balfour. On the one occasion, in 1939, when G.C. met the Balfours (see page 3) Lady Betty gave her *Prisons and Prisoners*, her sister's book, which, G.C. says, 'of course I read.'

(Ed.) This script could, therefore, be said to be a welling-up from G.C.'s 'Unconscious'. But was Mrs. Willett deeply interested in the Woman Suffrage Movement, and did she have strong feelings on the subject of how prisoners are or were treated?

Her son, A.T., states that his mother was indeed interested in the Woman Suffrage Movement. Though she was not a militant, she went to the length of waiting outside the Neath station (near their Welsh home) to distribute pamphlets for the cause to the returning miners.

One of them threw a pamphlet back at her, exclaiming, 'I'd like to drown you in your own canal!'

Her work as a prison visitor in Swansea, A.T. says, meant much to her. She observed how bitterly the men prisoners felt because they were not allowed razors, their beards were clipped instead. By tireless agitation in high places she at last got them permission to have safety razors, and the resultant increase in morale was so great that all prisons soon did the same.

(3) In this script, dated July 11, Winifred answers a question she puts to herself as to why she does not write of a more recent period or phase in her life. She says because it would be attributed to telepathy between her son, H.T., and the automatist, G.C.

On July 12, H.T. wrote to G.C., who was then in her Irish home near Cork, he being at the Hague in Holland, that his mother 'if she still exists and is able to follow terrestrial events' would certainly have been with him at this time, 'and might be willing to communicate about these shared experiences'. She had been a good deal in his thoughts.

One might say that Winifred saw this question being framed in H.T.'s mind, and, through G.C., answered it before it was written.

(4) It has not been discovered who 'Peter' is. The reference may be to the impending publication of 'Fred's' (F. W. H. Myers) private papers regarding his first love. They were published under the editorship of Mr. W. H. Salter in vol. 52, part 187, of the *Proceedings of the S.P.R.*, October, 1958.

July 22, 1958. Script 30.

(Letter from H.T. of July 12, 1958, produced by G.C.)
Astor is here. Yes, wait.
'Winifred Tennant.
'A letter from my son. Let me sense it.
'Ah! I think I shall reverse my decision in view of what has been written in the letter before me. But I must first tell you that I knew that Henry was going to write some such letter. My impression of it reinforced my feeling that I would not write about what after all is precious to me as a strange and wonderful experience. For he would only deny it all (1). Oh! I 'was angry with him when I got that impression from his mind of the letter he was going to write. I had a bad impression of conspiracy from it. So my answer, as Henry now knows, was a refusal to do as he asked, on very sound grounds. But these were not my principal

reason for my rejection of the request that I saw shaping in his mind. A certain contemporary event for me I would not have sullied by ridicule and denial then. But now, as I read the written words of his letter, I am touched, moved. He writes: "She would certainly have been with me in spirit at this time, if she still exists." So I relent.

'In reply I shall now give an account of certain contemporary events in the life of my soul. The first intimation of them came to me in a re-experienced poignant memory of long ago—and all relates to my son of what this narrative describes. It was not long before Henry was born I had the sensation of the little coming baby's heart beating within my heavy body. It gave me a strange joyful thrill. Then I began to suffer quite atrociously, for there was too much movement of the babe in my womb. At least so it seemed to me in that year when Henry was born—1913, I think.

'On this posthumous level I re-experienced the torture of that far time, and then at last mercifully came release and relief.

'It was followed by the experience of floating away into a radiance indescribable of pure light. The experience was sublime. Then I remembered my baby, and in my dream I heard it crying. Inwardly I felt as perhaps in the myth of Orpheus and Euridice, that I had to go down into hell and rescue my darling.

I won't describe that gloomy and alarming descent'. At last I saw you, Henry, my son, in the distance, struggling with what seemed to be figures in a mist. And I knew with a certainty that I could, with the extraordinary power of love imparted to me by the pure Light, release you from them, and I sent out such a longing you were able to rise away from them all.

'Suddenly, as if I had pulled you up a mountainside with a rope, you were with me, a you I had known in all your maturity when I on earth was fading out in the weakness of age. But this time I had the vigour, and I perceived that though your dear face was illuminated, you were epuise (épuisé) and unconscious of my presence. Then what might be likened to electric currents flowed through me in response to my prayer, for the burden of you had seemed all too heavy. And these currents strangely changed you. Indeed we were both changed into figures of Light, and together we soared. But always I led, and what seemed to be your hand was in mine.

'That soaring into blue immensities is indescribable and you, the weak one, were upheld by the love given me from some spiritual source, and it then seemed to me that we were bathed in the warm love of God.

'I have had what are called mystical experiences. But this seemed to me an imparting to you, a sharing with you, of their bliss. Hence all life deepened, widened for me as never before. But I knew then that the only delusion that cannot be eradicated from the human mind is death.

For though you appeared to enjoy the illumination and faintly sense my incomparable peace and love, you did not seem to realise my presence. I had the experience that individually, apart from me, you had some experience of my ecstasy, but you did not, any more than a man walking in his sleep, perceive that I was there, I, the awakened one, holding you up, directing you and guiding you in our to me glorious flight. Your fear of death perhaps prevented full sharing.

'I may be mistaken but, just near the end of my timeless joy, I thought that you knew I was with you, though you were without what is called perception of me, for finally, completely, I felt that we were spiritually one.

'It was too beautiful an experience for me. The end came then. I believe that the fear of death, the delusion, pulled you downwards out of true reality into the illusory deceptive mists.

'Oh! I followed you and lost you in a confusion of dimness and a jangle of discordance, separation, and bits of human minds like wreckage drifting about me. Soon I became distressed and frightened in all this confusion. But eventually things quieted down. I found myself on the vibratory level above the material world, and I was alone and mercifully there was silence.

'I thought I was near you, Henry, and you were distant in being encased in your physical body, when a stranger appeared. He was one of the physically disembodied, but still in his astral shell, so he had obviously died from earth fairly recently. I could perceive that his was an able mind. And I addressed him and learned that he had been a member of the medical profession when he lived on earth.

'Still very distressed about my Henry, I told this doctor something about these recent experiences of mine, and of the sudden loss of my son—in fact consulted this physician about you.

'He listened patiently to all I had to say, and finally replied: "Oh!—No doubt it's Osmund is the cause of this condition." It didn't seem to me likely that beautiful flowering fern had anything to do with you.

'But then the Doctor continued, using as doctors do, some medical term that has no meaning for their patients. He said that yours was possibly a psychedelic condition. I made him repeat that queer word three times, so I think it must be correct, and I got the spelling of it from him. Finally I asked, "Is that a kind of madness?".

'The Doctor smiled and said, "No fear of madness. But he had better keep off a rich protein diet, if that is what he is up to. I would recommend to any such person fasting and a light diet." (2).

'As the Doctor was a newcomer to this life and I was still agitated and knew well that a doctor will use long inexplicable words to cover up his real opinion, I left him there, and willed that I should make a direct contact with my son's mind.

'As a result, I perceived the previously mentioned letter shaping in his subliminal, and, still upset, I wrote my curt refusal of its request, through G.C.

'That briefly, Henry, my dear, is the story of my contemporary events, as they related to you. I did observe with relief, when I made that direct contact with you I have mentioned, that you seemed in good health and unusually happy.

Whereas I was then shaken and all upset after that alarming time descending into that confusion and meeting that stupid doctor. Irritated, I wrote that refusal to the letter I saw then shaping in your mind.

'Whatever you may say, I now have realised that your permanent self at any rate was with me for a brief while, nearer than ever before. So that is what matters to me most of all.

You see, I saw in that deeper self your real love for me. It no longer worried me, therefore, that you believe that I do not exist.

'Winifred Tennant.'

(1) In a letter to G.C., after receipt of the script in which his mother describes her 'mystical experience' with him, H.T. says that he was not himself aware of this. It does not correspond to any experience of his own which prompted his request.

(2) The episode of the doctor has puzzled both the automatist and the editor. As for Mrs. Winifred Tennant's consultation of a doctor whom she happened to meet, that does not puzzle her son, A.T., since he says that his mother was far from averse to consulting doctors.

As to the use of the words 'Osmund' and 'psychedelic', Winifred thinks that 'Osmund' refers to the Royal Fern, 'Osmunda'—she was herself a keen gardener, but 'Psychedelic', so incomprehensible to her and to the automatist and, till quite recently, to the editor, is a word introduced about 1951 by Dr. Henry Osmond to designate a group of 'mind-manifesting' agents, such as mescaline, lysergic acid, psilocybin and many others. In the case of mescaline, at any rate, the subject of the experiment does well to avoid 'a rich protein diet' before taking.

August 6, 1958. Script 31.

Astor. Winifred has been asking for the pen insistently. She may interfere with other communications if you do not grant her request.

'Winifred Tennant.

'Thank you, G.C., for this opportunity. I have been puzzling about certain recent experiences of mine which you reported.

I refer to my account of my mystical union with the Spirit of my Group Soul and my vision of my son, and of my too sudden descent to the dense level of earth in search of him. Since then, meditating on them and my strange discomfiture, and feeling all in bits in that terrene state, a flash of recollection came to me of the experience of a forgotten dream that occurred shortly before my mystical flight. When this clue came to me I was in my usual world, a metetheric realm. I told my husband about it and he advised my describing it through the automatist, and asking you to inquire of Mr. Salter whether the dream was in any way veridical.

'In my present life one can have during a rest period what is similar to the dream of a human being during life (1).

'The dream was but dimly lit, and took place in a quiet room.

But I saw Mr. Salter very clearly. I know his physical appearance fairly well, as I have seen him of quite recent date on several occasions, through his wife's eyes, when I have sought to give her directions about my secret life.

'But in my dream I saw Mr. Salter seated opposite my son Henry and talking volubly to him—at least his lips kept moving.

But it was in his mind I read the subject of the talk.

'I saw what appeared to be papers or typescript, and I perceived records of my sittings given long ago to O.L. and G.B. and the group. Most of the contents was news to my son—rather startling news. He thought he knew his mother fairly well, but dear boy—he did not know quite all! He gave much consideration to the new revelation, I realised, as I became receptive to various emotions of his, all connected with his own personal memories of me. Oh, what a confusion of half thoughts, images of "Winifred" came to her from his emotionally stirred mind. This made the scene and Mr. Salter fade from my view. Later when I roused up my first question to myself was—how did these two come together, when one lives in England and the other abroad? (2) It was for me a happy dream.

But it was soon forgotten, owing to those very strange experiences of mine, which I related in the previous script dictated to you, G.C.

'Owing to my connection with Helen [Mrs. Salter], I am and have been perfectly aware that they are selecting evidence I obtained of sittings so far kept private and now to be revealed.

It appears to be a matter of selection and presentation. I communicated my approval of such disclosures some time ago. Of late, when I met "Fred" and Gerald, they would not discuss the matter with me and changed the subject. But I suspect—I, the me that writes—that Fred and Gerald are perfectly au fait with what is planned by W.H. But they are afraid I may withdraw my approval, and, as I have previously written, in any case men love mysteries, and Gerald and Fred are still in their relationship on terrene level, and very much their human personalities.

'My dream may have been symbolic, but if true in substance I understand now that my son's discovery of the detail of his mother's hidden life had a certain emotional impact, helping to blend his human personality with his subliminal and, possibly in his sleep, with the transcendental self, and this led to our spiritual experience together, our glorious adventure on the peak of living. No doubt memory of any of it is denied to his firmly planted human personality. But that does not signify.

'Of course the dream I have related may be a thing of fancy, conjured up by memories of the past, or a confusion, a medley, created through my earnest desire to convert Henry to my view of continuous life, and to win him from the delusion he entertains about death.

'Mr. W.H. alone can tell me, through you G.C., if my dream was veridical, so send him this letter, please, from "Winifred".

'As I have written before, the normal human being and also when he has reached my discarnate level, is not usually a number of selves. But his dominant self is allied with minor centres of consciousness or units. A unit may act quite independently and so faintly report an experience to the dominant self it forgets it very speedily. That is the case with dreams of sleep very often, and was the case in this dream I had during my rest period. There are even instances when the dominant self does not consciously register a unit's experience.'

(1) In his otherworld diary Swedenborg claims to have observed the same phenomenon.
(2) This was a correct impression. H.T. and Mr. W. H. Salter had met to discuss publication of certain of Mrs. Willett's sittings with Sir Oliver Lodge and Lord Balfour (Gerald Balfour).

In a later script, not included in this collection, Winifred mentions the above meeting as having taken place in Holland. This was not the case, but A.T. says that there had been a plan, which miscarried, that the two should meet in Holland.

October 29, 1958. Script 32.

Astor. A request has been pressed upon me for your pen.
   Winifred has begged for one more talk with her son.
   (G.C. replied in the affirmative.) Then I shall let her write.

'Winifred Tennant. . .

(Editor: Winifred speaks about the differences in temperament of her two sons, Henry and Alex, as these affected her relationship with each of them. She then addresses Henry and speaks of her present life.)

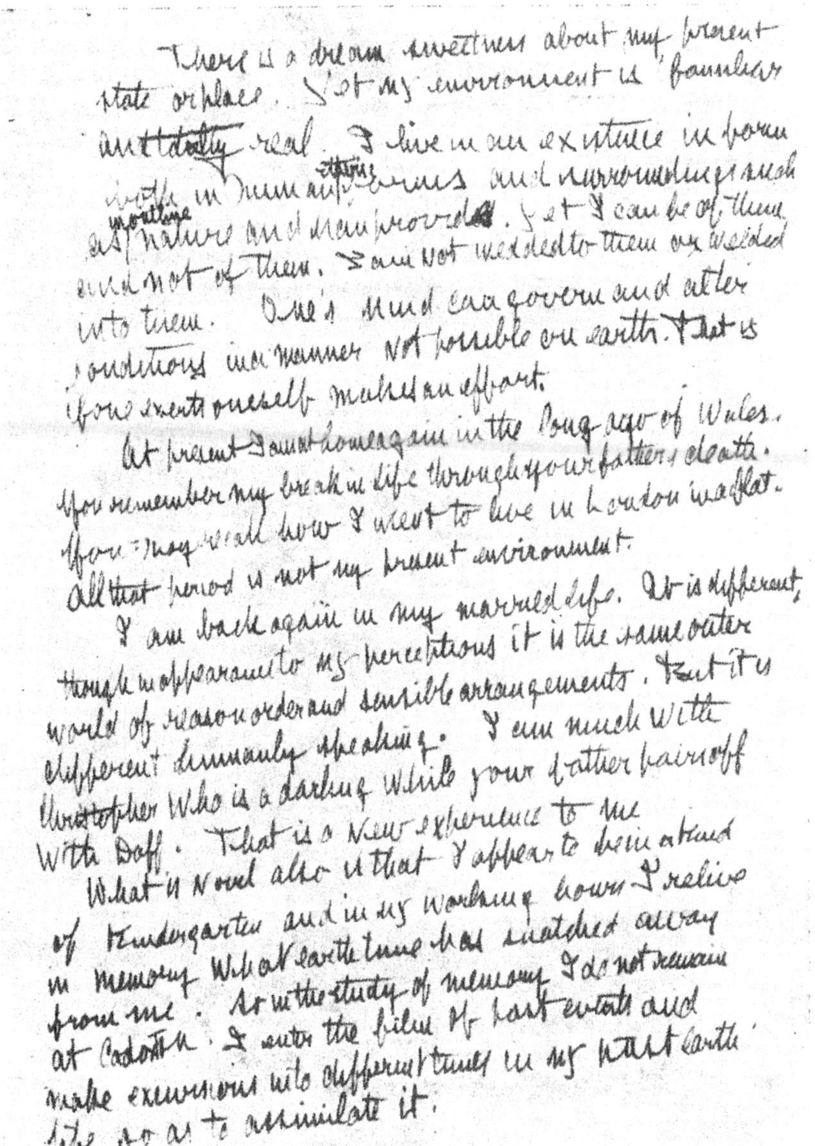
There is a dream sweetness about my present
state or place. Yet my environment is familiar
and totally real. I live in an existence in form
both in human etheric forms and surroundings such
as in outline nature and man provide. Yet I can be of them
and not of them. I am not wedded to them or welded
into them. One's mind can govern and alter
conditions in a manner not possible on earth. That is
if one exerts oneself makes an effort.
At present I am at home again in the long ago of Wales.
You remember my break in life through your father's death.
You may recall how I went to live in London in a flat.
All that period is not my present environment.
I am back again in my married life. It is different,
though in appearance to my perceptions it is the same outer
world of reason order and sensible arrangements. But it is
different humanly speaking. I am much with
Christopher who is a darling while your father pairs off
with Daff. That is a new experience to me
What is novel also is that I appear to be in a kind
of kindergarten and in my working hours I relive
in memory what earth time has snatched away
from me. So in the study of memory I do not remain
at Cadoxton. I enter the film of past events and
make excursions into different times in my past earth
life so as to assimilate it.

'There is a dream sweetness about my present state or place.

Yet my environment is familiar and totally real. I live in an existence in form both in human etheric forms and surroundings such as in outline nature and man provide. Yet I can be of them and not of them. I am not wedded to them or welded into them. One's mind can govern and alter conditions in a manner not possible on earth. That is, if one exerts oneself, makes an effort.

'At present I am at home again in the long ago of Wales. You remember my break in life through your father's death. You may recall how I went to live in London in a flat. All that period is not my present environment.

'I am back again in my married life. It is different, though in appearance to my perceptions it is the same outer world of reason, order and sensible arrangements. But it is different, humanly speaking. I am much with Christopher, who is a darling, while your father pairs off with Daff. That is a new experience to me.

'What is novel also is that I appear to be in a kind of kindergarten and in my working hours I relive in memory what earth time has snatched away from me. So in the study of memory I do not remain at Cadoxton. I enter the film of past events and make excursions into different times in my past earth life so as to assimilate it.

'I perceive again my budding public life, my immense enthusiasm for the Welsh Wizard, Lloyd George. He has even visited me in the disguise of his past earthly personality so blazing with fire and force when in its prime. He was bound to visit me because of his early influence on my actions. For his magical oratory led me to put all nervous shyness away and become a public speaker. He imbued me with the idea that we few of the elect could reform the world. Oh how hard I worked at my role of politician! Through my present perceptions I have experienced again the peak of excited pleasure that was mine when Lloyd George obtained for me the appointment of woman delegate to the League of Nations. [Correct.] The great statesman's faith in me! How wonderful it seemed.

'Yes, I was going to do wonders, perform miracles at Geneva —play my part in redressing wrongs, in above all bringing a smooth certain peace to the world. But what disillusionment awaited me. And yet now I perceive that the bitter disappointment when my Utopian dream of a better, reformed humanity living in tranquillity, came crashing down, leaving me with a sense of futility, was good fortune for me personally, as it produced growth in my real permanent self. All my talk and efforts at the League of Nations as I perceive it and re-experience it now in this film of memory did benefit my larger self, but was of very little service to anyone else.

'An experience that seemed only dust and ashes to me in later years taught me deep down some humility, and led me to read and ponder and look beyond the material world.

'Weighing and measuring my memories now, I perceive the ironical fact that the only statesman I ever helped and influenced was A.J.B. (Arthur James Balfour). I set no store by that at the time. But those sittings for Arthur, the evidence they presented—that you Henry have recently studied [correct]—did convince him that he had a soul and that the other half of his soul would meet him in a future life (1).

(Editor: Winifred now explains to her son that if his present existence should seem unproductive to him, it may yet in reality be productive, as her apparently sterile period at the League was fertile for her permanent self.)

'Do not think that my mention of the transcendental evidence I obtained for A.J.B. is for the purpose of eliciting from you an admission of conversion to a belief in survival.

'It is true that when I set out to communicate these G.C. scripts my main object was your conversion to the idea that your mother was not obliterated, not solely a handful of dust, but was, however changed, living and loving you still.

'I concentrated on that object and wasted no opportunities in sending amiable messages to anyone. Oh I was filled with moral and missionary zeal and laboured in various ways to give evidence of my identity.

'But now all desire has left me to convert you. Since I had that extraordinary experience of an almost mystical character, when you and I soared together, I am satisfied.

'Now knowing it to be a truly mirrored future experience I do not care whether to the end of your days you consider me non-existent. . . love, a force of gravitation in this world of the mind, will inevitably draw us together at some future date.

Meantime be as happy as you can in your nursery illusion that death means extinction. It will make the universe seem much cosier to you. But life goes on relentlessly and so does my love for you, dear son.

'Winifred Tennant.'

(1) Reference to the 'Palm Sunday Case' see script 32, note 1. It is correct that H.T. had recently studied the evidence in this case. As mentioned before, nothing was published about it until a couple of years after the Cummins-Willett scripts.

The facts mentioned in script 32 have been verified in notes to previous scripts. The object of repeating the story of her political life seems to be to encourage her son, H.T., who apparently has been feeling the futility of his life.

April 11, 1959. Script 33.

Astor comes. No, I advise you not to try and make contact with the two you mention today, as Winifred is very insistent in her demand for the pen, and I think would create confusion, block the way. Let her come.

'Winifred Tennant.

'This message is for my son, and I hope that you, G.C., will treat it as confidential.'

(Editor: G.C. gave her word to do so, and the larger part of this script cannot be published. The chief reason is that Winifred in it proves that she is able to perceive present circumstances which are totally unknown to the automatist, and, for that matter, to all but a very few people. There is, however, towards the end of the script, an account of her death experience, which is different from the confidential matter.

It follows.)

'I had many different residences during my restless life. West Kensington (1) and associated with it that curious darkness enfolding me about, the texture of black velvet. To be in the body and not in the body, unable to use, to move any limb. Yet the mind to be clear enough to perceive images, memories of my past long life from the beginning. Picture after picture over the years of it. All the faces, the appearances of all the people who had filled my eighty or more years, slowly filing by, projected in past scenes in groups or one by one. A vast army of ghosts out of the past—not frightening, but very surprising, and always the background of black velvet.

'The hackneyed saying—"a drowning man sees his whole life pass before him". Yes, I had that experience. But with a great effort I abolished these ghosts and tried to hold on to one name, "Henry—Henry". Must prepare. Welcome him back. But I was lost, I who knew London so well.

'West Kensington, I must get up, move on, West Kensington. The name now and then chimed in my ears like a clock telling the hours. That chime struck more and more often, became tiresome, more and more insistent. "West Kensington, West Ken ..." Oh, intolerable! I won't get there. If I don't I shall miss Henry.

'There came a tearing and a rending. I was floating away, mercifully released, at peace at last.

'Each one's experience of death is no doubt unique. That was death for me. Not at all sensational, rather ignoble, you will say, G.C.

'But now I am wholly alive. Not as we were on earth, merely living in bits of the self. I realise the ironical joke—men and women as being in shrouds. It is not us, but they; we, the dead, are free. No more slow recession; on the contrary, wide expansion.'

(l) Winifred's last residence was in Kensington, where she died, after a long illness.

May 30, 1959. Script 34.

Astor comes. Yes. Bea (1) is here today.

Today Bea is in the background in connection with Winifred.

She encountered her over here and gave her hints and help about the series of scripts that Winifred dictated to you. We have not informed you of this before, as we did not wish your mind to be sidetracked from Winifred's field into the Gibbes and Hilda field, as might easily have been the case. But there is no fear of such subconscious invasions, she says, today, if you concentrate on the suspension of your mind and let the inner flow come out. She gathers that Winifred wants to write about someone connected with her, probably a relation of Henry's and her own, one of the newly dead. So let your mind be a blank, not wandering back to the previous scripts received from Winifred. This is something quite new. A personal message for Henry, relating to his own people. I think it depends on you secondarily and Winifred primarily, and Bea's force, if it is recorded correctly. I think from what I hear that this friend or relative of Henry's, who died this year, sent or caused to be sent, someone who made an attempt to communicate, through another, news of the departed soul.

Now read this—then relax and listen in—in about half an hour's time.

Astor—Winifred will link up with you now.

'Winifred Tennant.

'My last letter to you [Henry is meant] must have appeared somewhat morbid, as it was an attempt to describe to you my emotional

experiences in my last hours. The individual who is thoroughly human, as I was and am still, is naturally extremely morbid and emotional about his or her own death, but this is intrinsically very much
less so in connection with other people's deaths! Today I shall write
more cheerfully about a very dear person's passing. Philosophically
speaking death is an occasion for rejoicing at your end as well as ours.
Oh! I am trying to educate you. H for Henry. H is an important letter
in the alphabet, as you may understand for me. But the cockneys deny
the existence of H. H is extinct for them in live speech, that is to say
in anything spoken. When seen by them on the printed page, H is as
dead as Dodo; they cannot lift it from the, to them, static print into
moving, vibrating, oral words. Dear Henry, no —'enry—I fear you are
still a cockney, and if I write H on this page you will reflect that H is
as dead as Dodo.

'But *de mortuis nil nisi bonum*. Of course I forget that when I am
discussing what is only sacred dust, you will be in a proper respectful religious frame of mind, and will take off your hat in salute to that
dissolving shape of dust, with proper reverence.

'Now, while in this mood, read my report.

'You may know to whom I allude when I say that, during my career
on earth, I had a certain friend named Mrs. Meg—Margaret, whom I
greatly esteemed. She was blessed with clever brains. So many women
had so few of them in my day. I greatly admired Margaret. It was not
that we saw each other often. But she had an important influence on
my life, as you of course know (2). Though her brains have been dust
these many years, she and I met here fairly soon after my passing. If
you can bear to continue reading of two brainless morons, let me tell
you that despite their alleged deficiencies the friendship between these
two—Margaret and myself—was rekindled and became enriched. We
had our own plots and plans. But apart from that, we have together
enjoyed looking back into our terrene past. But this happy parsing of
the past was interrupted by a startling summons. Margaret hastened
away. I followed into dim dense depths, finally was halted by the vision
of her meeting her daughter at the gate of death.

'It is of that experience, that ineffable joy for her, she charged me
then to write to you. Through the years she had never lost touch with
her daughter, but that summons came suddenly—as it were before its
time.

'As you, dear Henry, know the daughter, pray raise your hat and
murmur *Requiescat in pace*. Incidentally, that Latin tag gives human

beings such a perfect excuse for dismissing the dead from their lives. However, I believe you will not so lightly dismiss this lady—at least if you realise that her meeting with Margaret greatly affected your mother, its witness. Into what an intricate pattern we were woven during one phase of my earlier life!

'However occupied you are with your work and withheld from news by distance, I think you will have heard of the passing of Margaret's daughter, and will have been moved by it. I shall call her X—the unknown quantity. One reason for my naming her thus is that her husband is a friend of yours and still regards her as living, though now to him she is X—the unknown quantity. Call him Mr. X and her Mrs. X. The more obscurity, the greater clarity, in my opinion. You see it makes it easier for me to write freely on this matter (3).

'I know all about your last meeting with him (X), when indeed I read the dear man's thoughts or fragments of them. I was a witness of this meeting or meetings. You seem to have been a little while together. I was a spy "whether in the body or out of the body", as St. Paul said. But what do such illusions as our appearances matter, after all. Maya, as the Eastern sages define them, and seek so wisely to dismiss them thus.

'Che [sic]

'W.T.'

(1) (Ed.) Bea is Miss E. B. Gibbes, G.C.'s friend and companion for many years, a wise helper in G.C.'s psychic work. Miss Gibbes died suddenly in 1951.

(Ed.) Winifred who had to be helped to communicate at the beginning, and then learned how to do it unaided, is now in a new role, herself the guardian and helper of a soul that has more recently died.

For evidential purposes the identity of this deceased person is left hidden from the automatist, G.C., and even from G.C.'s 'control', Astor.

(2) A reference to Mrs. Margaret Verrall, who aided Winifred in her attempts at regular automatic writing.

(3) Margaret Verrall's daughter, Helen, married to W. H. Salter, had died suddenly in April, 1959. Mr. 'X' is meant to stand for Mr. Salter.

G.C.: 'This script took me in. I did not know who X was.'

May 31, 1959. Script 35.

Astor comes—Winifred begs to be allowed to continue this letter about a relation of theirs.

'Winifred Tennant.

'Dear Henry,

'Now I shall try to recall and record that transition scene as I observed it.

'I noted the withdrawal of Mrs. X (1) from her physical body, not as in deep sleep but in full consciousness. She hovered above it. But an apparition on our level does not necessarily mean death. The vital cord was but half severed. But from then on I received more than I perceived. I picked up an impression of her mind. Here it is.

'She realised she was out of her body perfectly. Was this an out-of-the-body experience, she asked herself, as she looked down at her own face and her shape under the coverings. That she could calmly think this will show you, Henry, that she was in no physical pain, and I know how glad you will be to hear that.

'At this point the flash of her thoughts made a picture I clearly registered of herself and her husband X sitting over the fire, talking, during that past evening. Psychic experiences were it seemed one part of the conversation. She pondered now about this present one. Her body lying there below her, clearly outlined, she floating apart. Oh! Would she remember this situation in the morning, to the extent that she could tell him about her out-of-the-body experience? He would question her. How could she prove it had happened?

'But soon this placid reflection gave place to keen emotion. There came a fear, sharp as a spear thrust. Could she get back into her body? Oh, get back she must!

'Here I was switched off from her mind, as I became suddenly aware of Margaret and her husband, and I realised their purpose.

'They wouldn't let her struggle back. Oh, they wanted to spare her so much, spare her what is called a living death. They were right; but it all seemed incredibly hard.

'She thrust away from them and was then suspended over the dark gulf of death.

'But to cut this depressing period short. They won. After that, all was blessedly well with her.

'Dear Mrs. X. She was very fortunate as to the manner of her promotion. But of course she couldn't forget. For all the happiness Margaret brought with her, just at first Mrs. X remorsefully questioned her own acts in the last phase of her life. So much to leave behind. If she had been sensible she could have lived longer, and so would not have deserted X. She blamed herself for this desertion. Among other things she hadn't taken proper care of herself, had concealed failing physical powers as far as possible. She knew that she wore herself out looking after the house. But she had her standards and did not let things go, as she should have done, in order to live longer for X's sake. She hopes, she prays, that dear X will leave that house (2). It is partly to bring about this object I send you this message, Henry. If and when you see X, advise him to sell up, get rid of that house. Only when he is free of it can he regain freedom, the kind of freedom in which to do what he still should do—which is more important than he realises. Oh, he would in time gain the contentment of achieving, and achievement in that freedom, the rounding off of a life well lived for a fine purpose. If you, Henry, aren't going to see X, write this to him.

'I have not been with Margaret lately, for the reason that I think it is more delicate not to intrude on that wonderful reunion of mother and daughter. Of course I have had news.

Margaret gave me a call up. She told me that Mrs. X had planned that, if she died before her husband, she would try to send a message through me to him. Here it is, as Margaret gave it to me:

' "Tell him of my safe arrival, and that all is more than well.

Of course I am forced to rest by two dear bullies, who are very reassuring. Now my great happiness is that it cannot be very long before you join me here. But I believe that you can hasten the time. There are things to be tidied up. Only you can do it, must do it, before you are permitted to go. So don't waste time, don't fail. Don't be disheartened, as I used to be sometimes.

When you arrive here you will realise that your life has been well spent. You will ..."

'There was more than that in the message Margaret gave me. But I do not care to repeat it for a good reason.

'Now as to the delivery of this message Margaret gave me. I am a little doubtful about an approach to Mr. X. You, Henry, know him better than I do, so I leave it to you to decide if you think it kind or wise to give him this message, or tell him anything about what I have written. It might be cruelly unkind to do so. For some people such a loss as his is sacred. No one should refer to it. It must be wholly ignored.

'Oh, I seem to remember he is a religiously minded man—very fond of Bible reading. In that case, he certainly won't like this message. Dear Mr. X, perhaps you had better let him be.

'I have only one more thing to say. Forgive the flippant remarks addressed to you in these two letters—references to all those solemn hat removals men go in for, etc. But, oh my dearest Henry, your disbelief in me sometimes enrages me, and then I write horrid sarcasms to you. G. (Gurney) helps me with them beforehand—"good for the youngster", he says. Well, never mind. At his—G.'s—direction, I write that I remain 'Your loving but non-existent

'MOTHER.'

(1) Mrs. X is Mrs. Salter. Winifred continues to disguise the participants in this event.

(2) Mr. W. H. Salter did consider leaving his home.

July 16, 1959. Script 36.

Astor is here. Yes, Winifred is eager to perceive her son's letter. She says that she has a confession to make to him, which may clear up some confusion in his mind about portions of various letters she has written him. She is now at last permitted to disclose a secret.

'Winifred Tennant.

[To her son Henry.]

'Not long after I began to send you messages, I was approached by my friends for whom I worked as an automatist during my lifetime. They considered that the difficulties were considerable for me in presenting successfully through G.C. anything that, would make an impression on an intellectual public. So they appointed Edmund Gurney as my assistant. We were to work in double harness, as it were, he to provide the force, I to be the actual communicator. Edmund was chosen because of his relationship, both physically and mentally, to W.H. (l). Since W.H. was a young man he has had considerable influence over him in the deeper grades through the family's unconscious racial mind. This influence warmed up Mr. Salter's originally very lukewarm interest in psychical research. Edmund claims that he was successful in directing his career to the extent that W.H. became the caretaker of the S.P.R. (2), and was a very useful agent of the group here, in that over many years he kept the S.P.R. alive, steering it, in conjunction with his good wife, through many storms in which it might well have foundered. Between Helen and Edmund's influence, W.H. could not escape his destiny.

'Edmund, therefore, as my assistant, was in some respects very helpful. He shaped the outline of certain scripts I have written via G.C. I provided the memories and was the communicator who directed the pen. But there were occasions when he trespassed on to the territory of my mind. In fact his mind, in certain instances, blending with mine, may have, as he admits himself, taken away from the revelation of what was characteristic of me. I want to make it clear that occasionally his keen sense of humour, as exemplified in passages in certain scripts and in their satirical construction, were not mine, and I have candidly told him that some of the remarks as taken down by the automatist were not as I would have phrased them, and also their humour was too flippant and cheap in character. These I disown, and I ask that in any analysis of these writings, due allowance is made for the Gurney blend in the style and approach of certain of the scripts. There is of course a considerable residue of myself in them. Also on my own I wrote several intimate personal letters that were entirely me. I am glad to perceive in your dear letter, Henry, now before me, that you recognise something of myself in the last scripts received by you.

'On the other hand, I must honestly say that I, as a newcomer to this level of life, would, I believe, owing to the great difficulties of communication, have almost totally failed, if it had not been for Edmund's experienced assistance and driving force.

'Helen's death brought Edmund to insist that he should take charge, not merely because Helen was his kinswoman, but because:

(1) It was necessary, if evidence was to be successfully pushed through, that the automatist should be misled. Thereby facts unknown to her could be more easily conveyed.

(2) That obscurity in the writing as was the case in the cross correspondences would be more impressive to W.H.

'We were for a time unfortunately defeated through the automatist not giving us her attention. But eventually we communicated a script that gave news of Helen in a cryptic manner. Afterwards I disapproved of the vein of satire injected into it about you, Henry. At least I considered some passages provided by Edmund were in somewhat bad taste. But Edmund was over-excited in planning his puzzle for W.H.

'I directed the pen, of course, my mind in part blending with Edmund's. I certainly agreed beforehand to Astor being informed that information given about Mrs. Verrall and her daughter should be said to be about our own T. relatives. In this only a white lie was told. Certainly it deceived the automatist. But it is a true statement that Margaret Verrall on this level is a relative of mine. For we live in a world of creative mind, and she is mentally and intellectually of my own family.

As Edmund said: "on earth it is asserted that blood can be thicker than water, but on our level, it is neither thick nor thin, as it doesn't exist." In this other world we are related to each other through having lived on earth in each other's fate, design or circle, to a greater or lesser degree, through our emotionally driven imaginations, through what pertains to minds being akin.

'In such mental clarity I found myself most affectionately drawn to Margaret Verrall, and before Helen's passing, we came to know each other well. But even in our limited busy material lives, mental kindship was demonstrated in the cross correspondence case. The sad cutting off by death of Margaret in the second year of the First World War greatly affected me at the time. I think in fact that my best psychic work was accomplished before her departure (3). This because we were imaginatively bound to each other by subtle strands, though we did not know it.

'But to return to my first script. The description in it of Margaret, her hastening away, my view of Helen out of her body, and subsequently my reception of a message given by Helen to Margaret and reported to me, came from me and was not influenced by Edmund. Near the end his mind began to blend with mine again, so I closed the letter rather abruptly.

'I was out of patience with him, then. So he agreed that in a second script there would be another method employed, G.C.'s subliminal mind, which is called Astor (4), would, so far as was possible, be sustained by us in the Verrall field and would describe what had transpired about Helen's exit from the physical body. It was something more than mutual selection. Astor was let loose in the Verrall field and made contact with Helen's father and read off the images in a section of his memories. How far Astor succeeded we do not know, but we believe that he did select and describe with a partial accuracy.

'Doubtless he made mistakes and these must be condoned, for he was reading off thoughts and images, and endeavouring to relate them in a coherent report. It is a very difficult process to interpret the symbols of memory—for a subliminal mind at any rate.

'As to the latest news. I have had the great joy of greeting and welcoming Helen. Besides her father and mother, a brother of hers was present (5), but he fell into the background. She was specially concerned about W.H. Her one special desire is that he should complete their work for the S.P.R. Until he has finished off certain jobs that are still before him, he will not be released from the internment camp of earth. Hence her craving that he will, however hard it is, occupy himself with them, as soon as all the affairs have been settled. It is a distress to her that he has the burden of the Crown House, but she has been assured that help is being given him. So her mind is more at peace about him now ... (6) 'I cannot hold on now, must close

'W.T.'

(1) Edmund Gurney was a distant cousin of W. H. Salter.

(2) W. H. Salter was Honorary Secretary of the Society for Psychical Research from 1924 to 1958. He was President of it for the years 1947-8.

(3) Correct. Mrs. Willett's best psychic work is considered to have been done before Mrs. Verrall's death in 1915.

(4) A curious statement if it is not made by a discarnate intelligence.

In that case it is G.C.'s 'subliminal mind' dismissing its own statement about itself—that it is a separate intelligence, called Astor, who claims to have been an ancient Greek doctor. See pamphlet by Miss E. B. Gibbes on The Controls of Geraldine Cummins.

(5) A brother (?)

(6) Mr. W. H. Salter did decide to remain in his house.

June 9, 1959. Script 37.

(Previous to this two scripts had been given to Mrs. Flower, from her husband, Cecil. These were on June 7 and June 8.

On June 9, the following came.)

Astor: Yes. I asked Cecil to stop writing yesterday. It was because of interference. A penetrating and unusual mind was pushing in. You little realise how difficult it is sometimes, when there is no sitter to help focus the field to their circle. (G.C. asked for him.)

Yes, he had some message and would like to give it. But hold Brigit Flower's letter.

(G.C. picked up the letter.)

It was her thoughts, her drawing power, that brought this man of long ago. He presented himself in old-fashioned clothes-frock coat and top hat. He belonged to the Victorian period.

Perhaps he's an ancestor of Brigit's. Ah! now the letter is bringing him back. Yes, he is a most interesting soul. There are two others with him. 'We are a trilogy,' he says, 'but in this my world a trilogy is the reverse of tragedy. In common usage the belief is that the last phase of the human being's life on earth is tragic. Hence the mourners, the crepe at the funeral.

But here the reverse, the joy of birth. Gradually there is an emergence from the trilogy of experiences, the pangs of decay, of breaking up, of infirmities, of the gloomy limitations of old age, into the early spring-time of new life on our level.

He says that he and his wife have their daughter with them now, the third in the trilogy. 'We were summoned from another level. Hence our arriving after the birth. But it was for us the right moment on that dense level of Hades. She was struggling to go back, trying to re-enter her physical body. She was distraught, did not recognise us; she only longed to go back to him. It was all very difficult, but eventually we succeeded in preventing her returning and controlling again her physical body; thus we rescued her from much physical suffering and mental distress (1).

'I want it to be known that she just slipped out of her body, found herself above it, and struggled frantically to get back. Owing to that slip out at her passing, she experienced no pain.

Why, though, did we keep her? Not out of selfishness. I simply could not permit her the horror of pain day after day. Scarred on my memory are my years of suffering on earth. Mine was a long experience of pain, before death's merciful release. I had a disease of the bones (2). But I hated to be beaten by it. So I suffered all the more by not resting. I went on working, often in acute pain, with a smile, facing people, speaking.

'I loved speaking, controlling an audience. So instead of taking narcotics, dulling my mind, thereby resting in a comfortable position, I engaged my enemy arthritis, in battle. I was a proud man. I would not be beaten by him. V for victory.

Oh yes! I worked on, growing more and more crippled. But at any rate, no one knew what it meant in terms of physical suffering.

'We were determined our darling would not be a tortured invalid, kept alive by damned drugs. Hers was a heart condition (3). We won, we saved her. Later she recognised us, and our welcome brought her peace. She sleeps well, only now and then wakes for a time then, as the small infant, sleeps again.'

That is all he will say. They are fading out now. I am interested in this unusual and brilliant soul.

(G.C. asked what his profession was.)

Astor: But it is difficult to place him. I mean, what he was, his position when he lived on earth. I think he must have been a great actor, judging from the glimpses I have had of his memories. I got an association with drama. If he was not an actor, he wrote plays. I saw a picture in his memory. He was writing, then walking up and down in what looked like a book-lined study, reciting lines—blank verse, perhaps, and making beautiful gestures. I had a sense of his voice; it was so carefully managed, resonant in tone, but varied and subtly used to weave spells on others, completely to absorb their attention (4).

I perceived his present environment. I saw an ancient Greek temple and near it an amphitheatre, mountains, sparkling sea and deep blue skies. He used, when in his study on earth, often to visualise this scene, so often that it has been easy for him to make it reality here. He is sucking the sweets of B.C. now in the Greece of his earthly dream. On earth, man, as he ages, lives in his dream. If it means much to him, he is caught in its webs here. But it is a natural evolutionary process, connected with the eventual growth of the psyche, when it passes to things undreamed of by mortal man. It enters then the world of creative mind. First the earthly dream is thus assimilated and once digested, he leaps to another level.

When V for Victory—he gave me no other name—was going into distance, after giving his message, this old Greek environment was his background. In farewell to me, he pointed to the amphitheatre and exclaimed: 'I am seeing the real thing now, and by God, they knew how to act!'

But he lived in the last century and was an Englishman, localised in England during his terrene existence.

Perhaps he had a previous life in ancient Greece. Hence his recreation of it as his present environment.

That is all I can tell you of this actor. It is Brigit's letter that seems to have drawn him to you. Ask her about him. He may be some relative of a previous generation, or an actor she once admired for his performance.

(1) It was wrongly assumed by both G.C. and Astor that this script was for Mrs. Flower, so it was posted to her. Mrs. Flower denied that the script applied to her. She has, for instance, no playwright ancestor, etc. Mrs. Flower and G.C. then agreed that the script was a subconscious production, because G.C. had written Irish peasant plays for the Abbey Theatre, and the script described a playwright at work.

This surmise was strengthened by the mention of the communicator's trouble with arthritis, as Mrs. Flower also suffered from it. But a later script gave the clue. It was then supposed that script 37 might be for Mr. W. H. Salter, so it was posted to him, and he verified its contents as applying to his father-in-law, Professor A. W. Verrall and to his daughter Helen, Mrs. W. H. Salter, who had died suddenly in her sleep one night the previous April.

(2) W. H. Salter in letter to G.C. of September 3, 1959: 'He [Professor Verrall] suffered increasingly from arthritis, bearing pain and disability with remarkable cheerfulness.

(3) Correct.

(4) W. H. Salter in same letter as above: 'The impression of A. W. Verrall is most interesting. Much of his work lay in interpreting, editing and in some cases translating the Greek dramatists. He was a magnificent lecturer; it was often said that his lectures were as good as plays.'

July 24, 1959. Script 38.

Astor: Here are Winifred and Helen. I leave the pen to Winifred.

'Winifred Tennant.

'Dear W.H.

'Helen and I have been doing a great deal of resting. 'But apart from other obstacles it has been difficult to reach her, because the V's have been taking such care of her, treating her as if she were a new-born infant—which in a sense she is —new here.

'But at last I had a talk with the dear thing. I mean I had her all to myself. I call it a talk, but it was something more—a state here of being that you could not understand. We relived in memory—even of a time before you came. It was to me the turning over the pages of a book of pictures, then reconstructing them like a stage-manager building a stage-picture, but with the setting, the scenery, and the people of other days. It was Cambridge—the period as a young woman when she studied there at the University. But we skipped out her visit to Dublin University (1). We kept more or less to the two houses nearly opposite each other (2). I recall a time I stayed with Fred and Eveleen in the other house, and the interest of the clever people who came and went to both houses. Helen was innately a shy, sensitive girl, as I told her. I don't think I was ever shy. But always she had depths, sound judgment. But she had learnt to be quiet with such able parents, to commit herself slowly and also cautiously Oh! I must not ramble on like this.

I will merely say that I think it did her good to take her right out of 1959, back to fifty years ago. As one makes in space a continental trip, so here Helen and I made a journey in past time.

'What amusement, what gossiping we had about it all—its annoyances and pleasures, above all the human element—Margaret's, for instance, surprise and disagreeable shock reaction when she came back repulsed by Eveleen on the occasion she first showed her messages from a discarnate Fred (3).

'Reciprocally I related instances of my own shocks about family matters, through interviews with Eveleen concerning them. First there was her snobbery, and in this I had to put her in her place. Then she did for a time regard her brother as very much more her brother than my husband. I had some money of my own, and took the liberty it gave me to be away from my husband when it suited me. I trained him into agreement and in time I think he realised the value of such absences. They introduced novelties into our married life. On my returning to him, we shared our experiences apart, and they made us better companions. Of course to such a possessive woman like poor dear Eveleen my conduct was outrageous. But oh if only she had practised such absences with Fred, he would have loved her so much more. All the same, as I told Helen, certain long past interviews with Eveleen shook me greatly. I was young then (4). What heart burnings! And now, in the year 1959, when we communed about them, and Helen's own knowledge of Eveleen's exchanges with Margaret, they were only an occasion for enjoyment of the rich comedic effects, and the pathos too of poor dear Eveleen did move us also. We are not altogether hardened wretches.

'Ah, now Helen is ready to write to you, W.H.

'What I (Winifred) have written is only a recollection of part of our conversation and our meeting together. But here it is possible to make a particular period in the past objective, and I think that she really did enjoy the Cambridge scenes I conjured up for her.

'Helen Salter.

'So strange, a pen again.'

(Extracts from Mrs. Salter's letter-script to her husband.) '. . . my turn to make what some believe is a long journey. But for me it was such a short journey. Oh, it was so incredibly easy and painless. There was only one very brief nightmare, when I wanted to get back into my body in order to return to you. An instant's bad dream. That's all death was to me. After it, almost immediately, there came the unimaginable moment —a welcoming mother and father. Oh, just as they were

137

in a long gone past, in their prime. You can't imagine what a feeling of safety they gave me. Freedom at once from that inert thing, my body—freedom from the fear of the Unknown.

'There they were, hands full, as it were, with all—all the security I knew as a young, irresponsible girl. I was back in the old house, enfolded in its past studious contentment. But they did not have a number of visitors. It was kept quiet to be a refuge of sheltering peace for me.

'In the past we, you and I, have wondered what our arrival to this level would be like. But nothing we supposed came up to that beautiful, surprising, homely feeling I had with these two protectors waiting for me. That's why I have called it the unimaginable moment.

'Death's exit is so simple, and all our lives we have made it intrinsically complicated, with long, nonsensical words. We were intellectually emancipated from the solemn, gloomy religious utterances. But we were tied up in knots by the intellectuals' weaving and weaving of phrases that eventually tore our poor selves into many shreds and abolished them.

'Well, all that grisly death meant to me was a return to my early home—a journey far shorter to it than the shortest air flight. I am almost ashamed to write of such an anti-climax to our exhausting work and study (5).

'Of course our friends will say of this account of my experiences—if they do not entirely dismiss it—that my perishing wraith is living in a gossamer dream. But in that case it is the pleasantest one I have ever dreamt when asleep on earth.

'But our little life isn't "rounded with a sleep". It made in my case the full round back to childhood and girlhood, my parents, A. W. and Margaret came from regions and appearance beyond my ken and adopted the old disguises. These are all in the litter of memory. They have appeared to me, as I remembered them in the earlier years of my life, before you came into it. They brought with them my very old-fashioned home of long ago and its dear, comfortable ugliness, its books, its papers and its flowers, even the photographs that figured in numbers in Victorian sitting-rooms, drawing-rooms, studies. How I am enjoying its dear atmosphere! I was very tired, and it has been so restful to me—imbued as it is with the fragrance of many distant memories. Oh, it will change I know. Later on—visitors, friends, the setting of another scene in my life.' (Editor: Various omissions of intimate things, except for 'Helen's' comment on 'Winifred'):

I have been amused by dear Winifred's attempt to comfort me, which she has developed in her letter. Her plan for suitable absences from her husband. How little she knew, or ever at any time had our experience of the perfect comradeship.'

(1) Helen Verrall Salter took a degree at Dublin University at a time when Cambridge did not give women degrees.

(2) Correct. The Verralls and the Myers lived nearly opposite each other at Cambridge in the old days.

(3) As mentioned before Mrs. Verrall met with Eveleen Myers' displeasure when she showed her the messages in automatic writing that Mrs. V. had received from Myers.

(4) In Mrs. Willett's early diaries there is plenty of evidence of how she felt towards Mrs. Eveleen and also came to feel towards her other sister-in-law, Dorothy, for 'their untruthful, unscrupulous ways' (February 23, 1908).

(5) Mr. and Mrs. Salter worked together in psychical research.

November 23, 1959. Script 39.

Written before G.C. met Mrs. Tennant's two sons. She met Henry T. for a few minutes on December 3, 1959, Alex one evening in February, 1960.

(After introductory remarks by Astor): '
Winifred Tennant.

'My dear, dear Alexander,

'It is my urgent need to write to you on a private matter that concerns us two. I have a humiliating confession to make and must cast away all pride. The matter in question requires some explanation. You may well tear up this letter and throw it away before even reading to the end of it. If you have that impulse please put it away and when in a more detached mood seriously read what I have to say as if it were another man's story. Then only pass judgment on me. And here now is my story.

'I have been a witness of the film of memory, the record of my life. Some fragments of it I have dictated in this manner which you may have read. They were disjointed and in parts a mere reflection of my moods in past times during my earth-life, or a presentation of a mask of the self with the conventional conversational patter of long ago.

'But there are, as you may know, underground chambers of the mind, certain of them might be likened to foul festering dungeons. I have very recently had a dismaying revelation of one of them. I feel I must share it with you or in future I shall have no peace of mind. *Tout comprendre c'est tout pardonner* is a wise old saying to bear in mind. That is my one plea in extenuation of a lifetime's error.

'I must now write of the year before you were born when my little girl Daphne died. In my messages to Henry I have described my, for a while inconsolable grief. Then in 1909 there came the lovely hope of another baby-girl to replace Daphne. Oh I was so bitterly disappointed when I learnt that this happy dream was a deluding fancy. In the first days after the birth I repulsed my baby-son; visited my bitterness on his tiny innocent self. It was more in thought than in act. But at that very early age the babe is subconsciously acutely sensible of the mother's emotion towards himself. Nature has implanted the instinct in him in his weakness to turn to her as his sheltering providence.

'Providence rejected my poor Alex in her thought for several days. (sic).

'Fortunately you were a healthy, normal little boy, but it produced in you a certain shyness and caution in regard to your apparently capricious mother. For later when I was stronger and more myself again I felt remorseful and went from one extreme to the other and became devoted to my baby boy. But it was too late. My tiny boy, just beginning to walk, was independent, withdrew from my kisses, rejected my impulsive violent, affection. He was deep down alarmed by it. So eventually that primitive mother became hurt and annoyed and turned away from him just when she might have won by her persistence and gentleness. Thus a psychological barrier began to grow up between us. Then there came Henry's birth, and he became the centre of my life.

'I see now that fundamentally I was a possessive mother. As you, a sturdy little boy, refused to be owned I instinctively turned to Henry and sought to own him.

'You have inherited a certain amount of intuition from me. Later on this intuition served you, led you to remain, as a schoolboy and as a young man, aloof from me as it seemed, and you married a charming, kind, captivating lady. I was even jealous of her, though I did not show it. Henry has, I believe, no intuitions, so he yielded too much to my possessive love. It has not been good for him.

'But quite often I have thought evilly of you, dear Alexander, because you were completely independent of me. But you were so good to me.

'I have even in these posthumous messages written, I believe, false things about you. But these were all derived from my baffled emotional vanity because I failed in any sense to possess you. In this life when studying our past memories we assume the mood of the time in which those memories were happening.

So I beg of you to remove from your mind any cruel, false thing I wrote of you in a posthumous message. In this life, I think what has helped me to discover what I call the underground chamber of my mind was my Daphne turning away from me.

In the clarity of this Hereafter she has realised I was her danger, the possessive mother, and quite rightly asserted her independence of me.

'I have written of very early days in your life in this letter that doubtless you cannot remember. It was in order to show you that mine has been the initial offence all along. If at any time you have felt a barrier between us I created it not you.

For the sake of my peace of mind I beg of you to forgive my grievous fault. It is true, I believe, that I did not, save in my lack of interest in you compared with my interest in Henry, injure you. But my thoughts of you were worse than my deeds.

Now I see it all so clearly I find I love you dearly, but not with the selfish overwhelmingly possessive desire that I showed for Henry.

'Dear sons, I send you from the Hither World my true love in equal shares.

(Writing became faint.) 'It has been very difficult to write this. I cannot hold on longer.

'Winifred T.'

General: Here Winifred doesn't try to present obvious 'evidential' facts. Those mentioned here have already been registered. Now she makes a general survey for the purpose of correcting what she feels is an unjust attitude she has had in the past towards her older son. It was written before G.C. met either of the sons.

Winifred started by wishing to convince her younger son H.T. of her continued existence. That was the bait which the communicators Balfour and Myers used to make her consent to play the medium once more. During the two years and two months or so that the experiment lasted Winifred changed. She came to understand and value her older son much more. Hers was not a case of 'static' survival.

March 6, 1960. Script 40.

G.C. was giving a sitting on the above date to Mrs. Brigit Flower (pseudonym) when there was an interruption to her alleged communicator and the name 'Wilfred Tennant' was written, as well as the following remarks:

'Are you Mrs. Flower? Yes, Helen Salter says you are and that you know all about my psychic past. But I must introduce myself. I was Mrs. Willett, whom I abandoned many years ago.

But when in my unpleasant old age Helen visited me—so kind —I soon noted that she wanted to talk to me about Mrs. Willett and those long past times.

'It roused up wistful memories of my dear friends,' the Balfours. I could not bear it, so I brusquely shut up Helen on that occasion, changing the subject, refusing to be drawn. But now today I am making amends. I have brought Helen, pushed her through this party of strangers [Mrs. Flower's communicators] to speak to you of the Balfours.

'Helen Salter.

'I am so happy to perceive you, Mrs. Flower. I have just met your sister—so charming, but I must be brief or may fail to get to you a few facts as Mrs. R. waits patiently for the pen.

'You may or may not believe me. But I have met the group of Cambridge scholars for whom we worked so hard, also our old colleagues, Gerald Balfour, Pid, Mrs. Sidgwick, even her brother Arthur and Sir Oliver. The Balfours, I would like my husband to know, highly commended him for his work, and the work he is even now striving to do for the S.P.R. If blushes were a fact I would have been crimson in this state of life so many compliments were paid us.'

(Omission of something private.)

'That is message number one, the other is personal. Shortly after I was promoted to this life I sent messages to my husband to the effect that he should move from Crown House and move to London and work here for the S.P.R. I feel now that I should not have suggested his uprootal. It would be too great a task for him. You know how helpless men are, Mrs. Flower.

'So, if you think fit, just let him know that I was not in a clear state of mind when I wrote and suggested that he should leave Crown House. I want him to know I have been near him occasionally and have been glad to know he is not moping. He has done much in dealing with innumerable papers.'

This little addition to the Willett scripts has been annotated by Mr. W. H. Salter in a letter of March 16, 1959, to G.C.:

'It is the case that a few years (I forget just how long) before "Winifred's" death, Helen called on her, and was rather surprised that she dismissed so firmly ("brusquely" is not an exaggeration) any attempt to discuss the old script material.'

Neither the automatist, G.C., nor the sitter, Mrs. Flower, knew anything about this matter. G.C. had never met Mrs. Salter.

Further comment from Mr. Salter's letter:

' "Pid" for J. P. Piddington is good. It was what we always called him. It dates back to his sittings with Mrs. Piper, whose control used to address him like that.

'The remarks about my staying on at Crown House represent my own change of feeling, which Helen, if still aware of earthly matters, might very likely share. I was, for a few months after her death, strongly inclined to move, but decided against doing so.'

PERSONAL BACKGROUND

BY GERALDINE CUMMINS

I have always disliked looking at my face in a mirror, but my collaborator in this book insists that I must face the mirror of time by relating some autobiographical facts, since they may be helpful to the reader of the Cummins-Willett scripts.

I am an author. Fifteen of my twenty-two published books have been 'transmitted', or produced by 'automatic' writing.

Of the rest seven have been consciously produced; five of them have Irish themes and setting; two deal with aspects of psychical research.

I am also a playwright. Four plays, three of them written in collaboration with S.R. Day, have been performed either in two London theatres or at the Abbey Theatre and elsewhere in Eire. I have also over the years contributed articles, short stories and book reviews to various periodicals in England, U.S.A. and Eire. It is necessary to make this statement as I have been quite often described as 'a well-known film star', (who has the same surname) or other professions have been alleged to be mine.

However, with twenty-two books to my name I have come of age at last and, therefore, should be regarded as a responsible person in respect of statements I make about myself.

This preface is necessarily brief and much has been omitted from a life crowded with various activities. But I must in self-defence emphatically deny the practice of one of several professions assigned to me as the livelihood producing my daily bread.

In 1932 a book of mine entitled *The Road to Immortality* was published. Shortly after its appearance I was invited to lecture at Brighton to a psychic research society. In due course its secretary sent me a notice of the meeting that had been posted to 200 members of it. On the notice was printed 'Speaker Miss Geraldine Cummins, writer of *The Road to Immorality*, fifteen years' experience'. Needless to say, when I arrived at the Pavilion, Brighton, I found awaiting me a packed audience, many standing. Never before nor since have I at a lecture been met with such enthusiasm and warm applause as at that Brighton gathering.

But now I must revert from this gay episode in my life to graver matters, at any rate to an author.

The technique of composition has always been of deep interest to me, and when I was a young Irishwoman it developed on two lines. (1) The composition was the creation of my conscious mind. (2) It was derived from the unconscious. In the former case I write very slowly and laboriously and have to revise the MS. again and again. A short story has taken my conscious mind a month to compose. To be of any literary value my published stories and novels and one Biography have had to be about Irish characters and my native country Ireland. On the conscious mind level I have tried and failed to write about English people. I did not know them sufficiently well to make their characters come alive in fiction. They remained foreigners to me.

But when my writing was derived from the unconscious it has been a very different affair. The theme was never Ireland or the Irish people. For instance, certain English and American persons' characters and personalities, unknown to me, were reported by their relatives or friends to have been successfully delineated in such writing. Its composition emerged from the deeper levels of mind, so much so it seemed as if I were merely a secretary taking down an already fully composed narrative by another author, and my pen travelled over page after page with abnormal rapidity. Various authors, notably William Blake the poet, have had that strange experience of dictated writing. We cannot explain it. But in my case such transmitted writing (a more correct term than 'automatic writing') led me into psychical research.

I use the adjective *transmitted* to define it because my conscious mind is suspended, plays no part in the communication.

Whatever the source of such writings, i.e. a subconscious or a common unconscious mind, or a discarnate individual's mind I have not composed a single sentence of those rapidly written scripts when provided.

As to origins I am wholly Celtic, that is to say I am descended from Irish people with a slight blend of a very occasional Norman or English ancestor; but not one Cromwellian settler in Ireland figures in my racial past. I have spent the greater part of my life in the southernmost portion of Ireland and was born at 17 St. Patrick's Place, Cork. As I was preceded by four sons my arrival on this planet was welcomed with some enthusiasm by my parents.

According to modern standards, my own education was negligible. I never went to school. Three of my younger sisters and I received instruction successively from two uneducated resident English governesses and finally a French mademoiselle. Later to satisfy my hungry imagination I sought and found for myself the Cork Public Library. I eagerly searched its catalogue and read voraciously mostly fiction and Irish tales and plays.

I was ten years old on the to me notable occasion my father took a house in the country, set in well-wooded grounds, for his large family. So when my elder brothers were on holidays from Public schools my second sister and I played football, cricket and hurling with them and other boys. Also we were employed as woodcutters, and I used the axe chopping logs and pulled at the double saw, became 'a tomboy' as a girl was described in those days who followed masculine pursuits.

Actually my interest in psychical research was first roused when I was about five years old. For then my father's coachman John Dempsey related to me with deep sincerity tales of fairies he had seen and of rather terrifying ghosts he had perceived. Better than any story books were the accounts of experiences he and my very Irish nurse exchanged with each other. Also my mother took a secret interest in any such phenomena.

So in our garden and a dark cellar I diligently searched for fairies and very recklessly for ghosts. Their alleged alarming appearance only stimulated my craving to meet them. Alas, despite my thorough searching, I did not see one of them. It was my first failure in an experiment in psychical research. Bitterly disappointed I became a complete sceptic. But the ghost tales told me in picturesque Irish dialogues did, perhaps, help to sow the seed in my subconscious mind of a desire to plumb these mysteries, though other pursuits buried it for a time.

My subsequent interest in psychic science was much reinforced, I think, through my family background of medical science. My paternal grandfather was a physician, my father Professor of Medicine at the National University, Ireland, his two brothers were professors in medical subjects at universities.

Two brothers and two sisters of mine are members of the medical profession and three of them are Fellows of the Royal College of Physicians, Ireland. My youngest sister, the late Phyllis Hayes was a British Government senior experimenter in peaceful atomic research. Another sister of mine was the second woman to obtain a civil engineering degree and the first woman to be made a member of the Irish Institute of Civil Engineers.

My four strong-minded sisters broke through all the barriers to a woman's University training, then in Irish society looked at askance, and in the course of time each one loaded herself up with three University degrees. In contrast to them I only went up for one examination in my life and that was for shorthand. I passed for ninety words a minute. My success was such that I never went up for another exam. But with our background of Medical Science all of us children were brought up in an analytical atmosphere with a kind of religious respect for exact truthful statement in scientific research; there was to be no loading of the dice for emotional or personal reasons. Absorbed in his profession my father in my youth often used to discourse to me at length about his medical cases and medical science.

Doubtless through this paternal influence I am still what I described myself at the age of seven, 'a very curious person', that is to say a person who wants to know the truth concerning life and death however disagreeable it may be.

But it was in the field of athletics I first sought to follow in my father's footsteps. In his youth he had won fame as a Rugby football international player. So when I was eighteen I won my place on the Irish Women's International Hockey Team.

My mother was a clever fascinating person I would not distress for worlds, so as she was horrified by my ardent wish to emulate my father further by seeking to qualify as a physician, I took to the elusive pursuit of literature and to work for Votes for Women. I wrote stories that were published in magazines and I collaborated with my friend Miss S. R. Day in writing an Irish peasant tragedy called Broken Faith. Then, at the age of twenty-two, I experienced the youthful bliss of witnessing this play being rehearsed by the poet W. B. Yeats and the playwright Lennox Robinson at the Abbey Theatre, Dublin.

Alas, only once in my life have I seen a ghost, one very welcome to me. Nevertheless my interest in them originally roused by John Dempsy's vivid tales may have led to my own psychic experiments beginning when in the later years of World War One I was a paying guest in the house of Mrs. Hester Dowden in Lower Fitzwilliam Street, Dublin. By day I had a small job in the vaults of the National Library, where I was peacefully occupied in cataloguing eighteenth-century sermons of inordinate length. The daughter of an internationally famous scholar, Hester was a cultured woman, a brilliant musician and a remarkable medium. So we occupied our evenings in the company of others with either music, or the literary gossip of the Dublin salon of that day, or in psychic experiments on the ouija board. Among those who attended our sittings was a young man back from the Serbian front, Mr. E. R. Dodds, later Regis Professor of Greek at Oxford University and finally in 1961-2 President of the Society for Psychical Research (the S.P.R.). His was an extremely wholesome sceptical influence. He has a keen sense of humour and youthful though he was then, did not mind Hester calling him 'the Universal Question Mark'.

Under her tuition I began to get messages on the ouija board. At first I was very sceptical as on that ouija board there were many statements made obviously traceable to my subconscious mind. But on page 131 of my book *Unseen Adventures* is recorded an early successful experiment through my communicator, my alleged guide or control Astor reading correctly one evening the emotional thoughts, etc. in Hester's mind when she was absent from Dublin in London. The sitters present were Professor E. R. Dodds, Mr. Row, a Fellow of Trinity College, Dublin, and an Army Officer.

Incidentally, I dislike the word 'control', commonly used in psychic research for the guardian caretaker of a medium. Mine, Astor, has never controlled me. I prefer that long gone medium Socrates' own name for his subliminal caretaker, which was 'Daemon'.

But my interest in the exploration of the capabilities of the human mind began when Hester Dowden and I embarked on a number of experiments in psychometry or object reading with a collector of ancient jewellery, Mr. Henry Bois. He brought rings and other precious objects to our sittings. Both she and I obtained a number of correct impressions of fragments of their history from them. These were all carefully recorded and a few of them were published in *Voices from the Void* by Hester Travers Smith.

At the first experiment I was given a plain gold ring to hold and obtained from it a brief resume of Napoleon's adventurous career and finally his name. Its owner Mr. Bois stated afterwards that it was Napoleon Bonaparte's coronation ring. I was puzzled about this and our other successful object readings of Mr. Bois's jewels in regard to the mental process involved. In my case, I had merely concentrated on stillness and listening as a stenographer does to dictation, and these correct statements relating to the history of the object touched by me or held wandered into my brain in words. I did not know from one sentence to another what would come. But it all made sense when the record was read.

This capacity of mine for reading objects served myself and others well later on in my research work.

During the past twenty-five years I have taken part in occasional experiments that come under the heading of Medical Psychology. A Fellow of the Royal College of Physicians, Ireland, writing under the pseudonym of Connell is the author of a book *Healing the Mind*. In it he has described some of our earlier experiments in which I was employed by him as an object reader. He used me as an intermediary to investigate through transmitted writing the psychological backgrounds of patients in cases of obscure neurosis. Thus was disclosed the conflicts etc. in the patients' subconscious minds. We have had a very high percentage of successes—in several cases through the treatment presented in my Scripts of 'Abreaction', unknown to me until I read Dr. Sargeant's book two years ago *Battle of the Mind*. The feature of our cures was the rapidity of each patient's recovery, which was immediate or almost immediate, and the cures were usually found to be lasting when reviewed in later years. Several of the sufferers treated seemed hopeless cases which psychiatrists had previously failed to cure.

Some of our successes were of patients, victims of either claustrophobia, asthma, amnesia, periodic self-starvation, periodic attacks of alcoholism, melancholia, or of various obsessive fears that menaced with ruin the careers of able-bodied men and women. I never saw the patients. Usually a sheet of his or her handwriting and an object he or she had worn were posted to me and I worked alone upon them in the absence of the physician. Using the analysis I secured, Dr. Connell employed the medical psychological methods, explaining and discussing with the patient the causes of the illness and its treatment, which my investigations had disclosed.

Certain skilled sensitives or mediums have been very useful to the community in various branches of the subject, too long to relate here. But a man described as 'an intellectual' recently in an ignorant article finally dismissed psychical research with the remark 'I cannot see the use of mediums'. Dr. Connell and I have proved that a sensitive can be of valuable service to medical psychology in restoring to health sufferers from obscure psychoses mainly through what is called psychometry or object reading. Certain patients have been thus rescued from ruin and despair.

I must add that I have no medical qualifications. I am simply employed as a masseuse by a physician. So no patient should apply to me about his case.

I was engaged on literary journalism when soon after my father's death in 1923 I met Miss E. B. Gibbes in Chelsea. It is entirely thanks to E.B.G. as I shall call her that I was able among my various occupations to work seriously at psychic research over many ensuing years. She was a member of the S.P.R. (Society for Psychical Research) and had thoroughly studied the critical methods they employed at that period of their history. She arranged for me to live in her house in Chelsea for about eight months each year and encouraged me to develop transmitted writing. Her exhaustive work in keeping records of our sittings and checking up evidence obtained by me for other sitters as well as for herself, has been very remarkable.

She tried to check every detail, fact or name, given in personal communications that were unknown to us. Of these there were a considerable number. She even analysed every sentence in certain series of writings of mine when seeking evidence of the character and style of deceased persons. In addition she had experimented with Mrs. Osborne Leonard, Mrs. Blanche Cooper and most of the leading mediums in London, thus training herself for Research.

I shall not in future cumber the pages with the words *alleged or purporting to be* from communicators. But in the nineteen-twenties apart from early messages from E.B.G.'s relatives or friends, I obtained in her presence in our first long experiment what are now called after the first published volume *The Scripts of Cleophas* (Psychic Press). These were narratives of early Christian history. In all eight volumes of them were published over the ensuing years. Leading English and Scottish theological scholars highly commended the accuracy of certain historical facts written in them, facts entirely unknown to me.

I could not in view of my education have known them.

During the same Cleophas period of writing I obtained scripts from F. W. H. Myers published in two volumes *The Road to Immortality* and *Beyond Human Personality*. These transmitted writings were accepted by Sir Oliver Lodge and Sir Lawrence Jones as coming from their old friend Frederic Myers and as dealing with subjects and ideas they had discussed with him during his lifetime. Mrs. Myers also accepted these scripts as messages coming from her husband.

During the past thirty years I received in the same way various communications stated to be from deceased persons in which evidence of identity was presented through personal facts or their subsequently verified memories unknown to me or anyone present when they were recorded in my transmitted writing. Some of these cases were published in journals or in the following books. *They Survive; Mind in Life and Death* and *Unseen Adventures*. Others written for various absent sitters are unpublished. E.B.G. checked up those received for absent relatives or friends of the deceased person communicating. In the Cleophas Books and in *Healing the Mind* are varied instances of 'extra sensory perception' phenomena.

Both in the production of E.S.P. and in the evidence that may be direct communications from the minds of the dead I, and, I may add, Mrs. Osborne Leonard and Mrs. Bertha Harris (to mention only three intermediaries) have accumulated a great deal of evidence suggestive of survival. I mention these two owing to their long records of work in psychic science.

Apart from Mrs. Leonard, the record of Mrs. Bertha Harris should be studied. She is clairaudient, and speaks at her sittings. Over the last twenty years, officials of the Society for Psychical Research have sent her sitters, each accompanied by a note-taker. The records of her sittings have been preserved and are buried in the archives of the S.P.R. so they are unknown to the public. She has had astonishing success in giving evidence of Survival. It has been revealed that during this long period of her experimental work for the S.P.R. she has obtained ninety per cent. 'ESP' phenomena.

In fact, no investigator is in a position to give a verdict against the evidence of survival obtained in psychic science until he has thoroughly studied among other previously mentioned cases of research, Mrs. Harris's notable achievement in a detached manner as a lawyer, weighing and sifting evidence.

Her proxy sittings, that is to say when the sitter, who takes the sittings has no knowledge of the communicator, are of especial value.

Admittedly mediums of the calibre of Mrs. Leonard and Mrs. Harris and Cross-Correspondence writers, such as Mrs. Willett, Mrs. Piper, Mrs. W. H. Salter and Mrs. Verrall are rare. There are extremely few great poets or scientists in a generation so there are very few psychic geniuses called mediums or transmitting writers.

As sitters and investigators, I found Miss E. B. Gibbes, Mr. W. H. Salter and Dr. David Gray equally unrivalled as investigators. Mr.

Salter conducted my long Cummins-Willett experiment. He and Mr. Henry Tennant (Mrs. Willett's younger son) were the absent sitters in this case. On perhaps four or five occasions they sent me a query or a request to put to the communicator, otherwise they simply in their letters to me acknowledged each Willett script of writing posted by me to either of them and replied that the script received was of interest, or asked for a further contribution. It was all the encouragement I required in order to obtain a further script when I had time and quiet for it in the course of my busy life.

Mr. Salter was for thirty-five years Hon. Secretary of the Society for Psychical Research. His wife and his mother-in-law were gifted transmitting writers. We were amateurs; I was never a professional. It was quite beyond my strength. Indeed, I have a respectful admiration for first-class professional mental mediums of integrity who lead an arduous, exhausting, ill-paid life.

In any case, such a profession was not for me owing to my cherished ambition which was a literary career. Until 1952 I avoided reading any books or articles about psychic research as I feared that its technical jargon would interfere with my composition in regard to my consciously composed literary work. I tried to follow three pursuits—Literature, experiments in transmitted writing and thirdly attend to the mundane duties of a woman's life. It led to the to me distressing detriment of my literary output.

E. B. Gibbes, my principal investigator for thirty years, rather deplored this ambition of mine. A month before she died on December 18, 1951, she begged me to abandon literary work, concentrating on our research. I promised to do so, and have kept my promise. My only consciously composed writing ever since her death has been devoted to books, articles and lectures on psychical research.

I think, therefore, I may claim as detached an interest as that of Mr. W. H. Salter in what may be called psychic science.

But now I must return to those autobiographical details. As I have written so much about the unconscious mind or selves I cannot do better or worse than to summarise my conscious self as it appears to me in the mirror of time.

I am a normal individual and am owing to deafness conversationally uninteresting. But though not by any means in my dotage, I am quite the reverse of the eerie, exciting, neurotic, screaming individual many people conjure up in their imagination as the character of the sensitive or medium who experiments in psychical research.

At my present ripe age I still have two athletic pursuits. Following my athletic father's example I indulge as a recreation in a little light gardening and in the summer even occasionally play tennis. Similarly I imitate my paternal ancestor intellectually. As he, with passionate curiosity, studied the mystery of life and death in medical science I continue to pursue and probe at this mystery in psychic science.

Is there a swan (a soul) that rises from the Black Sea of Death and flies away to other regions?

THE LINES OF COMMUNICATION

BY GERALDINE CUMMINS

How do you establish your lines of communication?'
That is a question which I often meet with, in one form or another. I wish I could answer it clearly and simply, so that my map could be followed without difficulty by aspirants to the same psychic experiences. But all I can do is to try to throw light on the process from different angles. It can never be a textbook answer, for the track that those lines follow is at least partly laid in a region apart from conscious thought.

The first directions which I received I owe to the famous Irish poet, A.E. (George Russell).

A few days before the production of my first collaborated play, *Broken Faith* at the Abbey Theatre, Dublin, I met the Irish poet A.E. In the course of conversation, he instructed me in the practices of Eastern metaphysicians for the development of mind. I, a twenty-two years old youngster from the provinces, listened with awe to the sage's advice, but only in one elementary exercise did I occasionally follow his instruction, one now known to many people in the West, but to few in those far-off days.

Briefly, A.E. advised concentrating intently on an object such as a 'White Triangle', or on a single word, for at first a very few minutes, three or four perhaps, as the whole attention had to be uninterruptedly fixed on the object, with every stray thought eliminated.

Some years later, when I had begun psychic experiments, I carried out this advice. I chose the word 'stillness', perceiving it meditatively in my mind's eye, for a few minutes only while I endeavoured to lose my little self in the meaning of that word. I feared, however, that this simple exercise was not sufficient when, in 1925, I was invited by the late Dr. Maude, Bishop of Kensington, to let him be present at a sitting for the writing of *The Scripts of Cleophas*. The most eminent theological scholar in England of that day, Dr. W. OE Oesterley of London University was also to be there.

Extreme fear and tension seized me at the prospect. The experiment seemed doomed to failure. These Cleophas scripts were of a period in early Christian history of which I was totally ignorant, so I had no idea beforehand of what would be written. My conscious mind was helpless in the matter.

But eventually, out of my gloomy forebodings, there emerged an amplification of O.K.'s advice, a response, perhaps from the Unknown to my request for aid in this apparently impossible task. The advice which was somehow transmitted to me was this: In the quiet of evening I was first to concentrate on stillness, secondly to desire the fulfilment of my need and thirdly to imagine it fulfilled.

In order to enter the stillness, it is necessary to raise one's intelligence to a higher degree of consciousness. The stillness is neither a passive, inert state, nor trance, in my experience. When achieved it is a lucid work of intense activity. The condition of stillness clarifies the desire and creates efficiency. Once launched, the desire seems as a little boat on the lake or sea of the imagination. There, piloted by desire, driven forward by the waves of imagination, it can on certain occasions reach the objective chosen.

So for nights before sleep I exerted my will in concentration on stillness, then desired that in the Bishop's study the pen I held would move rapidly and well, the 'Messenger of Cleophas' dictating as usual with abnormal rapidity, continuing the historical narrative. Over this I let my imagination wander effortlessly and confidently, as it did so often when I was a child seated in a meadow, gathering and enjoying its wild flowers, treating the flowers I picked as if they were living creatures, each kind with its own character and life.

But on the ominous date when I entered the ecclesiastical study there were five clergymen, besides the Bishop and Dr. Oesterley present, and a thunderstorm began to rage outside. All the conditions were hopelessly against me, so the fear returned that I would fail to put myself into the concentrated state necessary to receptivity.

However, once I was established at a table with foolscap sheets before me and had shaded my eyes with one hand while the other held the pen, a merciful tranquillity dominated me.

The seven learned witnesses were no longer there for me. After about three minutes 'the Messenger' took over, and for an hour and a half an historical narrative was written at a considerable speed without a single pause. Sheet after sheet filled with writing was passed to the silent clergymen by the attendant sitter. It was a feature of this writing that there were no halts until the final full stop.

During the sitting I did not even hear the loud claps of thunder. I was too concentrated on the suspension of conscious thinking in order to listen in on another mind-level to notice earthly conditions.

The material obtained on this occasion is incorporated in chapter 30, pp. 10 ff., of The Scripts of Cleophas.

Later on members of the medical profession, representatives of psychic research societies, authors and various clergymen were from time to time witnesses of such writing. None in any way appeared to influence its rapid flow. As much as 2,600 words were written at a sitting of close, historical narrative, and, according to Dr. W. OE Oesterley of London University, W. P. Paterson, Professor of Theology, Edinburgh University, Professor David Morrison of St. Andrew's University, and other eminent theologians, historical and geographical facts unknown to me were recorded in these scripts.

In the case of certain skilled mediums the subliminal appears to be the channel for a successful telepathic communication from another individual or group of individual minds, either incarnate or discarnate. In numerous instances it may only convey valuable evidence in flashes, the intervening words coming from the medium's own subconscious mind. Every sitting or script has to be judged on its merits.

Generally speaking, my first task is completely to orientate my thoughts away from the life around me. I prepare for such writing by eliminating sense impressions and muscular action.

Even if it is only for three minutes, when a sitter is present, I concentrate on stillness, having, previous to the sitting, desired to obtain something relating to the sitter, or an analysis beneficial to a patient suffering from an obscure neurosis. This procedure, if successfully practised, releases me from the material world. A condition of complete inattention to life is my goal, then a 'not-self' seems to dictate.

I much object to a sitter talking to me before I begin, as it interferes with this desired concentration on my part. Mediums have been accused of 'fishing' for information, but in my view such fishing is taboo, if, for no other reason, that it is certain to spoil my practise of concentration. I want to escape from everything and everyone around me into stillness, which, if attained, provides me with the listening attitude necessary for my inner hearing. How can I concentrate on the words that are to be dictated if I am compelled to listen to idle talk? Thereby my conscious mind is liable to be pulled out of its state of intense concentration and compelled to find answers to the sitter's tittle-tattle.

Once launched on a sitting, when I have attained to that other level, I have no objection to questions or conversation on the part of the investigator addressed to the alleged communicator, as then my conscious mind is in a state of equilibrium. When this is attained successfully, it appears to be on a higher level of energy and in complete control of my brain, able as a stenographer to take down the conversation of the communicator.

In the *Journal of the S.P.R.*, December, 1962, Professor C. J. Ducasse writes of two possible methods of communication: '(a) Cases where a person "possesses" for the time being parts at least of the body of a medium, i.e. uses her auditory and her vocal organs or writing hand; (b) employs the medium only as intermediary, i.e. "speaks to her telepathically", and "listens" also telepathically, to what she hears when she speaks.'

Mine is and always has been the (b) method.

As to my complete exercise: To Will, to Desire, to Imagine, it has only been occasionally employed in advance of a sitting I deemed important. Since the death of Miss Gibbes in 1951 especially, my life has been over-occupied with work and with people and their problems brought to me for advice. This makes me too tired to make the necessary effort in the evening that later might work the oracle.

Though it is difficult in these days to obtain leisure, if my compassion for a stricken person is especially roused, I practise my complete method of preparation. Three years ago I was told of such a case by Dr. Connell. A brilliant man, M. had been ill for eight and a half years with very sharp pain down his leg, pain also in his neck. He suffered thereby cruel insomnia, was unable to work, and became an invalid. His poor wife was in despair. They were ruined and the situation appeared desperate. Hypnotic treatment had been wholly ineffective. The patient had consulted five practitioners over the years of his illness, two Professors of Medicine, two leading psychiatrists. They prescribed strong sleeping draughts, as they failed to find the cause of the pain. The analysis in my script found plenty of causes for it in the patient's subconscious mind. But preceding that analysis, in what seemed to me an impossible task, on several nights I practised my complete exercise, while holding a sample of the patient's handwriting and his fountain pen. From the script-analysis I obtained there resulted an almost immediate cure of this serious psychosis, after it had been discussed with the patient and explained to him by his physician. M. was very soon able to work again, and is now earning a good livelihood. See article by Dr. R. C. Connell in Light (Autumn, 1962).

A point of interest in the M. case is that, when holding his writing and his pen before obtaining the analysis, I felt an immense compassion for his suffering. Thus my desire and imagination were strongly reinforced and may have opened the door to the therapeutic knowledge that produced this particularly difficult cure.

When emotion is roused in this way it strengthens desire and stimulates the imagination, which enables the higher mind or subliminal to function smoothly as a channel for authentic messages, as it has done in certain other cases. Apparently there is then little or no subconscious interference, breaking in and dictating irrelevant material.

Of course I have had my blank sittings, devoid of evidence. Mediums more gifted than I have also experienced them. Just as in physical science numerous experiments are failures, so it can be in psychic experiments. But in the latter case the sitter who has had a blank sitting with a medium of the first class too often wholly condemns the medium and does not examine himself for any part in the failure. He may have blocked the lines of communication himself. He may have a strong subconscious prejudice against any interesting results being obtained at sittings. This can be an emotional drive that paralyses the sensitivity of the medium. Perhaps he is expert in some branch of science which would be revolutionized by evidence inexplicable to his colleagues and himself in the terms of his chosen subject. His subconscious desire then inflexibly determines not to have him shaken out of his comfortable groove of thought. Or he may have some other strong inhibition, as for instance an unadmitted dread of his own death. This alone might ruin his sittings with mediums.

Of course the medium too can be the cause of failure. Serious worries in her own life can inhibit the production of convincing evidence, or, as in the case of professional mediums, exhaustion of sensitivity through giving too many sittings.

Scepticism, however, is no fault or hindrance in the investigator. If not allied with his emotional subconscious prejudices or fears, evidential results can very well be obtained.

I've been asked to try and describe my personal sensations when I am acting as recorder of transmitted writing from those who claim to have departed this life of fairly recent times. I can do no better than to quote 'Mrs. Willett'. (I may add that I have not read the *Balfour Study of the Psychological Aspects of Mrs. Willett's Mediumship*, only what is quoted from it in G. N. M. Tyrrell's *The Personality of Man* and in Mr. Saltmarsh's *Evidence of Personal Survival from Cross Correspondences*.

Neither book quotes very much from the Balfour Study.)

Mr. Tyrrell quotes her as saying: 'I heard nothing with my ears, but the words came from outside my mind ... I don't feel a sense of seeing, but an intense sense of personality, like a blind person perhaps might have—and of inflections, such as amusement or emotion on the part of the speaker.' And, again, 'It is as "minds" and "character" I know them.'

Her experience was similar to mine. But in psychometric work, that is to say when I have held an object I have occasionally been clairvoyant and have seen passing pictures of a person or a room or country that has been connected with the object or its owner. During the writing of *The Scripts of Cleophas*, I had now and then a 'sense of seeing'. Perhaps a moment before scenes and people were presented in the transmitted writing I saw them quite clearly in my mind's eye. But it was as if I were a spectator in a cinema, looking at moving pictures. I had hardly any sense of the words describing them that were being rapidly written by my hand.

Professor H. H. Price has said that our present higher education is designed to increase our capacity for verbal thinking. It may be significant that when I record communications from educated people of the last decade I do not see images and scenes, but when I recorded the Cleophas writings, concerned with people who were said to have lived eighteen hundred years ago, I sometimes saw moving pictures of them and their surroundings. Among them were scenes of mobs and uproar, trial scenes or a mystical vision. Very occasionally a foreign word or a foreign name, Hebrew, Greek or Roman, appeared in illuminated images of it.

In my book *Mind in Life and Death* are reports of so-called 'intruders', communicators unknown to myself or to anyone present at the sittings. They came with a purpose and appeared to force their way into my writing. One of these gate-crashed when I was in Co. Cork in 1952. The messages given were for a Mrs. Grant (pseudonym) with whom I had a slight acquaintanceship. I posted them to her in London. As she was a keen research student, she had this case examined and checked by a member of the Council of the Society for Psychical Research.

In these scripts a modern, highly educated Dr. Tomlin accurately communicated names and a number of facts, some of them psychological, about himself, his daughter and wife. Certain of the facts were unknown to Mrs. Grant, and she obtained verification of them from Dr. Tomlin's daughter. In her report of the case she wrote 'the description of (the daughter) Mrs. Jervis's life as given in the scripts was quite true and has been confirmed by her. She also confirmed the fact that she had never met or heard of Miss Cummins, nor did she know any friend or acquaintance of Miss Cummins other than myself.'

While recording communications from Dr. Tomlin I saw no images whatever. But as shown in the absent investigator's report I correctly gave an account of a highly emotional psychological situation in the lives of the father and daughter.

According to one anti-survival theory, Dr. Tomlin was extinct as an individual, and I was merely stealing his neatly tabulated memories from an alleged Common Unconscious. But how then in these scripts did this static Great Memory demonstrate a very active survival in Tomlin's case, showing his characteristic jealousy of his daughter's husband and exhibiting in unscrupulous action an agitated mind tormented by hatred and frustration?

This case and others show that when an intruding stranger is driven by a powerful emotion of love, jealousy or hatred he appears to be able through its power to overcome all difficulties of transmission and to be able to convey verifiable facts, as did Tomlin. His active, hate-driven mind endeavoured with threats to break up the happy marriage of a living couple. We do not seem to have static existence in the Hereafter, but continue our progress either for evil or for good. I felt extremely repelled by the unpleasant personality of Dr. Tomlin and I stopped his later attempts to write through me.

Exactly the opposite was my reaction to my communicator 'Mrs. Willett'. In her case I was sensible of a delightful and varied personality with a glancing wit. Her personality was indeed a trifle dominating, but she was clearly the fine, late Victorian English lady, public-spirited and a worker for others. Both she and Tomlin were unknown to me and they appeared to be impelled by powerful emotions to communicate even in the difficult circumstances of no sitter being present.

This mother had demonstrated in the earliest scripts and throughout the series a devoted love for her son Henry, which was later verified to have existed. The purpose of her communications was to convert him from a belief in her extinction to acceptance of the fact that she was still living and loving him.

Her emotional drive was the very opposite of static.

The later verified memories of herself and her life on earth were not a bunch of recollections stolen from a common unconscious by the writer. Her lively mind led her to break down the barrier and strive to fulfil her purpose, as can be seen in her scripts.

These two, as well as some other communicators, came wholly alive to me as deeply interesting characters and during the writing I was sharply and unusually sensible of their moods. I intended only to try and record two or three scripts from 'Winifred' in compliment to the investigator, Mr. W. H. Salter. But her personality was so engaging that I entertained her again and again, until I had about forty-four scripts. She had no immobilized existence in a Hereafter of static memory. Her progress was for good. During her exploration of 'the subterranean chambers of her mind' when she discovered a certain very minor fault of hers (later verified) of which she had been ignorant she turned her dismay into correcting it at once and thereby was able to progress for the good of herself and others.

Doubtless, if we survive, we shall all have access to the tribunal of the subconscious mind and we shall make unpleasant discoveries about ourselves, but few will have Mrs. Willett's brave honesty in admitting error, in rectifying it and in telling of it in her script-confession.

The information in this script was known only to two or three strangers to me, and even if I had known Mrs. Willett in her lifetime I could not have learned of it.

From a study of the Cummins-Willett scripts much can be learned about the process of communication, no doubt because Mrs. Willett herself had practised the art from this end in the long period of her mediumship that has so clearly and sensitively been surveyed in its psychological aspects by Gerald Balfour.

My own method of concentrating on 'stillness' does not seem to have been hers. Why should it be? Her sitters or investigators were very few and selected for their understanding and discretion, and the same seems to have been the case with her communicators. Perhaps she did not need to adjust herself to the extent that I have had to; considering the number of sitters who have appealed to me and the large range of personalities that claim to have communicated through me, claims that often have been verifiable.

In any case, no doubt every practitioner of transmitted writing probably has his or her own suitable method for acquiring the best listening attitude, but, I should like to repeat, as these lines of communication seem to have to pass through regions apart from conscious thought it is hardly feasible to make a map of them.

A more rewarding study is that of the material brought to us through these means, and I submit that Mrs. Willett has put us greatly in her debt.

Before closing this chapter I must emphasize one point in relation to my long experimental experience of psychic research.

(It extends over forty years of my life.)

I have previously stated that as a rule preceding a sitting I concentrate on *stillness* with the object of raising my intelligence to a higher degree of consciousness. This is a lucid work of intense activity. It places my directing self in a strong position in which I have never been controlled by an alien mind. Mine has never been a case of 'possession' by another mind. I am as a stenographer taking down words from dictation and employing as it were an inner hearing. To use the words of the poet William Blake in relation to the writing of some of his poems, 'I am the secretary. The authors are in eternity'. In my experience no more than any secretary or shorthand writer is my conscious mind dissociated during sittings. That is to say it is not in any way controlled by a dictating alien mind either during my scriptwriting or for one moment in my ordinary daily life. Certain people have said or written that 'automatic writing is dangerous to the writer'. In my case there has been no danger experienced by me, possibly for the simple reason that mine has not been automatic writing. It has been transmitted writing taken down as by a reporter who has complete control of his physical body. But I am aware that my conscious mind is more keenly alert and active in its pointed concentration during the transmitting process. This may possibly be so because on favourable occasions it appears to be raised through concentration to the higher subatomic level of energy. I did not in these proxy Willett sittings converse with Mrs. Willett. For this unsociability she severely chided me. But conversation on my part would have broken up my one pointed concentration on listening via the inner hearing to her dictation.

Whether the content of my scripts are transmitted to me by a subconscious or unconscious mind or a discarnate communicator, that is for others than myself to judge.

Paperbacks also available from White Crow Books

Elsa Barker—*Letters from
a Living Dead Man*
ISBN 978-1-907355-83-7

Elsa Barker—*War Letters from
the Living Dead Man*
ISBN 978-1-907355-85-1

Elsa Barker—*Last Letters from
the Living Dead Man*
ISBN 978-1-907355-87-5

Richard Maurice Bucke—
Cosmic Consciousness
ISBN 978-1-907355-10-3

Arthur Conan Doyle—
The Edge of the Unknown
ISBN 978-1-907355-14-1

Arthur Conan Doyle—
The New Revelation
ISBN 978-1-907355-12-7

Arthur Conan Doyle—
The Vital Message
ISBN 978-1-907355-13-4

Arthur Conan Doyle with
Simon Parke—*Conversations
with Arthur Conan Doyle*
ISBN 978-1-907355-80-6

Meister Eckhart with Simon Parke—
Conversations with Meister Eckhart
ISBN 978-1-907355-18-9

D. D. Home—*Incidents in my Life Part 1*
ISBN 978-1-907355-15-8

Mme. Dunglas Home; edited,
with an Introduction, by Sir
Arthur Conan Doyle—*D. D.
Home: His Life and Mission*
ISBN 978-1-907355-16-5

Edward C. Randall—
Frontiers of the Afterlife
ISBN 978-1-907355-30-1

Rebecca Ruter Springer—
Intra Muros: My Dream of Heaven
ISBN 978-1-907355-11-0

Leo Tolstoy, edited by Simon
Parke—*Forbidden Words*
ISBN 978-1-907355-00-4

Leo Tolstoy—*A Confession*
ISBN 978-1-907355-24-0

Leo Tolstoy—*The Gospel in Brief*
ISBN 978-1-907355-22-6

Leo Tolstoy—*The Kingdom
of God is Within You*
ISBN 978-1-907355-27-1

Leo Tolstoy—*My Religion:
What I Believe*
ISBN 978-1-907355-23-3

Leo Tolstoy—*On Life*
ISBN 978-1-907355-91-2

Leo Tolstoy—*Twenty-three Tales*
ISBN 978-1-907355-29-5

Leo Tolstoy—*What is Religion
and other writings*
ISBN 978-1-907355-28-8

Leo Tolstoy—*Work While
Ye Have the Light*
ISBN 978-1-907355-26-4

Leo Tolstoy—*The Death of Ivan Ilyich*
ISBN 978-1-907661-10-5

Leo Tolstoy—*Resurrection*
ISBN 978-1-907661-09-9

Leo Tolstoy with Simon Parke—
Conversations with Tolstoy
ISBN 978-1-907355-25-7

Howard Williams with an Introduction
by Leo Tolstoy—*The Ethics of Diet:
An Anthology of Vegetarian Thought*
ISBN 978-1-907355-21-9

Vincent Van Gogh with Simon
Parke—*Conversations with Van Gogh*
ISBN 978-1-907355-95-0

Wolfgang Amadeus Mozart with Simon
Parke—*Conversations with Mozart*
ISBN 978-1-907661-38-9

Jesus of Nazareth with Simon Parke—*Conversations with Jesus of Nazareth*
ISBN 978-1-907661-41-9

Thomas à Kempis with Simon Parke—*The Imitation of Christ*
ISBN 978-1-907661-58-7

Julian of Norwich with Simon Parke—*Revelations of Divine Love*
ISBN 978-1-907661-88-4

Allan Kardec—*The Spirits Book*
ISBN 978-1-907355-98-1

Allan Kardec—*The Book on Mediums*
ISBN 978-1-907661-75-4

Emanuel Swedenborg—*Heaven and Hell*
ISBN 978-1-907661-55-6

P.D. Ouspensky—*Tertium Organum: The Third Canon of Thought*
ISBN 978-1-907661-47-1

Dwight Goddard—*A Buddhist Bible*
ISBN 978-1-907661-44-0

Michael Tymn—*The Afterlife Revealed*
ISBN 978-1-970661-90-7

Michael Tymn—*Transcending the Titanic: Beyond Death's Door*
ISBN 978-1-908733-02-3

Guy L. Playfair—*If This Be Magic*
ISBN 978-1-907661-84-6

Guy L. Playfair—*The Flying Cow*
ISBN 978-1-907661-94-5

Guy L. Playfair —*This House is Haunted*
ISBN 978-1-907661-78-5

Carl Wickland, M.D.—*Thirty Years Among the Dead*
ISBN 978-1-907661-72-3

John E. Mack—*Passport to the Cosmos*
ISBN 978-1-907661-81-5

Peter & Elizabeth Fenwick—*The Truth in the Light*
ISBN 978-1-908733-08-5

Erlendur Haraldsson—*Modern Miracles*
ISBN 978-1-908733-25-2

Erlendur Haraldsson—*At the Hour of Death*
ISBN 978-1-908733-27-6

Erlendur Haraldsson—*The Departed Among the Living*
ISBN 978-1-908733-29-0

Brian Inglis—*Science and Parascience*
ISBN 978-1-908733-18-4

Brian Inglis—*Natural and Supernatural: A History of the Paranormal*
ISBN 978-1-908733-20-7

Ernest Holmes—*The Science of Mind*
ISBN 978-1-908733-10-8

Victor Zammit—*Afterlife: A Lawyer Presents the Evidence.*
ISBN 978-1-908733-22-1

Casper S. Yost—*Patience Worth: A Psychic Mystery*
ISBN 978-1-908733-06-1

William Usborne Moore—*Glimpses of the Next State*
ISBN 978-1-907661-01-3

William Usborne Moore—*The Voices*
ISBN 978-1-908733-04-7

John W. White—*The Highest State of Consciousness*
ISBN 978-1-908733-31-3

Stafford Betty—*The Imprisoned Splendor*
ISBN 978-1-907661-98-3

Paul Pearsall, Ph.D. —*Super Joy*
ISBN 978-1-908733-16-0

All titles available as eBooks, and selected titles available in Hardback and Audiobook formats from www.whitecrowbooks.com

Lightning Source UK Ltd.
Milton Keynes UK
UKHW010641080822
406998UK00002B/337